Y0-BEK-597

Managing Development in a Global Context

Managing Development in a Global Context

O.P. Dwivedi
University Professor Emeritus, Department of Political Science, University of Guelph, Canada

Renu Khator
Professor of the Department of Government and International Affairs, and the Provost and Senior Vice President at the University of South Florida, USA

Jorge Nef
Professor of Rural Extension Studies and International Development University of Guelph, Canada and Director of the Institute for the Study of Latin America and the Caribbean (ISLAC) of the University of South Florida, USA

palgrave
macmillan

First published 2007 by
PALGRAVE MACMILLAN
Houndmills, Basingstoke, Hampshire RG21 6XS and
175 Fifth Avenue, New York, N.Y. 10010
Companies and representatives throughout the world

PALGRAVE MACMILLAN is the global academic imprint of the Palgrave Macmillan division of St. Martin's Press, LLC and of Palgrave Macmillan Ltd. Macmillan® is a registered trademark in the United States, United Kingdom and other countries. Palgrave is a registered trademark in the European Union and other countries.

ISBN-13: 978–0–230–00005–6 hardback
ISBN-10: 0–230–00005–3 hardback

This book is printed on paper suitable for recycling and made from fully managed and sustained forest sources.

A catalogue record for this book is available from the British Library.

Library of Congress Cataloging-in-Publication Data

Dwivedi, O.P.
    Managing development in a global context/O.P. Dwivedi, Renu Khator, Jorge Nef.
        p.   cm.
    Includes bibliographical references and index.
    ISBN-13: 978-0-230-00005-6 (cloth)
    ISBN-10: 0-230-00005-3 (cloth)
    1. Economic development–Social aspects. 2. Civil society–Developing countries. 3. Developing countries–Social conditions. 4. Developing countries–Social policy. 5. Human capital–Developing countries. I. Khator, Renu. II. Nef, Jorge. III. Title.

HD75.D885 2007
338.9009172'4–dc22

                                          2006051552

10   9   8   7   6   5   4   3   2   1
16   15   14   13   12   11   10   09   08   07

Printed and bound in Great Britain by
Antony Rowe Ltd, Chippenham and Eastbourne

Contents

List of Tables

Preface

Managing development in a global age: some unavoidable questions

Development administration – often referred to as development management – is now over half a century old. It has exhibited paradigmatic shifts and epistemological crises. It has evolved over the years into a self-confident and mature field. As it expands in scope and sophistication it has also become more interdisciplinary. This coming of age of what we once called a "fence around an empty lot" has given us a perspective to explain and understand the problems faced by developing nations worldwide. A key question remains: Will the new development management offer a liberating and dignified perspective for the future, or will it be just an instrument of elite control as the new managerialism of an inequitable world order?

This volume is the result of a collaborative effort by the three authors to respond to a fundamental question: How can societies manage progressive social change in an age characterized by globalization and growing uncertainty? It is eminently an interpretative exploration into the history and circumstances of the human predicament at the turn of the twenty-first century, and as such it combines both structural explanation and phenomenological understanding of such predicament. The book is also a demonstration of teamwork. The three authors who joined their efforts to bring this undertaking into fruition had realized that they thought very much alike when it came to the field of development, and the challenges faced by it. During 2005–6, we had an opportunity to engage in this exploration at the University of South Florida (Tampa, USA) where we were able to exchange our varied experience and insights. It is these experiences and insights that we wish to share with those who like us have toiled in this field for decades and with those who are to follow in our footsteps. Our combined experience put together in this volume provides a unified and systematic treatment of the subject. The analysis presented here attempts to critically examine both the range of changing patterns of political and administrative culture, as well as the collateral effects of development policies, reforms, and globalization faced by developing nations.

In this sense, *Managing Development in a Global Context* is an intro-spective reflection into the meaning of development, security, and social technology, complementing and expanding upon our research and field experience of over thirty years as global citizens. As such citizens we straddle two intellectual traditions. One is that of the "center" where we received our doctoral education, respectively at Queen's (Canada), Purdue (USA) and the University of California (USA). The other is that of our ancestral homes in the global South, where we grew up, did our undergraduate and professional studies and where our basic perceptions and primary orientations were formed.

Two of us, Dwivedi and Khator, received our basic educational train-ing in India while Nef is a product of the Latin American intellectual tradition. This combination of diverse experiential and intellectual traditions has led us through numerous collaborative academic ven-tures in the last two decades. A fundamental search has been our exploration of the interplay between development, administration, ethics, and technology from a broad, global and interdisciplinary perspective. This is our first tripartite undertaking in a book form add-ressing the above-mentioned issues and epistemological concerns.

We are putting these ideas together primarily to share our collective experience with the new generation of young scholars at the beginning of the twenty-first century. It is primarily aimed at and dedicated to advanced students who will take on the new challenges of academic and professional life in a significantly different context from the one we have lived under. This generation will be undoubtedly the one to face challenges of development management and governance in an interdependent world of high risk and mutual vulnerability, but also one full of opportunities.

We individually and collectively acknowledge an intellectual debt to several of our teachers and intellectual mentors: J. E. Hodgetts, John Meisel, Frank Lee Wilson, William McLauchlan, Harold D. Lasswell, Paulo Freire, and Richard Harris. These teachers taught us most of what we know of public administration, development, management, and teaching itself. For us, it is a noble educational legacy indeed, com-bining Political Economy, Management, and Ethics. We are also indebted to our numerous students, many of whom have gone into forging successful academic careers of their own, in particular to Lisa Fairchild, Erin Steurer, and Nanita Mohan who worked hard to help us with the collection of information, doing research, and giving us related help. Finally, we the authors would like to thank Ms. Jennifer Nelson of Palgrave Macmillan who initiated this book project, and later continued by Ms. Hazel Woodbridge. Finally, we take the responsibility for our views and analysis, and what is said but particularly what is unsaid in this volume.

Onkar P. Dwivedi
Renu Khator
Jorge Nef

Introduction: Managing Development in a Global Context

This book is largely an interpretative examination and analysis of the role of management and organization in human development. It will explore the historical record; the current global, regional, and national characteristics of present developmental and managerial dilemmas; and possible future scenarios. Of particular interest is the analysis of the relationship among mutual vulnerability, human insecurity, and de-development. In this sense, our work brings into question many of the prevailing linear and unidirectional understandings of development, management, politics, and globalization. One of our concerns is how to connect the copious amount of theoretical literature and the various practices in order to understand development as a long-range process involving continuity and change. We also examine the development-management challenges facing both the global South and its wealthy but equally vulnerable Western counterpart.

Our collaborative text has been the product of years of analysis, critical reflection, and "decantation" on our part, bringing together teaching, sustained research, and over sixty years of collective field experience as development consultants. In this brief introduction, we outline the main themes of the book. We also define basic terms, such as development, well-being, management, and globalization, and lay out the conceptual framework of the volume that will unfold and expand in subsequent chapters. We will attempt to straddle a conceptual and analytical void in a broad-ranging, though systematic, way by examining the complex interrelationships between management and administration, on the one hand, and development and globalization on the other.

Our understanding of development goes beyond traditional definitions centered on spontaneity, economic growth, and the GNP. It

1

encompasses a myriad of interrelated and reciprocating environmental, economic, social, and political attributes (Heady, 1979). It also relates to matrices of cultural preferences, values, and ethics. In the final analysis, we are looking at development as the spread and consolidation of the material, natural, and spiritual well-being of people and nations. For us, this well-being is not just a mere actuarial aggregation of indexes and arcane parameters. At a structural level, well-being means most people being able to live in a safe and sustainable environment, now and in future generations. It also means sharing in the material benefits of their labor, in an equitable and persistent way. It implies nurturing networks of social support and solidarity that permit living without want and anguish and experiencing positive interpersonal relations characterized by care and compassion. It also means empowerment and living freely without discrimination, violence, fear, and abuse (Prescott-Allen, 2001). Lastly, it means a set of values, practices, and cognitions that permit people to take charge of their own future and learn from error, so as to provide for environmental sustainability, equitable economic prosperity, social safety networks, peace, and enlightenment. In this sense, development is more than a matter of chance. This is where the connection between induced development and management is important, for development is essentially a historical consequence of human agency.

The concept of management is used here to encompass a whole array of social technologies, practices, and organizational modalities, by which people pursue collective objectives (Kettl, 2000). We are particularly emphasizing one aspect of such management: public management, in the sphere of the *res publica*, the public interest and the political system, whether domestic or international. The term "development administration" is used to mean a style of management and organization in which the state assumes a leading role in facilitating economic prosperity, creating conditions for political development and nation-building, and expanding its role in social security, education, and welfare functions (Dwivedi and Nef, 1982). Finally, globalization, a very ambiguous and loaded term itself, is seen as a multidirectional and open-ended process of economic, social, political, and cultural inclusion, of homogenization and amalgamation (but also exclusion, differentiation, and fragmentation), with multiple impacts upon different peoples and regions. Globalization, as a term, also implies an interdependent and interacting world; it refers to how events, issues, and challenges in one part of the globe affect other parts (Kiggundu, 2002). Ever since development paradigms, under the guise of neoliberalism, have revived the idea of spontaneity and the "invisible hand," globalization has been perceived as an automatic and almost inevitable agent of history.

The history of development management and that of development theory and practice are dotted with policy failures and operational mishaps. This lackluster record can be explained partly by how development administration, and its multiple mutations and reincarnations, has been a field replete with theoretical and practical contradictions. On the whole, development has been persistently conceived as a strategy to bring about Western-style modernization, "progress," and democracy to otherwise poor, underdeveloped nations in what was once referred to as the Third World. More recently, the realm of development management has been extended to the now "transitional" societies of the former socialist "Second" World. As such, it has primarily been an effort by neocolonial elites to morph alien societies by transferring capital, values, and know-how from the Northwestern core to its periphery. Using a language much in vogue today, this strategy is eminently conceived as a soft form of "regime change" *for* "them," but by no means implemented *by* "them," "down there."

Here lies a fundamental paradox: globalization and development for the non-Western world is neither progressive in its effects, nor is it really global, let alone universal. At best, it represents a narrow, albeit dominant, ethnocentric view of the way things ought to be, as prescribed from the vantage point of non-critical outsiders in the developed world. Since its onset in the late 1940s, development mongering has been constructed largely on three conceptual and policy axes. One is the awareness of an accelerated process of decolonization, independence, and "indigenization" of postcolonial nations – in Asia, Africa, the Middle East, the Pacific, and the Caribbean – following World War Two. The other epistemological and political assumption has been that the experience of reconstruction, development (and containment) of the Marshall Plan in Europe could be transplanted to the above-mentioned postcolonial societies. Most important, development had been conceived as a softer side of counterinsurgency in the context of the pervasive Cold War.

Most of the ideas and policies that configured a body of thought and practice over the years evolved from the above circumstances. These materialized in national and multilateral institutions and programs: the UNDP, US AID, Canada's CIDA, the Swedish SIDA, and the United Nations Development Decades (which began in 1961) and a myriad of national development plans and agencies. Critical reflection on these issues led to reform efforts, such as the New International Economic Order under UNCTAD, and to numerous environmental and socioeconomic summits including the World Social Forums (Argyriades, 1988). This leads us to a second paradox: After all this rhetoric and activity for over five decades, disenchantment and disappointment is pervasive in all quarters. Dissatisfaction has ranged from the transnationalized and influential elites, to the disenfranchised masses conspicuously left out, or worse, negatively affected by these policies (Nef, 2002).

What went wrong? Seen from a systemic and historical perspective, it appears that at the threshold of the twenty-first century most people on the planet are confronted with a complex crisis of enormous proportions. The crisis is one of reciprocating dysfunctions in the global ecology, the economy, the society, the polity, and the culture. It is unprecedented in its velocity and magnitude. It is apparent that current styles of development and their management structures have either contributed little to crisis-alleviation, or worse, have been a major ingredient in the generalized insecurity and mutual vulnerability that exists. For the last three decades at least, the highly integrated global economic order has been moving from crisis to crisis, with widespread poverty, misdistribution, unstable growth, and sociopolitical upheavals. The human cost has been borne disproportionately by those least materially endowed to withstand the calamity. Worse, in a sort of global butterfly effect, the entire world has become more vulnerable. Social safety networks and communities have suffered the brunt of dislocation, displacement, and erosion: a dramatic devaluation of social capital. Despite a hope for genuine democratization and peace worldwide following the collapse of the Berlin Wall – and much rhetoric – the bulk of the people on the planet are increasingly disenfranchised from the political process and unable to attain non-violent and manageable levels of conflict-resolution. The political crisis is seen by some as a crisis of democracy; not just one of failed conflict management, or one of "over-participation." Rather, it has been a wider breakdown of legitimacy, transparency, representativeness, inclusion, and effectiveness. Finally, there is a crisis of culture – in values, learning, and ideas – underpinning a structural crisis of material civilization, affecting environmental, economic, social, and political processes. The impact of these negative synergies on development options, and on the organizational and managerial instruments to attain development, is dramatic. The "end of liberalism" and Keynesianism and their replacement by neoliberalism and the associated strategies of New Public Management have not brought about more successful recipes than the "orthodox" developmentalist strategies they pushed aside (Bouckaert and Pollitt, 2003).

This book is divided into four sections, containing a total of eleven chapters. Part I provides a theoretical and historical perspective on the issue of managing development in a global age. It is subdivided into five chapters. Chapter 1 is a mapping expedition of the history of development from the early 1950s, through the Cold War and its aftermath. It examines the politics and economics of development aid, policy failures, and the emergence of a unipolar world with trade liberalization, globalization, and the emphasis on democratic governance. With the onset of the third miillennium, and that of the UN Fifth Development Decade, it appears that many of the assumptions of development, administration, and globalization that we took for granted have become porous.

Chapter 2 deals with the transformation of the notion of development and its discourse from national, to international, to finally the notion of "global development." It examines how interconnected movements in the world economy, technology, and culture have converged since the 1960s to create a tendency toward internationalization and globalization of production, power, and communications at an unprecedented rate.

These global economic forces have decidedly affected the nature of development discourse, and the very nature of development itself. They have also impacted the operation of its public organizations, and their management. For it is at the level of governance and policy-making that transnationalization, globalization, and even deregulation occur. Foreign aid and structural adjustment packages and conditionalities attached to debt management have had the net effect of enhancing centrifugal and denationalizing tendencies. These, combined with crises of governance, fiscal insolvency, and the erosion of legitimacy, have also impacted development and democratic politics. As globalization substitutes for development, and the global idiom becomes the new all-encompassing *mantra*, people's security – environmental, economic, social, political, and cultural – has become increasingly precarious. This discussion sets the stage for the analysis of exclusion.

Chapter 3 explores how development strategies, administrative practices, and power relations have combined to hamper the delivery of public resources intended for those who need it most (namely the rural and urban poor), and exclude them from development. As there is the global poor, there is also the global rich, and the super rich, with little in between. Development, globalization, and management certainly are not class, gender, or ethnically neutral. In fact, the benefits and the burdens are unequally distributed among various socioeconomic groups. Poverty is not just a matter of limited accessibility to wealth and opportunity, but is essentially a political problem of disenfranchisement and exclusion, rooted in exploitation. Thus, political, economic, and social insecurity are closely, though not fatally, interconnected. These insecurities, in turn, are contingent upon a culture – and pedagogy – of insecurity. Globalization, far from bringing in universal democracy, has meant by and large the process of gradual (and at times sudden) de-democratization and loss of popular power, as the state becomes increasingly dependent on external constituencies and conditionalities.

Contingent labor, job and income insecurity, regressive redistribution, and the decline of unions have brought about pauperization in areas of the world where labor absorption through outsourcing from abroad has not been possible. Meanwhile, globalization has benefited regions where the pool of labor is massive and cheap (such as in China and India). But outsourcing has not necessarily helped the poor in these regions, nor labor elsewhere.

Chapter 4 examines the question of development for whom and who benefits from it. In this respect, the collateral damage extant in common developmental wisdom needs to be re-examined from the perspective of those who are either not affected or, more importantly, negatively affected by development. Left alone, the situation could at best reproduce a generally skewed status quo, or at worse threaten those lacking power and influence. These impact biases are even more pronounced when it comes to modernization and induced development. What we call the issue of inclusive vs. "exclusive" development has become an ethical and operational consideration in development management and international cooperation. Gender and ethnic dimensions have been very slowly incorporated into development discourse and practice, though the extent to which these factors are effectively considered remains a subject of controversy. An important aspect of this analysis is the recognition of the necessity for a multidimensional treatment of exclusivity–inclusivity, combining gender, class, ethnicity, and spatial-territorial dimensions of the phenomenon, as they relate to different forms and styles of development and globalization.

Chapter 5 explores two interrelated questions. One is the extent to which there is congruity between unrestricted world trade, on one side, and human rights observance and environmental protection on the other. The second question is more institutional in nature; it concerns the adequacy of the current international mechanisms to harmonize property rights and accumulation by the rich with the sustainable livelihood and dignity of the workers and protection for the global commons. Massive trade and the efficient organization of labor for production are among the leading technological advances of our age. They have also entailed huge costs for people and the environment. Globalization, as conceived today, is primarily about trade and the way to generate greater productivity through the extraction of surplus. It is also about new forms of finance and capital accumulation. Proprietary rights, royalties, and the like have taken an ever greater component of global transactions – concomitant with a displacement of material production – away from the industrial counties and into those regions whose comparative advantage (or incomparable disadvantage) is a seemingly unlimited supply of cheap labor. Outsourcing has become the most prevalent form of production. As previously mentioned, technology is neither gender, nor ethnic, nor class neutral when it comes to development. Its dominant trademark has been to reduce the cost of labor, rather than reducing human toil.

Perhaps the most significant feature of globalization is its reliance on freer trade. Fueled by technological advances, world trade is not only intensifying but is fast transforming the social and cultural fabric of even the most remote regions. Its sole global manager, the World Trade Organization, has been expected to be more sensitive to developing countries' needs than its predecessor, GATT. But, like in the GATT, in the "rule-based" WTO not all members are at the same level of industrial development, and do not share the similar historical experiences produced by industrialization.

Part II examines contemporary paradigms of development and globalization. It is divided into two chapters. Chapter 6 tackles the continuities and changes from the ideas of Development Administration to New Public Management. The former, Development Administration, as a field of study, has been the center-piece of Western comparative public administration. It was tightly tied to its old moorings largely with its still value-laden Northern universalistic design that assumed a single, "rational," competitive, and capitalist world economy. It postulated a number of "principles": pyramidal administrative structures, procedural and financial accountability, the management of human resources, central–local relationships, the departmentalization of ministries, the centrality of parastatals, and smooth linkages with civil society and grassroots groups. All this professional "deontology" was based on practices created and developed in the North, and subsequently transferred to the South.

New Public Management (NPM) was motivated by the paramountcy of modern management principles and private business enterprise in the United States and, to a lesser extent, Japan and Europe. On the whole, it retained – under a seemingly more relativistic mantle – some of the same presuppositions and basically the same ideas of the Administrative Reform Movement it replaced. The empirical source of the "new" managerial know-how have been the generally large and, until then, seemingly efficient transnational corporations. Western academicians coined the New Public Management idiom to refer to a "leaner and meaner" state in the 1990s. The new concept emphasized training, professionalism, customer-orientation, ethics, productivity, responsiveness to the changing demands of business, and global-mindedness. The aims were to reduce bureaucracy and inertia in government and infuse risk-taking and entrepreneurship. Incidentally, these were some of the same values celebrated by the "old" Administrative Reform Movement in the earlier twentieth century – the predecessor of Development Administration. While the West celebrated the "retreat of the state" in the midst of the economic boom of the 1990s, most developing nations faced deprivation, corruption, and retardation in social capital formation. This was often attributed to "subjective" factors, namely that the values of NPM were not embedded in local culture and traditions and therefore its rituals and practices did not bear the expected fruits. In Chapter 6, a number of broadly comparative and operational questions will be addressed: (a) What changes in administrative structures, culture, and behavior have occurred in the "Other World" as a result of economic and political reforms in the past two decades? (b) To what extent do the administrative systems in these regions increasingly present legal-rational characteristics? (c) Are these systems of public administration becoming more efficient and/or effective in delivering services? (d) Is there a noticeable tendency of government agencies to become more, or less, client or service oriented? (e) What is happening to public trust, accountability, and probity and, more specifically, what is the role of corruption in this process? (f) Finally, the perennial question: what has been the extent of public administration's contribution to national and regional development under these auspices?

Chapter 7 examines the notion of sustainable development as an alternative paradigm, by focusing on the debate between rich and poor countries concerning what priority ought to be placed on poverty alleviation and environmental protection. The idea of sustainability in development has fundamentally changed the content and scope of the discussion about styles and effects of development. To begin with, it has challenged the intellectual construction centered on economic development, with the result that the pursuit of economic growth is no longer the core value of development strategy. The history of environmentalism started in June 1972 when a gathering of world leaders took place in Stockholm to discuss environmental issues in a systematic and comprehensive manner. Until then, the physical setting was treated either as an unchanging backdrop for all kinds of unrestricted human activity, or as an almost inexhaustible resource for human exploitation. For the first time questions were asked about global pollution as a mutual problem and its relation to poverty and affluence. The summit in Stockholm also raised questions about the global and generational responsibility shared by the wealthy North in degrading the environment. Finally, the Stockholm sessions confronted various issues pertaining to international responses to environmental problems: the need for all nation-states to abide by international agreements and conventions. In addition to these questions, a clear divide between the poor South and the rich North became visible.

When the 1992 Earth Summit took place in Rio de Janeiro, the world was significantly different from the one that existed in 1972. During those intervening twenty years, the Cold War had ended, the Soviet Union (that had boycotted the Stockholm Conference) was no longer a player, and global markets were expanding at a rapid speed. Moreover, scientific and technological advances had brought nations together. The internet had boosted the power of epistemic communities and many environmental disasters had taken place outlining the futility of national borders to address environmental problems. There was also a reconceptualization of the relationship between environment and development provided by the Brundtland Commission (1987). Most importantly, the end of the decade brought the realization that environmental protection could no longer be regarded as a luxury of the rich. Rather, environmental factors had to be integrated with economic and social issues. Thus, when another gathering of world leaders took place in Johannesburg in 2002, there was a general agreement that the three main pillars for a sustainable world – environmental protection, human development, and economic well-being – could not be kept separate. The complexity and scale of contemporary environmental issues – and of those related to sustainable development – does not permit an exclusive division among nation-states, with their respective sovereignties. The challenge has been how to reform and reinvent the existing world systems to secure a firm place for future generations.

Part III focuses on how current issues and challenges affect the nature of managing development. It is divided into three chapters. Chapter 8 examines the globalization of administrative culture in light of both structural circumstances and development paradigms. Here, the culture of an organization is treated as a kind of "mental software": a set of embedded practices, desired states, and values. Administrative cultures everywhere reflect the distinctiveness and complexity of the various regional, national, and local realities (including their unique historical experiences); their forms of insertion (subordination or domination) into the system of regional and global relations; and their levels of development and fragmentation. An administrative culture is the result of a process of immersion, acculturation, and socialization. There are structural "push factors" or "drivers" that affect the style of management. Some of these factors are implicit and induced through policies, like taxation and education. Most of them, however, are implicit and often invisible preconditions within society. Meanwhile, the circumstances of administering a nation have been increasingly defined by parameters outside the confines of the developing nations themselves.

Administrative culture is understood here in its broadest sense as the modal pattern of values, beliefs, attitudes, and predispositions that characterize and identify any given administrative system. The possibilities for effectively managing development and attaining "good" governance start with the congruity between the culture, the context, the structures, and the functions of entities charged with the task of nation-building and development. The profound and critical understanding of indigenous culture, traditions, and styles of governance is crucial for policy-making and prescription. This discussion sets the stage for the subsequent chapter.

Chapter 9 addresses another challenge: the one posed by the contradictions between governability and governance that underpin the notions of deficit democracy, corruption, and accountability. Is good governance an illusion, or is it an ideology to justify Western superiority? Or, to put it another way, why have so many nations failed to become efficient and effective entities after half-a-century of decolonization and international assistance? And why has corruption emerged as allegedly one of the greatest threats to good governance and sustainable development in lesser developed nations? We introduce the topic of governance, in its often contradictory normative and empirical dimensions. We consider the catchphrase "good governance" used by various bilateral and multilateral agencies and, in doing so, we explore the perceived "obstacles" to such governance. In the chapter we also analyze the impact of corruption on the developmental process, and discuss broader ethical issues emerging from governance and transparency questions. Corruption is complex and involves the interface of public and private interests. It is also systemic more than merely episodic, with cultural and structural predispositions, encompassing the abuse of power, privilege, and a significant lack of accountability. It is not only found in the form of "underdeveloped" petty and manifest transgressions, as when officials demand bribes. There is wholesale corruption too: massive and largely covert and "stealth" corruption, as in the developed world. In the chapter we will also examine the complex interrelationship among development, institutionalization, security, corruption, and globalization. We will specifically explore the proposition that corruption and development are inversely related and that globalization entails a reduction of corruption. Finally, we will deal with the issue of deficit democracy as a challenge for good governance – and an alleged contributor to corruption – and suggest some interpretative and general propositions to mainstream discourse in the study of development.

In Chapter 10 we will analyze the ethical dimensions of development and governance, which are not often addressed in a systematic manner. While ethics and values have always been present in the developmental debate, the normative principles shaping development theories and models have been seen as independent from the values and standpoint perspective of their creators. There is no human action which is not susceptible to blame and praise, or deemed good and/or bad by somebody. When the global mental map was constructed as being configured by three worlds of development – First, Second, and Third – this division was loaded with explicit and implicit value judgements. In the 1950s and 1960s, the newly independent countries were referred to as "backward," "undeveloped," "lesser developed," or "underdeveloped." The terms "developing" and "emerging" were included later. This was a value laden characterization, yet it was rarely recognized as such. Even the term "development" has ethical connotations, as it normally conjures up images of a progress from small to big, poor to rich, and bad (or undesirable) to good. All of these connotations suggest that development as a theory or process has never been devoid from ideological and ethical underpinnings. In this chapter, in addition to differentiating between "ethics *of* development" and "ethics *in* development," issues such as religion, culture, and values, which make up the ethical foundations of development, are discussed. Other relevant and related questions are examined: (a) One is the ethical implications of development challenges in the rapidly globalizing context of the twenty-first century. (b) Another is the extent to which Western theories and practices of development and governance (their basic concepts, assumptions, and beliefs) are really the only value-free options for the entire world. (c) A third question is the significance and ethical implication of indigenous knowledge and alternatives, looking at things like human security, basic needs, the eradication of poverty, and the protection of human dignity. (d) A fourth issue is assessing whether the current crisis of governance faced by many developing nations, and the West itself, is precisely a consequence of the inability of Western thinking to incorporate the substance of other non-Western developmental experiences into the prevailing conceptual mold. In this chapter we will examine these factors as an often contested and conflicting territory where policies and clashes of culture occur. We will discuss the implications of this clash of cultures for development, management, and globalization beyond stereotypes and caricature.

Finally, Part IV, Chapter 11, the last section of our book, takes a retrospective and a prospective view of the analyses and findings made in the previous sections. Our intention here is to integrate the various strands of the discussion and attempt a concluding commentary and a set of suggestions for further analysis. The discussion offered in this chapter, as a part of our concluding arguments, is an attempt to highlight the problems faced not only by developing nations, but by the whole world. It is also a plea for bringing about a sustainable global order; one where the well-being of humankind – the "well-being of nations" – is paramount, where the worst forms of poverty can be eliminated, the status of women and those generally excluded can be improved, and children all over the world can be educated in the foundations of freedom and change. In the final analysis, peace means much more than the absence of war; without justice peace will always be precarious. For as long as a portion of humanity remains insecure, in an interdependent world, this insecurity will affect global security. Security by and for people must be based upon sustainable and equitable development. This central objective in the Millennium Goals can only be achieved through good governance – in both the South and the North. It means above all respect and sensitivity to local customs, indigenous culture, as well as spirituality; thereby bridging the gap between North and South and building a new, more holistic and multicultural course in human history.

References

Argyriades, Demetrios (1988) "The Administrative Problems of International Organizations," in Peter I. Pararas (ed.), *Mélanges en l'honneur de Phedon Vegleris*. Athens: Sakkoulas, vol. 2, pp. 477–90.

Bouckaert, G. and C. Pollitt (2003) *Public Management Reform: a Comparative Analysis*. Second edition. Oxford: Oxford University Press.

Dwivedi, O. P. and Jorge Nef (1982) "Crises and Discontinuities in Development Theory and Administration: the First and Third World Perspective," *Public Administration and Development*, 2, pp. 59–77.

Heady, Ferrel (1979) *Public Administration: a Comparative Perspective*. New York: Marcel Dekker.

Kettl, Donald F. (2000) *The Global Public Management Revolution: a Report on the Transformation of Governance*. Washington DC: Brookings Institution.

Kiggundu, Moses N. (2002) *Managing Globalization in Developing Countries and Transition Economies*. Westport, Connecticut: Praeger.

Nef, Jorge (2002) "Public Administration and Public Sector Reform in Latin America," in Guy Peters and Jon Pierre (eds), *Handbook of Public Administration*. London: Sage Publications, pp. 523–35.

Prescott-Allen, Robert (2001) *The Wellbeing of Nations: a Country-by-Country Index of Quality of Life and the Environment*. Washington DC: Island Press.

Part I

Theoretical and Historical Perspectives

1
A History of Development and Development as History

Development as a concept and as historical narrative

Any assessment of development requires a distinction be made between two interrelated, though distinct, issues. On the one hand, development refers to an actual historical and material occurrence: a significant change in the economic, social, political, and cultural conditions affecting large groups of people. On the other hand, development can be conceived of as a construct, mental picture, or theory about such change. This polisemic but distinctively Western concept of development as progress has evolved: from the Augustinian notion of the ascent of humanity from the City of Man to the City of God guided by divine providence, to the ideas of progress in the Enlightenment, to social evolution, modernity, and the unfolding of human potential. There are many theories of development but until the mid-nineteenth century, real development occurred largely without explicit theories, let alone prescriptions for its inducement.

In practice, human development has been a complex, convoluted, never-linear process. The inscribed and excavated history of the world – that is, the long-range development cycle – has been characterized by the rise and fall of civilizations in a pattern of emergence, expansion, and decay. In other words, development, de-development, and underdevelopment are part of an inextricable and unfolding historical process. If development is equated with the dubious term "civilization," and with material culture, such "development," then, has been occurring for a long time. And so has its opposite. Early empires in Mesopotamia, the Nile, the Mediterranean, China, India, and Rome extended their cultures, power, and wealth under the mantle of civilizing

17

otherwise "barbarian" peoples. Something similar occurred with the expansion of Islam and the Crusades during the Middle Ages. These civilizing drives, for all their universal pretensions, were nevertheless relatively confined in scope; for all their claims of universalism they were not truly global.

The Spanish re-Conquest in the late fifteenth century followed, in general, a similar trajectory and was driven by the religious motive of Christianization and the more mundane quest for wealth and territory. What was novel about it, however, is how the expansion and configuration of a unified Castilian empire under Ferdinand and Isabella in 1492 did not stop with the expulsion of the Moorish kingdoms of southern Spain. In a sense, the re-Conquest was a precursor of the early stages of the so-called discovery, and subsequent conquest and settlement, of the New World laying across the Atlantic. It also started a mercantile rivalry for global hegemony between two naval and commercial global superpowers: Spain and Portugal. With both Christian kingdoms fighting for supremacy over the global monopoly of sugar and spice, the foundations were laid for a form of global imperialism, one in which the papacy acted as mediator and regulator. In fact, the *Bulla Intercaetera* of 1493, issued by Pope Alexander VI and formalized in the Treaty of Tordesillas (1494), divided the world into two spheres of influence. The eastern hemisphere, beginning 370 leagues west of Cape Verde, was to be Portugal's domain. The hemisphere to the west of this line would be Spain's. This meant the Spanish crown (with the exception of Brazil that was at the east of that circumpolar line) had control over the New World, while Portugal dominated the trade routes in Africa, India, and Asia.

This embryonic global regime provided the foundations for an evolving world system whose *de facto* and *de jure* characteristics took shape in the mercantilism of the seventeenth century. In the 1600s, the Netherlands displaced Portugal, and England had made an ever growing dent into the Spanish empire – an empire upon which "the sun never set." Power, prestige, and wealth were heavily dependent on a center–periphery arrangement. In such an arrangement, colonies would provide labor, cheap and abundant raw materials (cotton, sugar cane, tobacco, cocoa, sisal, spices, and minerals), as well as markets for European-produced consumer goods for elite consumption. The plantation, the mining town, or the cattle ranch became the new features of this trading and production system. Growing labor shortages produced by the decimation of the local populations in the New World were addressed by the slave trade. Global production, trade, and distribution were dramatically globalized. Specialization and the international division of labor produced a self-perpetuating and expanding system of unequal exchanges, based upon the trading of commodities and the super-exploitation of workers.

This mode of global accumulation set in motion the process of "development" in modern Europe, while conversely laying the foundation for the "underdevelopment" of the conquered and colonized territories in the Americas, Africa, and Asia. The collapse of the highly sophisticated Aztec and Inca empires in the sixteenth century, and the decimation of the pre-Columbian Amerindian way of life, was paralleled by the impact of the slave trade in East and West Africa, the conquest of India in the eighteenth century, and the subjugation of China in the nineteenth century. Highly advanced and complex civilizations were uprooted: from being "traditional," to use the jargon of the colonizers, to becoming "backward" in the process of being modernized and civilized.

While the issue of "development" was not directly addressed in the emerging mercantilist and classical economic literature of the mid-to-late eighteenth century, notions such as prosperity and the "wealth of nations" appeared prominently. The mercantile policies of Colbert, Campomanes, Campillo y Cosío, in the seventeenth and eighteenth centuries, as well as those of late eighteenth-century free trading theorists such as Smith and Ricardo, explicitly linked prosperity to trade. Both camps disagreed radically on the issues of protectionism and the role of government, but trade was seen by both as the main source of prosperity. Much of this literature also recognized the association between labor, value, productivity, and capital formation, with the latter two directly related to wealth and national power. It could be said that with the emergence of classical economics (or what was termed "moral philosophy" at the time) there was a clear understanding of the question of economic growth (the "wealth" of nations) and its conditions, including comparative advantages, trade, competition, and the like.

Of course, even the most progressive of economic and political thinkers in the eighteenth and early nineteenth centuries paid little attention to issues of labor, exploitation, or even the notion of "nature." The latter was conceived as something to be conquered, an obstacle to be overcome and over which humans had dominion. Humans, as laid out in Scripture, had a manifest destiny vis-à-vis nature and the so-called "lesser breeds without the law." In fact, the very term "exploitation" was used at first with a positive connotation: making nature productive (as a resource) and tame for human benefit. The concept was made synonymous with the Enlightenment notion of "progress." The idiom "exploitation of labor" only entered common usage as a sort of metaphorical equivalent to natural resource exploitation – a critical and moral reference of the downside of liberalism and the industrial revolution. The American and the French Revolutions may have been over the "rights of man," understood as those of the bourgeois Third Estate, vis-à-vis aristocratic privilege, but they were largely silent about socioeconomic equity.

In the nineteenth century, the associated meanings of progress, development, and growth were firmly established in mainstream intellectual and conventional discourse. Development (literally meaning "unfolding") and growth were understood as spontaneous occurrences, where rational market and individual forces based upon comparative advantages would lead to prosperity and a "modern" way of life. Clearly, this teleological view of history assumed the existence of a preordained pattern of stages, whether implicit or explicit, leading to an unfolding of the modern as a final stage. *"Laissez-faire"* represented a scientific position and an article of faith: progressive, stable, and orderly change. Increasingly, this discourse blended with the emerging notions of social evolution, as in Herbert Spencer's sociology. Only utopian socialists, the likes of Fourier, Owen, or Saint Simon, or subsequently "scientific socialists," like Marx and Engels, insisted on the distinctively exploitative nature of capitalism and the dysfunctional and catastrophic nature of economic cycles.

This is not to say that there were no economic thinkers and practitioners that believed that progress and modernity could be directed and accelerated by government intervention and planning. There were nineteenth-century examples, such as Paraguay under the militarist regimes of Vicente López and his son, Francisco Solano López, and in Brazil under the guidance of the Viscount of Mauá, where induced industrialization took place. Most notable, however, was the successful example of Wilhemian Germany, under the unifying Prussian control of Prince Otto von Bismarck and influenced by the writings of economist Georg Friedrich List. Nation-building, modernization, authoritarianism, and industrialization combined under a project of induced development and modernization, changing the nature of the development game from spontaneous to government directed. Meiji Japan, inspired by the Prussian example, followed this lead. By the 1890s, the once-feudal Nippon had become an industrial giant, challenging European predominance in Asia, and in subsequent years beyond its regional confines.

Most important, however, was the reinvention of socialism under Lenin in the new Soviet Union. Marx had envisaged the collective ownership of the means of production as something almost naturally emerging from the contradictions of advanced capitalism. Socialism was a way to redistribute the prosperity and surplus value generated by the exploitation of labor, turning the tables on, and expropriating, the bourgeoisie. That the first socialist revolution took place in a huge, backward, and sparsely industrialized country like Tsarist Russia presented the dilemma of growth versus distribution. Planned development – Lenin's "New Economic Policy" (NEP) – under the Soviet regime became a conscious strategy to catch up by means of further exploiting the workers and postponing the establishment of communism. From a productive point of view the Soviet model paid off. In less than half a century it had been able to transform a decaying empire into a military and industrial superpower, albeit at tremendous social and environmental cost.

But induced development, as suggested earlier, has not been, by any means, the exclusive domain of socialism. In the 1930s, and at the heels of the Great Depression, European fascism, Latin American populism, and the American New Deal applied Keynesian formulas based upon planning and the Administrative State to survive the economic slump and prosper. The American experience with the New Deal under the F. D. Roosevelt administration is of particular importance in this discussion. Not only was this model successful through the early period of economic hardship (1930–4), World War Two (1939–45, for the US since 1941) and the subsequent postwar economy, but it provided a blueprint for the international challenges of the postwar era.

The origins of developmental theory and discourse are found explicitly in the experience of post-World War Two European reconstruction under the Marshall Plan (Sanger, 1969: 179). Development practice was born under the sign of the Cold War and its subsequent study and theorizing has been the bearer of this legacy ever since. The relationship between development and containment, articulated in President Truman's Point Four program in the late 1940s, and in the early 1960s in the Colombo Plan, the Alliance for Progress (1961–9), and in the United Nations Development Decades (since 1961), gave development theory and praxis a distinct ideological and controversial flavor. In this sense, development became a surrogate for counterinsurgency: plainly a counterrevolutionary strategy (Nef and Dwivedi, 1981: 12).

The underlying reasoning was that social turmoil and revolutionary activity were greatly facilitated by poverty and inequity. Therefore, distributive justice *per se* was not an ethical imperative, but a means to prevent radical social change. In turn, equity was seen as contingent upon an expansion of capabilities, and growth a fundamental condition to preserve the status quo. Stanley (1961), in a book sponsored by the Council for Foreign Relations in the US, explained it this way:

> The future of underdeveloped countries in Asia, Africa, and parts of Europe and the Americas is a vital matter for the future of Western civilization, including, of course, the security and the way of life of the American people. Economic development of these areas in cooperation with the West is a necessary part of the conditions for Western survival and for the survival in the world of some of the West's most important contributions to human progress . . . Should the Communist power bloc, however, succeed in bringing most of the underdeveloped countries into their orbit and cutting their links with us, the effect in our security would be enormous. (Stanley, 1961: 3–4)

This same rationale underscored the above-mentioned Colombo Plan and, even more so, President Kennedy's Alliance for Progress (1961) (Levinson and de Onis, 1975). In turn, the other superpower, the Soviet Union, after chastizing foreign aid as a form of imperial bribery, turned actively to financing and providing technology for development in Third World nations. After the Eisenhower administration rebuked Egypt's President Nasser and refused to support the hydroelectric complex in Aswan, Premier Khrushchev eagerly provided massive assistance (Mason, 1997). The aid package, like that of its Western counterparts, was also linked to military assistance in weapons procurement and training. This allowed the USSR to wield considerable influence in the non-aligned movement, just emerging from the Bandung Conference of 1955. Soviet aid to Africa and other Third World nations, such as India, the Arab world, and even Iran, then a US pawn, was soon to follow. These policies culminated in massive support for Cuba, after its revolution (1959) and the subsequent confrontation between Premier Castro and the United States.

Multilateral development efforts, implemented through the United Nations, its functional agencies (ILO, FAO, WHO, UNESCO), and the UNDP were formally at "arm's length" from dominant Western donors. Yet, they carried out programs with a heavy Eurocentric and US-centric conception of development. This was also true of regional organizations such as the various development banks in Asia, Africa, and Latin

America. In turn, the pseudo multilateral agencies, like the World Bank (by and large the most important international source of IGO finance) and the IMF, unabashedly pushed pro-Western, market-oriented policies under the guise of aid. The very concept of development as teleology was automatically translated into the deontology (or means) of foreign aid.

Since the UN's First Development Decade, various and powerful discourses opposing Western orthodoxy have emerged. Terms and concepts such as "another development," "basic human needs," "appropriate technology" (Schumacher, 1973), "gender and development," "microcredit," "environmental sustainability," "sustainable livelihoods" (Thompson 2001),[1] and "human security" (Nef, 1999) have been employed when analyzing Western development models and their far-reaching effects.

However, these challenges to the hegemony of modernity and Western ideology have been, time and time again, effectively deconstructed, homogenized, and trivialized. In sum, they have been rendered harmless by a bureaucratic and intellectual culture embedded in the practices of bilateral and multilateral agencies. At present, the resilience of the modernization discourse resides in the mantra of restructuring, transition, and globalization. International development studies today, like Development Administration in the not so distant past, has become largely a "fence around an empty lot" (Nef and Dwivedi, 1981: 12).

Even a cursory look at the history of development illustrates how, since the Cold War, the concept of development has become highly politicized and increasingly devoid of substantive meaning. This emptiness of the development idiom became prevalent irrespective as to whether a country was a client of the West, or the East, or found itself in the increasingly anti-Western non-aligned movement. Some forms of bilateral aid, as in the case of Sweden, attempted to remain at the margins of developmental bipolarity. Yet the bulk of bilateral assistance was unequivocally related to the explicit pursuit of one or another socioeconomic and political development models (Jaguaribe, 1968)[2]: national capitalism, socialism, or a "mixed economy."

Undoubtedly, the politicization of development practices has profound ethical implications. First, any development strategy will identify and define possible allies and opponents, friends and foes, and will chart the political alliances that support and oppose development efforts. Second, the choice of strategy in a sense also constructs and predetermines both "winners" and "losers" in the development game.

Third, it presupposes the presence of external constituencies (Nef and Bensabat, 1992: 77) for and against development options. Fourth, these constituencies, beyond their level of contribution, have a controlling interest in the content and course of development projects. Fifth, external aid packages increasingly become a built-in "carrot and stick," clientelistic device, geared to rewarding or punishing Third Word elites for their compliant or defiant behavior toward dominant actors. As many critics have posited, aid has not only been confused with "development," but it has also evolved into a subtle form of imperialism (Hayter, 1974: 15–24).[3]

For Escobar, the very notion of development, as a Western ideological construct, encapsulated the purpose, the practices, and the subjects of the process (Escobar, 1984: 370). In so doing, it also defined a dominant–subordinate structure of expert knowledge reinforcing economic, political, and technological elite control (and clientelism) extant in development practices. This "culture of development" generated its own ethical foundation. It established the predominance of Western values, ideology, religion, language, morals, and standards, to which peripheral peoples could aspire but never fully achieve. Moreover, development and development assistance were rewards for good behavior. In this sense, in Freire's terms, the pedagogy of development was largely one of oppression, not of liberation (Freire, 1971).

While the discourse of development and development assistance was couched in benign and idealistic terminology, in apparent contrast to the brutal realism of the Cold War, its practical effects were, more often than not, quite the opposite of what development theorists and practitioners had promised. The "development-of-underdevelopment" thesis of those espousing a dependency perspective (Frank, 1992) was reified in the foreign aid field even more dramatically than in the realm of foreign investment. This pervasive double standard configured a profound ethical breach as a deceiving practice hiding either strategic/ military goals, economic gain for the aid-givers, or both. The poor record of development and its associated problems – including the inability to effect change, enrichment at the cost of the poor, the collateral damage of modernization, the hypocrisy of foreign assistance, and the absconding of development funding by corrupt and parasitic elites – are direct results of this contradiction.

The accumulation of "horror stories" regarding development created a predisposition, not only in the public at large but also among scholars, to perceive it in an increasingly negative light. As far as the world scenario is concerned, the end of the Cold War and the collapse of the "other side" made development assistance less glamorous and development-as-counterinsurgency increasingly irrelevant. The result has been an ontological and ethical void where buzzwords and conceptual pyrotechnics have substituted for development – and human dignity.

International development: conservative versus critical predilections

The study of international development is the result of a juxtaposition of several conceptual traditions, or "cultures."

One of these traditions is the general field of development, where theories of growth (subsequently, development economics and economic development) (Higgins, 1959), political development, and modernization prevail. Almost without exception, the intellectual bases of this tradition have been derived from the logical-positivist and highly linear disciplinary tenets in economics, sociology, and political science, each of them dominated by Western thinking. References to diffusion, "trickle down," the particularistic–universalistic and agrarian–industrial dichotomies – articulated in Parsons' "pattern variables" (Parsons, 1967) and much earlier on in Spencer's evolutionary sociology – are prevalent in this discourse. These tenets are predicated on the assumption of an objective and value-free social science. The fundamental ethical implication of this posture is that the guiding principle in the study of development is "normative neutrality." That is, theory, research, and findings are to remain detached from politics and ideology. Some critics have characterized this stand as a compelling "ideology of non-ideology" of which the ultimate political effect is the justification of the status quo. The continuity of a "conservative-liberal" synthesis in political thinking (from Cold War liberalism down to neo-institutionalism and public choice) finds its correlate in the conservative predilections of economic theory (Myrdal, 1957), and the tendency of contemporary sociology to go "micro," to cast away political sociology, and abandon structural and critical thinking.

In the specific realm of political science, the equation between political development and participatory democracy, a normative ideal of the 1960s, had been displaced in the 1970s by a definition emphasizing order, institutionalization, and authority (Cruise O'Brien, 1972). Under the rubric of the *Crisis of Democracy* (Huntington, 1975), participation in the "input" side of politics was seen as the major impediment to governability at the "output" side, eventually leading to chaos, praetorianism, and mob rule. The same was true of the ideological shift regarding social mobilization and the belief that economic growth could, of its own, bring greater equality. A pervasive form of Machiavellian political conservatism increasingly replaced the liberal-democratic hybrid of the postwar years. The ethical implications of this definition of political development are quite straightforward. The need for order and the maintenance of property relations override human rights and due process: liberalism and democracy, liberty and equality end up in contradiction. Subjects replace citizens.

Under the mantle of alleged ethical neutrality, conventional development theory and praxis have also exhibited a distinct missionary and moral perspective, building models and creating prescriptions for induced socioeconomic change. A most compelling formula representing the marriage between economic science, Western manifest destiny, and militant anti-communism – and a cornerstone of development orthodoxy – was Walter Rostow's *The Stages of Economic Growth: a Non-Communist Manifesto* (1960). Politically, Rostow was a liberal economist, an advisor to President Kennedy, and an early architect of the administration's policy in Vietnam: the archetype of a Cold War liberal. He was also known to be a highly moralistic man. So was the case with his associate, Robert McNamara, in both of his incarnations: as the "hawkish" Secretary of Defense and as the latter-day "dove" President of the World Bank. What Bodenheimer (1970) called the "ideology of developmentalism" was essentially a messianic form of anti-communist social engineering reproducing a postcolonial discourse. In it, the world order and the very ontology of development *for* poor nations was seen from Northwestern eyes (Berger, 1995).

Conservative realism vs. Cold War liberalism

Another tradition came from the "international" component of development theory, namely the highly ethnocentric and hard-line perspective of International Relations. Schooled under the mantle of "realism," most International Relations analysts ignored the Third World; a few among them saw development primarily as a goal and as a tool of foreign policy. The latter was perceived as conditioned by the objective parameters of bipolarity and the pursuit of national security. Development policies, in a Cold War context, were equated with bilateral foreign aid. Its role was the spread of modernization in client states, basically as a means to enhance the donor's national interests.

For the more liberal students of the multilateral realm of international organizations – where the more palatable term "cooperation" was widely used – international development was understood primarily as capital and technology transfers between North and South. A persistent belief in this regard was the notion of "mutuality" (Pearson, 1969), enthusiastically endorsed by Prime Minister Pearson of Canada and the framers of the United Nations' First Development Decade. Multilateral and regional agencies ostensibly mediated these center–periphery interactions. From this perspective, development assistance was simultaneously a moral imperative, a necessity for enhancing enlightened self-interests, and a means of peaceful change in peripheral societies.

The involvement of the Soviet Union in the development assistance game added a centrally planned perspective to an essentially Northern domain. Regardless of whether the assistance was bilateral or multilateral, the prevailing view was that the development of the South (alternatively referred to as the Third World, or as developing, underdeveloped, lesser-developed, backward, or poor) was contingent upon the international system, not the countries themselves. Thus, the periphery was portrayed not only as having the (Northern-defined) problem of underdevelopment, but also as being *the* problem itself. Conversely, the center was construed as not only having the solution, but also *being* the solution. The ethical implications of this view are obvious: to develop, the LDCs had to be Westernized. This could be done either by replacing their "traditional" structures and institutions or, more so, by changing their value system and culture away from agrarian "amoral familism" (Banfield, 1965) and into a modern, industrial, achievement-oriented existence.

As the Cold War drew to a close, the realism of the "nuclear theologians" and the National Security doctrine appeared to fade into the background. An integrated consensus theory of international regimes came in the form of Keohane and Nye's (1977) "complex interdependence." For its followers, global transactions, as in von Hayek's neoclassical notion of "catalaxia" (Hayek, 1976: 5), constituted a web of essentially cooperative economic relations, heavily centered on trade and elite networks. Trade liberalization and deregulation, and the construction of business-controlled transnational regimes, not aid or cooperation, were seen as the engines of development. Admittedly, the notion of complex interdependence, which gave ideological justification to the Trilateralist, or Davos' views of the world, was constructed with the explicit purpose to counteract both conservative realism and "radical" dependency theories (Keohane and Nye, 1977). In this essentially neoliberal view of world politics, the main historical agent had shifted from the "prince" to the "merchant" (Nerfin, 1986), but, in the same manner as its predecessor, at the expense of the citizen and the bulk of civil society. Ethically, a neo-materialism of the right becomes a dominant discourse. In it, the "objective" laws of the market define the logic and preferences for maximizing individual choices. What is real is rational, what is rational is real. Systemic welfare is a function of the aggregate equilibrium of these rational choices.

Development and area studies

A third intellectual tradition came from area studies, or more specifi-cally, developing area studies. As in the case of the previous two tradi-tions, the origins of area studies are found in post-World War Two circumstances. For the United States, the occupation of Germany and especially Japan had forced a banding together of all disciplines and the emergence of interdisciplinary area studies. It also led to generous financing of research centers in universities. Subsequently, private foundations such as Rockefeller and Ford – especially the latter's Foreign Area Studies Fellowship Program, created in 1952 – were instrumental in laying the groundwork. However, it was not until the National Defense Education Act (NDEA) of 1958, that area studies became insti-tutionalized. Area studies linked the need to know by the defense and security establishments, academia, and the government (Pye, 1975: 13), all this in a charged bipolar context.

Decolonization conflicts in Africa and turmoil in Asia and Latin America gave impetus to the expansion of these initiatives under the rubric of developing area studies. In line with the model of the military-industrial complex, academia provided sophisticated intelligence analysis for the national economic, political, and military elites. This maximized the pursuit of the national interest, and the idea was that it would contain communism, while at the same time facilitate the development of foreign countries to maintain prosperity and harmony at home. The model of multidisciplinary centers soon spread through-out North America and Europe. Latin American, Asian, African, and Middle Eastern studies emerged side-by-side to accompany the research and teaching of developed areas, such as European and Eastern Euro-pean studies.

Over the years, development and area studies programs and centers converged with the developmental dimensions of politics and econom-ics and with the foreign aid policy component of International Rela-tions and International Studies. The result was the emergence of international development programs, where the above-mentioned traditions coexisted without a meaningful epistemological or ontological – let alone ethical – synthesis. Governmental financing largely facilitated this convergence. The creation of agencies for international development (US AID, CIDA, IDRC, SIDA) came to provide potential sources of project funding, and the pervasiveness of the "international development" idiom encapsulated theory and practice overseas.

Development theory and development practice converged with administrative and managerial theories and practices after the end of World War Two. The result of this convergence was the Marshall Plan. This model of reconstruction and development, and its Keynesian assumptions of induced modernization, were subsequently applied to bring prosperity and democracy to the emerging nations resulting from decolonization. The context of this approach was the rigid bipolarity of the Cold War, when both camps competed for more than simply the hearts and minds of people. For the West, confronted with what appeared then as the unstoppable march of history, development became a form of counterinsurgency to prevent destabilization on the other side. By the early 1970s, during the United Nations' Second Development Decade, this orthodoxy had run its course. Neoliberalism replaced the Keynesian recipes, while new views of public sector management, such as New Public Management (NPM), displaced the old notions of the Administrative State.

As neoliberalism displaced some of the old Keynesian presuppositions, increasingly the very notion of development has been pushed aside. In its place, the term "globalization" gained support among business elites, politicians, and their institutional intellectuals. This topic will be addressed in greater detail in the next chapter. What is persistent, however, is that irrespective of these shifts in theory, ideology, and, above all, prescriptions; the human predicament has followed its own often haphazard course. So has development discourse. The new phraseology still contains the same *telos*, ethnocentric biases, and sense of manifest destiny and imperial intent that its predecessors had. The new facade, however, is trilateral more than unilateral, as it includes Europe, Japan and the globally integrated business elite. As we head into the UN Fifth Development Decade, it appears that many of the assumptions of development, administration, and the world order we took for granted do not hold true any longer. What has persisted, however, is a system of unequal exchanges that under any name is objectively harmful to the security of most of the inhabitants of the planet.

References

Banfield, Edward (1965) *The Moral Basis of the Backward Society.* Chicago: Free Press.

Berger, Michael (1995) *Under Northern Eyes: Latin American Studies and US Hegemony in the Americas 1898–1900.* Bloomington: Indiana University Press.

Bodenheimer, Suzanne (1970) "The Ideology of Developmentalism: American Political Science Paradigm-Surrogate for Latin American Studies," *Berkeley Journal of Sociology,* 15, pp. 95–137.

Cruise O'Brien, Donal (1972) "Modernization, Order, and the Erosion of a Democratic Ideal: American Political Science 1960–1970," *Journal of Development Studies,* 8, 4 (July), pp. 351–78.

Davies, Susanna and Naomi Hossain (1997) "Livelihood, Adaptation, Public Action and Civil Society: a Review of the Literature," IDS Working Paper 57. Institute of Development Studies, University of Sussex, Brighton, UK, July.

Escobar, Arturo (1984) "Discourse and Power in Development: Michel Foucault and the Relevance of His Work for the Third World," *Alternatives,* 10, Winter, pp. 370–400.

Frank, Andre Gunder (1992) "The Development of Underdevelopment," in Charles Wilber and Kenneth Jameson (eds), *The Political Economy of Development and Underdevelopment.* Fifth edition. New York: McGraw-Hill, pp. 107–18.

Freire, Paulo (1971) *Pedagogy of the Oppressed.* New York: Herder and Herder.

Goulet, Denis and Michael Hudson (1971) *The Myth of Aid: the Hidden Agenda of the Development Reports,* New York: IDOC Books.

Hawkins, E. K. (1970) *The Principles of Development Aid.* Harmondsworth: Penguin.

Hayek, Friedrich (1976) *Law, Legislation and Liberty: a New Statement of the Liberal Principles of Justice and Political Economy,* Volume II: *The Mirage of Social Justice.* Chicago: University of Chicago Press.

Hayter, Teresa (1974) *Aid as Imperialism.* Harmondsworth: Penguin.

Hensman, C. R. (1975) *Rich Against Poor: the Reality of Aid.* Harmondsworth: Penguin.

Higgins, Benjamin (1959) "The General Nature of the Development Problem," in Higgins, *Economic Development: Principles, Problems and Policies.* New York: W. W. Norton, pp. 3–24.

Huntington, Samuel (1968) "Political Development and Political Decay," in Robert Kebshull (ed.), *Politics in Transitional Societies: the Challenge to Change in Asia, Africa and Latin America.* New York: Appleton Century Crofts, pp. 288–93.

Huntington, Samuel, Michel Crozier, and Joji Watanuki (1975) *The Crisis of Democracy. Report on the Governability of Democracies to the Trilateral Commission,* Triangle Papers No. 8. New York: New York University Press.

Institute for Development Studies (IDS) and DFID, Livelihoods Connects (2002) "Frequently Asked Questions on the Sustainable Livelihoods Approach," June 20, pp. 4–15, www.livelihoods.org/enquirydesk/enquiryfaq.html.

Jaguaribe, Helio (1968) *Economic and Political Development: a Theoretical Approach and a Brazilian Case Study.* Cambridge, MA: Harvard University Press.

Keohane, Robert and Joseph Nye (1977) *Power and Interdependence: World Politics in Transition*. Boston: Little, Brown and Co.

Lappe, Frances Moore, Joseph Collins, and David Kinley (1980) *Aid as Obstacle: Twenty Questions About Our Foreign Aid and the Hungry*. San Francisco: Institute for Food and Development Policy.

Levinson, Jerome and Juan de Onis (1975) *The Alliance that Lost its Way: a Critical Report on the Alliance for Progress*. Chicago: Quadrangle Books.

Mason, Mike (1997) *Development and Disorder: a History of the Third World since 1945*. Toronto: Between the Lines.

Myrdal, Gunnar (1957) "The Conservative Predilections of Economic Theory and Their Foundation in the Basic Principles," in Myrdal, *Rich Lands and Poor Lands: the Road to World Prosperity*. New York: Harper and Brothers, pp. 137–49.

Nef, J. (1999) *Human Security and Mutual Vulnerability: the Political Economy of Development and Underdevelopment*. Ottawa: IDRC Books.

Nef, J. and Remonda Bensabat (1992) "Governability and the Receiver State in Latin America: Analysis and Prospects," in A. Ritter, M. Cameron, and D. Pollock (eds), *Latin America and the Caribbean to the Year 2000*. New York: Praeger, pp. 161–76.

Nef, J. and O. P. Dwivedi (1981) "Development Theory and Administration: a Fence Around an Empty Lot?" *Indian Journal of Public Administration*, 27, 1, pp. 42–66.

Nerfin, Marc (1986) "Neither Prince nor Merchant: Citizen – An Introduction to the Third System," IFDA Dossier No. 56, Nov.–Dec., pp. 3–28.

Parsons, Talcott (1967) *Sociological Theory and Modern Society*. New York: Free Press.

Pearson, Lester (Chairman of the Commission) (1969) *Partners in Development. Report of the Commission on International Development*. New York: Praeger.

Pye, Lucian (1975) "The Confrontation between Discipline and Area Studies," in Pye (ed.), *Political Science and Area Studies, Rivals or Partners?* Bloomington: Indiana University Press.

Rostow, Walter W. (1960) *The Stages of Economic Growth: a Non-Communist Manifesto*. Cambridge, MA: Harvard University Press.

Sanger, Carl (1969) "Pearson's Eulogy," *International Journal*, 325.

Schumacher, Ernst Friedrich (1973) *Small is Beautiful: Economics as if People Mattered*. Vancouver: Hartley and Marks.

Stanley, Eugene (1961) *The Future of Underdeveloped Countries: Political Implications of Economic Development*. New York: Praeger.

Thompson, Anne (2001) "Food Security and Sustainable Livelihoods: a Policy Challenge," *Development*, 44, 4, pp. 24–8.

2
Globalization and the Transnationalization of the State[1]

Globalization

Since the 1960s, reciprocating transformations in the world order have converged, resulting first in growing internationalization and subsequently the globalization of production, power, and communications at an extraordinary rate. In addition, the penetrability of boundaries brought about by the Cold War, combined with the emergence of transnational corporations, has induced a weakening of national sovereignty in all but a small group of powerful nation-states. And even in some of these very same dominant nations, internationalization and regionalization have produced a kind of limited statehood. These same forces have also affected the nature of the development process itself and that of the public and private organizations that manage this development.

The momentous transformation of the world system affecting both its overall structure (polarity) and those of its constituting regimes, referred to under the generic and contested term "globalization," is rooted in several changing and interconnected circumstances. These could be grouped into three main categories. The first set of factors is the deep and long-range changes effected by an age of pervasive technology (Nef et al., 1988). In this case, we are referring specifically to the multiple and far-reaching innovations in the exchange of information and knowledge that have occurred since the end of World War Two. The second set of factors affecting global systemic change involves alterations in the ideological-political matrix, which define the cultural polarities in the system. More specifically, we are referring here to the sharp divide between Marxist-Leninism and liberal capitalism, which characterized the Cold War, followed by the sudden disappearance of one of these ideologies in the late 1980s. From this alleged "end of history" there emerged both the hegemony of neoliberalism and the cultural fundamentalism permeating the supposed "clash of civilizations." The third and perhaps most important set of circumstances are those related to alterations in the economic fabric, or basis of the world order: the transformation of world economics from international trade and finance among nations into global and transnational economics. The nature of trade itself has also been altered, from the predominance of the tangible and "visible" manufactures and commodities of the past to the "invisible" trade of intangible services, derivatives and the like.

Technology

Over the course of the last fifty years, the development of technology has increased exponentially. It has affected the nature of the world system in two ways. One is the impact of technological innovation upon the instruments of war, both hard (like weapons) and soft (military doctrines and organizational modalities). The other effect of technology on the world system involves the dramatic improvement in the speed and reach of communications and transportation. Information, finance, goods, people, and troops have become more mobile than in any previous period of human history. The development of military and industrial technology since World War Two to the present reduced the time and space limits of world politics. What were once international relations – understood as "politics among nations" – progressively and unavoidably has become global politics (Blake and Walters, 1976). In this context, domestic concerns are nowadays so intertwined with "external" factors as to make the distinction between what is national and global merely semantic. The long-range effects of technological permeability on the territoriality of nation-states, and upon the very idea of sovereignty, have been overwhelming.

Ideology

However, more important than the technological changes mentioned above have been the transformations of the ideological parameters since the end of World War Two. The period between 1945 and 1989 was defined by a clash of two cultures: liberal capitalism and state socialism. The semantic foundations of this binary and Manichean worldview conveyed an inescapable logic: alignment as either friend or foe. Its corollary was a rigid ideological bipolarity between two incompatible camps which permeated national boundaries.

The emergence of Third World nationalism expressed in Bandung in 1955 was a reaction against this sharp ideological schism. Yet, non-alignment and the attempts to separate North–South issues from East–West confrontations, paradoxically increased a proclivity for clientelism, entangled alliances, and ultimately facilitated the transnationalization of peripheral states. Foreign aid, the international transfer of technology, manpower training, planning and administration, and the all-pervasive presence of military assistance during the Cold War increased reliance on external constituencies. Peripheral elites were integrated into a global structure by means of manifold linkages of complex dependency (Nef, 1983, 1986). This dependency, beyond its economic implications, manifested itself in political and cultural spheres.

This patron–client structure was developed by both power blocs, creating structural conditions built into the nature of nation-states that persevered even after the demise of the USSR. Bilateral dependency relations, irrespective of who occupied the center, have had a tendency to persist. External constituencies have become, and remain, an intrinsic part of the political alliances that participate in the internal public policy process. There have been also significant multilateral forms of transnationalization. These result from the development and expansion of international law and international organizations and because of the need for regional security. Furthermore, the Cold War legacy of collective defense and collective security, not to mention a complex body of international contract law based on trade, has further limited territorial sovereignty. In most parts of the world – the United States being the most noticeable exception – the centrality of past elite nationalism has been displaced by elite internationalism.

Correspondingly, in an increasingly unipolar world, a global ideology with hegemonic pretensions has gained predominance among the core sectors within the Group of 7 (now, with the inclusion of Russia, Group of 8) countries. This ideology is Trilateralism (Sklar, 1980), which is merely another name for neoliberalism. Substantively, the cultural software of this "New International" is distinctively free-trading, elitist, and monistic. The Trilateral view has a wide appeal to the affluent, globally integrated, and modern elite sectors in what used to be called the Third and Second Worlds. Its intellectual antecedents are partly rooted in nineteenth-century social Darwinism and partly in the messianic universalism of neoclassical economics.

Economy

The two central polarities that emerged since World War Two among *national* actors – between North and South and East and West – were replaced, after 1989, by a single core–periphery axis of relations. The

Western core, the First World, remained as it was: an interdependent and stratified bloc of dominant trading partners. Yet, the other two worlds collapsed into one heterogeneous conglomerate including "newly industrializing," "developing," "poor," and the "transitional societies" of the former socialist camp. As said earlier, the core–periphery conflict occurs *mainly between social sectors* within both the developed and the lesser-developed societies. It takes place between transnationally integrated and affluent elites and their related clienteles and a large and fragmented conglomerate of subordinate sectors at the margins of the modern and integrated global society (Sunkel, 1973).

In this more interconnected world, poverty is spreading faster than ever before in this, the most prosperous age in human history. The problem is clearly not one of production, as the world economy continues to grow faster than its population, but of distribution. While there were 157 billionaires and about 2 million millionaires in 1989, there were also 1.2 billion inhabitants of the planet living in absolute poverty, including 100 million living without shelter (Brown, 1993). A 1993 UNDP report noted that the wealthiest 20 percent of humanity received 82.7 percent of the world's income. The historical trend is even more revealing. While in 1960 the income differential between the better-off 20 percent of the world's population and the bottom 20 percent was a ratio of 30 to 1, in 1991, that distance had more than doubled to 61 to 1. By 1997, the income gap was 74.1 to 1.[2] If one examines these figures in terms of the acceleration of inequality, in the 31-year period, the distance between rich and poor was expanding at an average rate of 6.6 per year; a very fast pace indeed, compared with both population and income growth. In the six-year period between 1991 and 1997, the gap was increasing at 20.2 percent per annum – over three times faster than in the previous period. This means that income concentration is occurring at an accelerated speed, and so are global socioeconomic inequalities.

As of 1991, the same global elite also controlled 80 percent of world trade, 95 percent of all loans, 80 percent of all domestic savings, and 80.5 percent of all global investments. They consumed 70 percent of the world's energy, 75 percent of all metals, 85 percent of its timbers, and 60 percent of its food supplies. In this context, the global middle sectors are shrinking considerably, since the 20 percent of what could be called the world's middle class only received 11.7 percent of the world's wealth (Robinson, 1994). In aggregate terms, this means that by 2002–3 the wealthiest 20 percent of the world accounted for 86 percent of all private consumption (Bright, 2003: 9). Meanwhile, between one-half and two-thirds of the African population live in a state of permanent destitution. It has been estimated that in this decade average per capita incomes fell by about 3 percent per year in sub-Saharan Africa and by about 1.3 percent in the highly indebted countries (IDRC, 1992). The cumulative figures of economic decline for the "lost decade" (1980–90) are 25 percent for Africans and 10 percent for Latin Americans.[3]

But restructuring has not been limited to the lesser developed countries in the South. There has been a drastic restructuring of the "transitional" Eastern European economies. The movement to capitalism in the formerly centrally planned economies of the East has resulted in declining productivity, diminishing living standards, and an extremely unequal distribution of income (UNDESP 1993). About one-half of the poor in the North now live in Eastern Europe and in the territories of the former Soviet Union. They include social categories virtually non-existent scarcely a decade ago: homeless people and beggars. In North America, where a government-sponsored, radically regressive distribution of income has been underway, the proportion of the American population living below the poverty line was 13.5 percent in 1990 and had risen to 14.2 percent in 1991; a 5.2 percent increase in one year. In 2004, the figure was 17 percent (UN 2004: 150). Canadian figures, though not as extreme as in the US, reveal a similar trend.

The myth of the global society

There has never been a real global society. Nor has there existed a defined global social regime. What does exist is a social construction: an image of social interactions encapsulated in terms such as the "global village" or similar allegories. There is, however, a rapid process of globalization, expressed in an increased mobility of elites, and circulation of communications and capital across national boundaries conveying and strengthening that image. Perceptions of the global village are grossly distorted by unique First World experiences. Yet, for most of the world's population, despite claims of an emerging cosmopolitanism, the globalization of social life means hardly more than the virtual reality of canned media and the advertising of products. Thus, when we talk about the global village, we are referring to a relatively small portion of humanity: the affluent, the powerful, and the informed, the privileged who really possess a transnational character. The bulk of the world's population, while affected by the planetary character of communications, production, distribution, and accumulation, does not partake in the benefits of a new social regime. Rather, the negative consequences of internationalization have a greater impact on the lives of most people than the promises of a unified and nurturing global social order. Migration is perhaps the only and often illegal form of integration of those less affluent and privileged. However, despite alarmist scenarios that portray "hordes" of Southern people pouring into Europe and North America, the figures remain relatively small when compared with the movement of capital and goods, and with the inner migration between countryside within lesser developed countries.

Francis Fukuyama, in answering the question "is globalization really a euphemism for Americanization?" candidly replied:

> I think that it is, and that's why some people do not like it. I think it has to be Americanization because, in some respects, America is the most advanced capitalist society in the world today, and so its institutions represent the logical development of market forces. Therefore, if market forces are what drives globalization, it is inevitable that Americanization will accompany globalization. (Fukuyama 1999)

While internationalization has meant an increased freedom of movement for capital, and for those who possess it, labor mobility is not an intrinsic characteristic of the present system, unless we count as mobility the bits of low-wage labor incorporated in globally traded goods. For most workers and for the unemployed, globalization means hardly more than the old notion of international division of labor: capital "shopping" for cheaper wages in various national markets and relocating there as a function of lower costs. It is much more likely for the affluent to go South than for those in the periphery to visit the center, or even be allowed in, other than through the fortuitous routes of illegal immigration and exile. A myriad of economic, political, legal, regulatory, and security factors prevents them from doing so. Thus, to talk about a global social order is, at best, an illusion, when so many are limited by the accessibility to resources and the means to acquire mobility. However, there are a number of interconnected factors that constitute global trends affecting the quality of social life in otherwise eminently national and subnational societies. This globalization manifests itself in a number of specific and interrelated trends: population growth, hyper-urbanization, the decline of communities, migration, and refugee flows.

What seems to be taking place all over the world is a process of transnationalization of elites, going on side-by-side with a process of growing disintegration of national societies and local communities. The internationalization of the "low-wage economy" has increased the social marginalization, polarization, and social disintegration of the wage and salaried sectors, while conversely facilitating the formation of new global elites. In addition to the manifold linkages provided by international networks, the international integration of global elites is facilitated by communications technology, global finance, trade, and transportation.

At the other side of the equation, there is the decimation of organized blue-collar labor. This tendency follows a generalized pattern to deindustrialize the centre and internationalize a new form of transnationally integrated manufacture. Meanwhile, as the pressures for restructuring the administrative state, the educational establishments, and the workplace multiply, white-collar sectors also begin to decline. To a large extent, the processes of globalization and structural adjustment have brought about the demise of the middle class and the mesocratic values associated with it: family life, nationalism, and "civic duty." To paraphrase Antonio Gramsci, the crisis consists in that the old is dying and the new cannot be born. The implications and causes of social breakdown are global, though their manifestations are quite specific to each concrete society. Acute disintegration of existing structures, and the weakening of solidarity, make smooth social adaptation to externally induced changes extremely difficult. The legacy of economic restructuring is an acute social decomposition with profusion of morbid symptoms in the center and the periphery: unemployment and underemployment, marginalization, addiction, alienation, and crime. For those unable to acquire extraterritorialities, quality of life tends to decline considerably; poverty and personal insecurity become endemic.

A backward glance at the future

The historical and structural circumstances of the neoliberal economic order are defined by three fundamental structural parameters, the common denominator of which is global macroeconomic restructuring. The first is the end of the Cold War and the collapse of the socialist "Second World," construed as a victory of capitalism. The second contextual parameter of this new order is the disintegration and further marginalization of the Third World. The third parameter is economic transnationalization on a scale and depth unprecedented in human history. The most crucial ideological trait that underpins the present global regime is the pervasiveness of neoliberalism as a hegemonic and homogenizing discourse. At the heart of this discourse there is a distinctive ethics of possessive and predatory individualism with very few moral constraints, consequential or otherwise, which effectively justifies any means to maximize profits. Whether under the spell of monetarism, or the so-called "Trilateral" doctrine (Sklar, 1980), neoliberal economic thinking has not only displaced socialism but practically all manifestations of structuralism and conventional Keynesianism. Most important, however, are the entrenchment of inequality and the devaluation of labor as guiding principles of economic life.

The formal decision-making structures of the global economic regime are clearly recognizable, encompassing the General Agreement on Tariffs and Trade (GATT) and its successor, the World Trade Organization, the International Monetary Fund, the World Bank, the various regional banks, the Organization for Economic Cooperation and Development (OECD), the Group of 7 (occasionally Group of 8 if we count Russia), and the established major trading blocs: the EC, ASEAN, NAFTA, and MERCOSUR. The still evolving and incomplete Multilateral Agreement on Investment (MAI) is another complementary set of rules: a charter of rights for finance capital. This global structure finds its correlate inside the internal mechanisms of macroeconomic management within nation-states, namely, the ministries of finance, treasury boards, and central banks. The formal linkage between global and domestic management is provided by international agreements and external conditionalities attached to fiscal, monetary, and credit policies – especially those of debt management. This linkage is, in turn, reinforced by common ideology and professional socialization on the part of national and international experts.

Through these devices, world economic elites manage their interests and negotiate regulatory structures to serve their common interests and maximize profits. As Huntington rather cynically put it:

> Decisions . . . that reflect the interest of the West are presented to the world as . . . the desire of the world community. The very phrase "the world community" has become the euphemistic collective noun (replacing "the Free World") to give global legitimacy to actions reflecting the interest of the United States and other Western powers . . . Through the IMF and other international economic institutions, the West promotes its economic interests and imposes

on other nations the economic policies it thinks appropriate. (Huntington, 1993)

But harmony and predictability at the level of the transnational core do not necessarily translate into security at the base. As production, finance, and distribution in a rapidly globalizing economy become transnational, so does mass economic vulnerability. After the years of worldwide prosperity during the 1960s and the 1970s, instability and exposure have become endemic. The effects of economic insecurity, manifested in poverty, unemployment, and sheer uncertainty, are felt by the bulk of the population in both the center and the periphery. Economic globalization under the prevailing formula has disenfranchised people from fulfilling their basic human needs: access to food, health, housing, and employment. It has caused social polarization within and across national boundaries. It has contributed to the emergence of a new center and periphery no longer based on geographical regions, but on political and economic groupings in both the North and South. On the one hand, there is the highly transnational core of affluent, mobile, and influential individuals in the First, Third, and former Second worlds. On the other, there is the heterogeneous and fragmented majority of the inhabitants of the planet – in all the "worlds of development" – who are effectively marginalized and disenfranchised from the global village. As the process of globalization under the banners of neoliberalism advances, the proportion of those in the "other world" increases; so does the probability of human insecurity and mutual vulnerability.

There is a great deal of optimistic triumphalism among those who espouse the present orthodoxy. From the perspective of its supporters, the inherent superiority of this global project has been demonstrated by the collapse of Eastern Europe, the disintegration of African societies, or Latin America's "lost decade" while the West has prospered. Yet, the sharp schism between two worlds – "this" and "the other" – and the conflict between an expanding "Western" elite civilization and an increasingly fragile, unstable, and besieged global and domestic periphery, offers a scenario of violent confrontation: a new phase of World War Three. The growing squalor of the many, which makes the prosperity of the few possible, has intrinsically destabilizing effects. It is a direct threat to everybody's security.

The world predicament, with reciprocating and multiple environmental, economic, social, political, and cultural dysfunctions, points in the direction of a new global crisis. Its scope and magnitude are potentially much larger and deeper than those of the global meltdown of the 1930s. This time its gravity is determined by a condition of mutual vulnerability. This means that in a highly interdependent world, the strength of the total configuration is largely conditioned by its weakest links. The evidence gathered so far on the unfolding Asian, East European, and Latin American crises indicate that the world's core nations are very much at risk, especially those who lack the power and the resources to shelter themselves from unemployment. Social safety nets, already under pressure from budget cuts and structural adjustments, are insufficient to accommodate those white- and blue-collar workers falling by the wayside. As a result, the overwhelming majority of the population is exposed. The "Fordist" social contract of labor relations has finally broken down.

At the same time, the prevailing cultural software, with its fixation on automaticity and "natural" self-correction, precludes decisive intervention to prevent and reverse the tide. The anti-planning bias is an ideological cul-de-sac, one which privileges and serves the interests of those espousing the kind of short-term social Darwinism which precisely brought about the crisis. It also serves as an ideological justification for the ultimately self-destructive proclivities of a predatory and non-productive speculative sector.

Despite rhetoric like Margaret Thatcher's famous "there is no alternative" (TINA) principle, neoliberalism and globalization – far from being a fatal, natural-like phenomenon – are mainly the result of policy decisions by states and increasingly transnationalized elites in order to establish new rules, often under the guise of deregulation, that benefit these very same elites. To understand the dynamics of globalization it is essential to examine the transnational integration of elites and that of the state itself and the concomitant processes of national disintegration of civil societies. For it is at the level of governance and policy-making that transnationalization, globalization, and deregulation occur. As the state becomes more and more a vehicle to articulate the interests of a transnationalized and affluent constituency, it increasingly becomes a receiver state whose major function is to extract resources from the excluded majorities and redistribute these upwards. Foreign aid and other structural adjustment packages and conditionalities have had the net effect of enhancing centrifugal and globalizing tendencies. These, combined with crises of growth, fiscal solvency, and legitimacy have also impacted development and democratic politics in a negative way. Despite the claims of advancing global democracy and the end of history, many societies, including some once hailed as developed, are beginning to show increasing symptoms of stagnation and decay. As globalization substitutes for development as the new all-encompassing mantra, people's security – environmental, economic, social, political, and cultural – becomes increasingly precarious.

The paradox is that there exist intelligence and planning mechanisms – a "hardware" of sorts – at the national and international level for policy and program planning that would help to overcome the crisis. What does not seem to exist, and this is likely the Achilles' heel of the present global order, is the conceptual "software" and political determination to grasp the bull by the horns, so to speak. But this is not irrational: it makes perfect sense from the perspective of the powerful and the wealthy. It seems that in their enthusiasm for tearing down the authoritarian enclaves of "really-existing socialism," those who talked about freedom and the open society demolished the foundations of democratic planning and social equity. In so doing, they brought about another kind of triumphalist economic determinism: "really-existing capitalism."

References

Blake, D. and R. Walters (1976) *The Politics of Global Economic Relations.* Englewood Cliffs: Prentice-Hall.

Bright, Chris (2003) "A History of our Future," in Chris Bright et al., *State of the World 2003.* New York: W. W. Norton.

Brown, L. (1993) "A New Era Unfolds," in L. Brown et al. (eds), *State of the World 1993: a Worldwatch Institute Report on Progress towards a Sustainable Society.* New York: W. W. Norton.

Clarke, Tony (1998) "The Multilateral Agreement on Investment." Document accessed at http://www.nassist.com/mai/mai(2)x.htm (November 17).

Fukuyama, Francis (1999) "Economic Globalization and Culture," *Technology and Society Document*, internet version (February 1), http//www.ml.com. woml.forum.global.

Huntington, S. (1993) "The Clash of Civilizations?" *Foreign Affairs*, 72, 3, pp. 22–40.

International Development Research Centre (1992) *The Global Cash Crunch: an Examination of Debt and Development.* Ottawa: IDRC.

Nef, J. (1983) "Political Democracy in Latin America: an Exploration into the Nature of Two Political Projects," in David Pollock and Archibald Ritter (eds), *Latin American Prospects for the 1980s: Equity, Democratization and Development.* New York: Praeger.

Nef, J. (1986) "Crise politique et transnationalisation de l'État en Amérique latine: une interprétation théorique," *Études Internationales*, 17, 2, pp. 279–306.

Nef, J., J. Jokelee Vanderkop, and Henry Wiseman (1988) *Ethics and Technology: Ethical Choices in an Age of Pervasive Technology.* Toronto: Wall & Thompson.

Robinson, William (1994) "Central America: Which Way After the Cold War?" *NotiSur*, 4, 8 (February 25), pp. 1–9.

Sklar, Holy (1980) "Trilateralism: Managing Dependency and Democracy: an Overview," in H. Sklar (ed.), *Trilateralism: Elite Planning for World Management*. Montreal: Black Rose, pp. 1–55.

Sunkel, O. (1973) "Transnational Capitalism and National Disintegration in Latin America," *Social and Economic Studies*, 22, 1, pp. 156–71.

The Toronto Star (1998) "Rich get richer as wage gap widens," Thursday, October 22, A1.

United Nations (1992) *Human Development Report 1992*. New York: Oxford University Press.

United Nations (1994) *Human Development Report 1994*. New York: Oxford University Press.

United Nations (2004) *Human Development Report 2004*. New York: Human Development Report Office.

United Nations Department of Economic and Social Development (UNDESP) (1993) *Report on the World Social Situation 1993*. New York: United Nations.

3
Poverty and Sustainable Livelihoods

This chapter explores the issue of poverty and how conventional ways of managing development have not only failed to extricate the poor from their predicament, but have generally excluded them from development altogether. It also analyzes both the conditions of economic insecurity and the nature of the global economic regime that manages and nurtures such conditions. To approach these tasks in a systematic way, we will concentrate upon the relationships among poverty, livelihoods, and globalization.

For our purposes, poverty can be defined as a situation in which "someone experiences a fundamental deprivation – a lack of some basic thing or things essential for human well-being" (CPRC, 2005: 5). Livelihood refers to "people, their capabilities and their means of living, including food, income and assets" (Chambers and Conway, 1991). In turn, globalization, as discussed in Chapter 1, means, in very general terms, "the increasing integration of economies and societies, not only in terms of goods and services and financial flows but also of ideas, norms, information and peoples. In popular use . . . the term . . . has come to mean the increasing influence of global market capitalism or what is seen as the increasing reach of corporate and financial interests at the global level" (Birdsall 2002: 2).

The nature of poverty

Poverty is the most conspicuous symptom of economic insecurity. Other economic symptoms that affect people's security and livelihoods include slow or stagnant growth, huge indebtedness, deteriorating terms of trade, and unemployment. Many, including most development economists, international organizations, and NGOs, see poverty as the principal economic and social problem in the world. Indeed, it is undoubtedly the major challenge for managing development. The key issue of real economic development (and conversely, underdevelopment), more than the size of GNP, GDP per capita, or the rate of growth, is Seers' (1977) question: "What's happening to poverty?" The paradox is that poverty is persisting and spreading in the most prosperous age in human history.

Recently, neoliberal elites, their institutional intellectuals, and the agencies that manage the global economy have made claims regarding a decline of international disparities. However, the long-run historical trends, as shown in Table 3.1, are quite revealing.

These figures point at an entrenched structural bias in the material distribution of assets and liabilities in the world system. In the words of Geoffrey Garrett, "globalization . . . has squeezed the middle class, both within societies and in the international system" (Garrett, 2004: 84).

Poverty is not just a matter of material deprivation and limited access to wealth and opportunity. It is a complex problem of disenfranchisement and exclusion, generally rooted in powerlessness and exploitation. Broadly speaking, it is a state of insecurity and "ill-being," where material want is reinforced by numerous socioeconomic, cultural, and political circumstances that drive people into, and perpetuate, the cycle of poverty. In this sense, it implies a situation and a process that creates vulnerable, insecure, and unsustainable livelihoods, in which political, economic, and social insecurity are closely, though not univocally, interconnected.

Table 3.1: Global income distribution, 1960–94

	Share of global income (%)		
	Richest 20%	*Poorest 20%*	*Ratio of the richest to poorest*
1960	70.2	2.3	30:1
1970	73.9	2.3	32:1
1980	76.3	1.7	45:1
1989	82.7	1.4	59:1
1991	85.0	1.4	61:1
1994	94.0*	1.2*	78:1

Source: UNDP (1992); figures for 1991 are from UNDP (1994). *1994 figures are estimated on the basis of the 1997 UNDP *Human Development Report*. After 1991 the distribution calculations ceased to be regularly reported and published.

These various structural manifestations of insecurity, in turn, are maintained and reproduced by a culture and "pedagogy" of insecurity. Culture here is understood as a set of shared psychological orientations towards the self, others, and their circumstances (Almond and Verba, 1989). In the specific case of the "culture of poverty," the latter involves more than the values, myths, and beliefs of the poor – and the adaptive/learning processes by which poor people cope with, and rationalize, their poverty. It is also primarily reflective of the ideologies and doctrines by which the privileged members of society justify and generate poverty. As socially constructed representations, attitudes such as cultural atavism, racism, class and gender biases, or categorical imperatives, reproduce and rationalize the material and political conditions underpinning poverty.

The dimensions of poverty

On the surface, poverty can be seen as a situation of low income: many operational definitions of it use terms like "living on less than a dollar a day," "people below one half of the median income," and so on. However, while low income is an important indicator of the actuarial valuation of deprivation, there are issues that are more basic to poverty than merely low income – and these issues are distinctively physical and sociopolitical. These refer to a poor quality of life and an inadequate capability to sustain one's livelihood. Most significantly, these inadequacies entail very limited accessibility and coverage, as well as low quality of such capabilities. In other words, the material indicators of poverty involve a series of interconnected symptoms. These comprise, among others, short life expectancy, high infant mortality, hunger and malnutrition, stunted anatomical growth, disease, unemployment and underemployment, inadequate housing, unsanitary conditions, absence of safe and clean water, environmental deterioration, lack of education, and exposure to multiple manifestations of violence (Sen, 1993).

There are also "social" liabilities that are both contributors to and consequences of poverty: discrimination, exclusion, stigmatization, abuse, and hopelessness. Low income is merely the tip of the iceberg of economic insecurity. It correlates strongly with all these manifestations of deprived well-being, but of itself the concept of low income fails to portray the complex, dynamic, and multi-sided nature of the poverty phenomenon.

National accounts are often unable to convey the essence of poverty. Not only is it hard to capture material and social situations in one single economic measurement, but also its operationalization presents some significant technical problems. One of the most common of these is the unreliability of the statistics and surveys upon which data are based. There are more mundane and procedural issues as well, such as currency convertibility, the accuracy of the methods to calculate purchasing power parity, and the degree of realism involved in comparing figures with numerous caveats. The bottom line is that numbers should be approached with a degree of skepticism.

With this warning in mind we can examine the figures. Recent estimates put the world's poor at over 1.39 billion, out of a population of 4.97 billion (CPRC, 2005: 9). This is slightly over 28 percent of the world's population. Historical analyses, such as those undertaken by Surendra Patel (in Meier, 1970), have suggested that in the period between 1850 and 1960 the development gap between industrial and non-industrial economies has expanded with progress. For most of the twentieth century, the gulf between rich and poor people, as well as between "rich" and "poor" nations, has steadily increased. In recent years, neoliberal economists and ideologues have questioned the growing gap hypothesis. The fact remains, however, that since Gini indexes were first calculated there has been ample evidence of this polarization.[1]

Some analysts have distinguished three groups regarding the dynamics of poverty and poverty transition: (a) The first is the non-poor, comprised of those who remain above the poverty lines[2] – from the super-rich to those who merely get by – and who, short of a societal dislocation, are generally secure. (b) The second group is the transitory poor, fluctuating between occasional poverty and non-poverty and who are relatively vulnerable. (c) Finally, the most vulnerable are the chronically poor, including those who are always poor, and those who are usually poor. "Chronic" poverty here refers to the poorest of the poor: people who are in extreme, persistent, and often inherited poverty. These three categories correspond to levels of vulnerability regarding food and health security (Nef and Vanderkop, 1989: 2). Pauperization is a process by which people who are transitorily deprived fluctuate in and out of poverty or occasionally experience severe downturns, and they always face the risk of falling into chronic squalor.

Current estimates put the global number for the chronically poor between a low figure of 298.3 million and a high figure of 421.7 million, ranging between 24 and 34 percent of the world's poor. Although poverty and wealth are often seen as opposites, the dynamics of wealth and poverty generation are more complex than a simple linear relation. Poverty, in terms of the quantum and intensity of deprivation can move at a different rate and direction to those of income generation. Under conditions of economic deterioration, the absolute and relative numbers of those unable to afford a basic "basket" of goods and services can, predictably, increase. However, absolute and relative poverty also expands under conditions of economic growth. For instance, during the recoveries of the mid-to-late 1980s and the mid-1990s in North America, employment creation failed to keep pace with economic reactivation. This type of recovery without employment gains is also noticeable in Latin America, after the so-called lost decade. The deleterious effects of pauperization have more of an impact on sectors already vulnerable (like women, the young, the elderly, minorities, the unemployed), as they are more strongly associated with existing income disparities and powerlessness than with composite levels of prosperity.

The average global per capita income in constant dollars by the end of the twentieth century was over US$5000 per annum; this is 2.6 times that of 1950 (UNEP, 1999). In 2005, the GNP per capita had risen to $8753. According to an analyst: "The year 2004 was a milestone in the world economy, which grew 5.1 percent – the fastest in nearly three decades" (Jimenez, 2005: 1). However, world poverty has not been reduced, either proportionally or absolutely. The number of those below this threshold in 1993 was around 1.3 billion people; about a quarter of the Earth's population. Today's ratio is roughly the same. The same author explains: "Despite rapid economic growth, income disparities are in-creasing across regions and within countries. As world output doubled during the last two decades, income inequality worsened within 33 countries. With one in every five people in the world surviving on less than $1 a day, poverty continues to afflict significant parts of the world population" (Jimenez, 2005: 3).

The largest absolute number of the world's poor (almost 1 billion), are in the Asia-Pacific region. Yet, the highest proportion and the fastest growing rate of poverty have occurred in sub-Saharan Africa, where at the turn of the century half the population was estimated to be poor. In Latin America, estimates made in the early 1990s put the figure at well above 100 million, and growing. In Eastern Europe and the former Soviet Union, a decade ago, the "new poor" had risen dramatically to 120 million people. Most significantly, in the industrialized countries of Europe, North America, and the rest of the G7 nations and the OECD during the same period, 80 million people remained below the poverty line (UNDP, 1997). In the US, the proportion of the population living under that line has fluctuated between 12.5 and 14 percent. Income distribution figures are even more revealing: "In 1979, the top 1% of the US population earned, on average, 33.1 times as much as the lowest 20%. In 2000, this multiplier had grown to 88.5" (Hogan, 2005: 1).

Poverty, distribution, and globalization

As suggested earlier, the relationship between globalization, development, and poverty is by no means a simple and uncontested one. Rather, it is pregnant with ideological implications. This is further complicated because the very concept of globalization has become an all-encompassing, almost metaphysical force representing both "progress" and Western-style development. Two basic schools of thought have produced diametrically opposed theses regarding this relationship.

According to Birdsall, "a debate continues to rage about the merits and demerits of market-led globalisation for the poor" (Birdsall, 2002: 2), with relatively sharp demarcation lines. One side includes most mainstream economists, international financial institutions, globalized financial managers, government elites (ministries of finance and central banks), and the development establishment of experts and consultants. They generally support the proposition that globalization has little to do with any increase in world poverty and inequality. Instead, they advance the thesis that globalization has closed international inequalities and the poverty gap. They argue that it is "the people least touched by globalisation, living in rural Africa and South Asia, who are the poorest in the world" (Birdsall, 2002: 2).

The other side of the debate includes "most social activists, members of non-profit civil society groups who work on environmental issues, human rights, and relief programs, most of the popular press, and many sensible, well-educated observers" (Birdsall, 2002: 2) For this group, there is clear and conclusive evidence that globalization benefits the rich, and that means rich countries as well as the rich people within rich and poor countries. There is also evidence that it has deleterious effects upon the bulk of the population in poor countries, and especially for the most vulnerable sectors in both the South and the North.

Scholarly backing for the pro-globalization thesis is provided, among others, by the works of Sala-i-Martin (2001), Dollar and Kraay (2002), and especially Firebaugh and Goesling (2004). The core of their thesis centers on three assertions: (a) worldwide income inequality has been declining steadily since at least the mid-1970s; (b) this decline is, to a great extent, the result of industrial globalization of large and once extremely poor countries like China and India; and (c) poverty has been reduced as a consequence of such globalization. A report commissioned by the Norwegian government (Melchior et al., 2000) echoes, in general terms, the tone of the poverty-reduction hypothesis, and argues for the adequacy of using country differentials and purchase parities as a good way to adjust conventional measures of inequality.

On the other side of the debate, Milanovic (1999), the UNDP (2002), Weller and Hersh (2002), and Wade's critique of Firebaugh and Goesling (2004), challenge the above assertions. Broadly speaking, the "anti-globalization" counter-thesis centers upon three arguments: (a) Given the sheer size of India and China, overall GNP per capita increases in those countries would affect the distribution among other countries. Thus, changes in the Lorenz curve are more the results of the incidence of large populations in rapidly industrializing countries than improvements of real income disparities. (b) The second argument is that while income differentials among countries may have shown a small decline in recent times, this does not mean that internal income disparities within countries have decreased. For instance, income differentials have grown significantly within China, in all of Latin America, in the former socialist countries of Eastern Europe, as well as in North America. The proponents of the critical view argue that neoliberals overvalue the decrease of international disparities at the expense of in-country inequities. (c) Thirdly, as Nobel Laureate in Economics Amartya Sen has noted, globalism should not be judged by small changes in income inequality but by its ability to provide the poor with a fair share of growing planetary resources (Sen, 2002; CGRIS, 2005: 6).

Sen, as well as Birdsall (2002), suggest also a broader way of looking at the conundrum. In their opinion, even if there may be evidence that global inequality was not rising, the reduction is at most slight, and the historical legacy of distributional skewness so prolonged, so pronounced, and so entrenched as to produce and sustain structural poverty. Thus, the record is not sufficiently unproblematic to assert that globalization has had a beneficial impact in reducing either maldistribution or, most importantly, poverty. The corollary is that without regulatory and redistributive efforts, globalization – and market liberalization – are unlikely to have a direct positive impact in reducing poverty; especially its worst and chronic manifestations. From this perspective, globalization, even if not clearly a part of the problem, is certainly not the solution. This is especially the case since the rules of the game are stacked against the poor, as the powerful create and use them to benefit themselves (Birdsall 2002: 6). The rules need to be changed to allow the poor to improve their lot.

The factors of poverty[3]

There are numerous factors that drive and perpetuate poverty. Among these, the most common are low investment, low productivity, resource scarcity, long- and short-term boom-and-bust cycles, indebtedness and conditionalities, deteriorating terms of trade, a hostile international environment, structural unemployment, lack of democracy, political instability, widespread violence, corruption, environmental collapse, and natural disasters. The stress on people's livelihoods comes from acute and often combined manifestations of these factors.

Since at least the 1930s world depression, one of the most repeated and ubiquitous beliefs has been that economic security, measured by poverty-reduction, is attained through growth. Short of a radical redistribution of wealth and income, the standard recipe for such growth has been enhancing the wealth of nations (capabilities) through increases of the marginal capital/output ratio. This means essentially domestic savings or foreign investment. In fact, development theory and specifically modernization theory were constructed on the inextricable and causal relationship between the expansion of per capita income and the improvement of sociopolitical conditions. Conventional wisdom also postulated that once the society's overall level of goods and services increased in relation to population, a form of automatic "trickle down" of benefits was bound to occur. Given their level of income, the rich in this equation have a built-in greater propensity to save (or not to consume), than do the non-rich, whose income largely goes into needs satisfaction. In theory, assuming that savings equals investment, this would eventually translate into more expansion, more jobs, more and better salaries, and improved social and overall living conditions. The latter, in turn, would reduce social antagonisms and bring about a stable democratic order.

This mode of reasoning took for granted that wealth and poverty were at opposite ends of the economic continuum, each being the reciprocal value of the other. Thus, if wealth, defined as per capita income, increased, poverty would then decrease accordingly, and so would all its negative social and political consequences. The practical experience of the postwar boom corroborated this reasoning. The

Marshall Plan and most of the induced development and international assistance schemes since 1947 reflect this mode of development thinking. Between the late 1940s and the late 1970s, most industrial economies experienced a prolonged period of prosperity, low unemployment, and a consumption boom. North America, Europe, the South Pacific, and parts of Asia led the way. The global demand for raw materials triggered a unique pattern of commodity-based expansion in the peripheral former colonial regions. In Latin America, the post-recession import-substitution industrialization (ISI), boosted by the war and reconstruction-driven export expansion, brought about rapid and sustained growth.

Yet, this allegedly normal scenario of prosperity proved to be the exception rather than the rule. Since the 1970s, the ever more integrated Bretton Woods global economic order created in 1944 began moving from crisis to crisis, revealing the persistency of widespread poverty, increasing skewness in distribution, and unstable growth. Even in the shorter interludes of economic expansion, poverty grew in scope and intensity. The wealth of nations could not be seen as synonymous with the well-being of nations. Development, globalization, and the bulk of the managerial, endogenous, and external bilateral and multilateral schemes to deal with poverty had proven not to be class, gender, or ethnically neutral. These inner contradictions were less apparent and acute when economic capabilities expanded. If capabilities grow to meet or surpass expectations, distributional conflicts between "haves" and "have-nots" will tend to decrease.

However, disguised under the Keynesian induced consumption boom, the benefits and the burdens had not been equally distributed among various socioeconomic groups. Nor did the development and globalization game occur on a level playing field. Rather, the rules of the game, as was the case with the Bretton Woods system, turned out to be biased in favor of some actors at the expense of others. Without continuous growth, a situation which is altogether unsustainable, conflict is inevitable. This is where politics as conflict-management comes in.

Governance and poverty

One common claim, rooted in the end-of-history and globalization theses, has been that of a post-Cold War world of expanded democracy. The issue of democracy, or rather lack of democracy, is of fundamental importance for poverty reduction. Policies, more than the automaticity of hitherto invisible hands and trickle-down effects have a fundamental impact in creating equity or inequity. Globalization, far from bringing in universal democracy, has meant, by and large, a process of gradual (and at times sudden) disenfranchisement, corporatization, and de-democratization – to paraphrase Michels, a kind of global "iron law of oligarchy." As discussed in Chapter 2, many states have become increasingly dependent on external constituencies and conditionalities; this undermines sovereignty and the responsibility of their governments to their constituencies, and to majority rule.

Contingent labor, job, and income insecurity, the persistence of regressive redistribution and taxation, and the decline of labor power and solidarity have brought about pauperization in areas of the world where labor absorption through outsourcing from abroad has not been possible. Meanwhile, globalization has at least temporarily benefited regions where the pool of labor is massive and cheap (such as in China and India). Not even in Mexico, Central America, Central Asia, or Eastern Europe are there any more viable alternatives. On the whole, outsourcing, as a way to increase profits by slashing the cost of labor, has largely resulted in a "race to the bottom" regarding wages and salaries.

In the developed world, chiefly in the United States, outside the protection of a still robust but weakening welfare state and particularly the military industrial complex, blue- and white-collar workers have been hit hard. In most semi-developed countries, after the illusion of *maquiladora*-like employment faded away (as in Mexico and Central America) job losses, unemployment, and income declines have been the order of the day. In the final analysis, the lure of development and the benefits of globalization have remained elusive to a significant majority of the world population. Despite Gini index fluctuations and minor inequity reversals among nations, the net effect has been so far greater concentration of wealth among the very rich and deepening inequality throughout the world.

This is not to say that globalization and development will necessarily result in benefits for the few and great losses for the majorities. What is apparent is that the current modality and style of management of both development and globalization contains dysfunctional characteristics. Once again, the issue of regulation, both national and international, needs to be re-examined in light of the costs and benefits – especially whose costs and whose benefits – of the above-mentioned style of globalism.

Since 1961 the lesser developed economies of Africa, the Americas, Asia, and the Middle East have gone through at least four United

Nations-sponsored "development decades." However, not much development, let alone catching up, has taken place. From a long-run historical perspective, it appears that periods of generalized prosperity are indeed abnormal and that economic crises, volatility, and uncertainty are more the rule than the exception. This has an immediate effect on the dynamics of world poverty.

The last two decades have been characterized by a bimodal pattern of crisis and recovery. Between the early 1980s and the 1990s the world economic system experienced a phase of decline and disarray. Stagflation, unemployment, indebtedness, and declining opportunities were traits commonly associated with a state of generalized crisis. After 2000, however, the world economy experienced a significant upturn. The driving force of this recovery was decisively led by the expansion of two Asian giants: China and India, two countries that account for nearly 40 percent of the world's population. Even during the preceding contraction, when the world economy was experiencing low and negative growth rates, both economies were outperforming all other countries, with annual growth rates of 10 percent for China and 5 percent for India. Irrespective of the rate of expansion, in both periods the accumulation of wealth has continued unabated. First sluggishly, and then at a faster pace, the global GNP has steadily increased. In the mid-1980s a new global regime of economic management was in place. Its hub was the World Trade Organization (WTO) that replaced the old General Agreement on Tariffs and Trade (GATT).

However, despite greater institutionalization, many of the features of crisis persist, for most people in the planet. Growth, prosperity, and the domestic and global economic order appear to have worked to the advantage of those who control political power, capital, and production. To ascertain the nature of economic insecurity and its victims and beneficiaries, a number of its symptoms must be examined. These traits are multiple and are often interconnected. At any rate, one should bear in mind that the impact of expansion and recession does not affect an entire population in the same way. Rather, since inequalities are cumulative and economic vulnerability affects various sectors of the population differently, development and underdevelopment tend to be class, gender, age, ethnically, and regionally sensitive.

Expansion, contraction, and poverty

The 1970–90 recessive phase of the global economy exhibited two principal features. One was the slowing down of the rapid economic expansion of the postwar years, from the late 1940s. The other was an entrenched structural crisis. Since 1974 there have been four recessions. The first two, in 1974–6 and 1980–1, were a direct result of oil price increases. During these years, rates of growth in personal income dropped sharply worldwide but remained on the positive side. The 1990–2 and 1998–2000 recessions, resulting from broader structural transformations in the industrial economies, were deeper and much more severe than their predecessors. Between 1990 and 1992, the average global growth rate in per capita income, in fact, did not merely slow down but even became negative: an annual average of 1.1 percent decline of the GNP per capita for 1990–2 (Brown, 1993).

The declines in per capita rates of income in Africa and Latin America during the worst years of the so-called "lost decade" (1991 and 1992) were, respectively, 0.9 and 0.8 percent. In Africa, per capita incomes were lower in 1992 than in 1971, and in Latin America they were worse than a decade earlier. In terms of the pace of deterioration, however, the once relatively affluent centrally planned economies of Eastern Europe were the most severely affected by the downward spiral.

However, aggregate figures fail to convey the disparate regional and intra-societal impacts of reduced incomes. For instance, the international Gini coefficient, used to measure income disparities in a range between 0 and 1, rose from 0.69 to 0.87 between 1960 and 1989, "an intolerable level that far exceeds anything seen in individual countries" (UNDP, 1992). Dramatic as they are, these numbers do not show the pre-existing and expanding enormous inequalities. Nor do they show the actual growth of poverty, since as mentioned earlier, and contrary to widespread developmental mythology, such poverty is not just the reciprocal value of wealth.

Poverty and indebtedness

A related major contributing factor to macroeconomic insecurity has been expanding and insurmountable indebtedness. In 1970, according to World Bank figures, the total external debt of all debtor nations was equivalent to 14 percent of their GNP and 142 percent of their annual export earnings. In 1987, these figures had climbed to 51.7 and 227.9 percent, respectively (IDRC, 1992). Debt crises directly affect employment, consumption, and credit in the less affluent countries. In industrialized states, the exposure of lending institutions has led to uncertainty and severe internal dislocations. Financial institutions, attempting to reduce exposure, normally transfer the debt burden to the public sector through government-sponsored insurance schemes or simply pass on losses to their customers at home. Ultimately, the burden falls on the shoulders of salaried taxpayers, those who cannot take advantage of the shelters created to protect the business elites. Most countries have debt burdens (mostly to foreign creditors) larger than their annual GNP, and many of them cannot generate enough export earnings to pay principal and interest, or to maintain basic imports.

As a liquidity problem, the foreign debt crisis in the periphery translates into equally burdensome indebtedness and vulnerability in the center. This is a manifestation of mutual vulnerability. As credit tightens or as economic recession sets in, material production tends to decline. Bankruptcies of the most heavily indebted firms ensue, bringing about a chain reaction: more defaults, unemployment, and shrinking consumer demand. This, in turn, feeds the spiraling downturn in productivity. Extreme economic concentration and economic decay are the consequences. An overextended public sector is frequently singled out as the major cause of public indebtedness. Whereas irresponsible spending and misdirected use of public funds are probably a direct and manifest cause of indebtedness in most countries, its root causes vary considerably. For instance, in the case of the largest debtor country, the United States ($7.85 trillion, or $26 500 per capita),[4] the huge government deficits (between $294 and 368 billion for FY 2005) can be traced back to the combination of deep tax cuts for the corporate sector and extensive overspending in wars and arms races, and generally huge military expenditures. This latter combination, incidentally, drove the former Soviet Union into bankruptcy.

In other countries, increases in the cost of basic imports (such as oil), growing interest rates on borrowed capital, declines in the value of exports, government inefficiency, corruption, and costs sunk into existing projects played a major role. Likely, the overall debt problem is a combination of all of these. Yet the debt crisis is specifically the consequence of national revenues – especially exports – being unable to keep pace with increasing interest rates (IDRC, 1992) and imports. In a way, the debt crisis was created by high interest rate monetary policies in the developed countries – policies that were designed to fight the stagflation of the late 1970s and early 1980s (Sheppard, 1994).

Another side of the debt crisis is the use of credit policies by Western elites and their governments to turn the tables against the newly found "oil power" of the Organization of Petroleum Exporting Countries (OPEC) and the commodity cartels it inspired throughout the Third

World. The West "won" the "credit wars" of the 1980s; credit resulting from recycled petrodollars generated by the 1970's "oil crisis." The enormous profits created by soaring prices between 1973 and 1980 accumulated in the hands of transnational corporations, the likes of Exxon, Texaco, Shell, BP, and Standard Oil, and the ruling sectors in the oil-producing countries: Brunei, Indonesia, Iran, Kuwait, Libya, Mexico, Nigeria, Saudi Arabia, and Venezuela. Petrodollars were transformed into long-term deposits in major Western banks, which, in turn, peddled them at low, yet floating interest rates. Third World political and economic elites in both the oil- and non-oil-producing nations were particularly enticed by the availability of easy international credit. High indebtedness was the consequence of expanded financial availability. When oil prices sharply fell in 1981–2, on the eve of the Iran–Iraq war, borrowers were saddled with unmanageable debt burdens.

The inability to meet debt payments resulted from the double impact of declining export values for primary commodities, including oil, and higher interest rates. Credit restriction by means of high interest rates, geared to fight inflation, was the trademark of a new monetarist policy relentlessly pursued by the central banks in the major industrial nations. This maneuver had tangible short-term financial and political benefits for the ruling sectors in the West. It had, however, disastrous systemic effects. It further destabilized an already vulnerable periphery, bringing about severe balance-of-payment deficits. The tight money policies also wreaked havoc among middle and lower-income earners in the center. The credit squeeze sent a second shockwave through salaried sectors barely recovering from the earlier impact of high energy prices and stagflation. This economic onslaught facilitated the restructuring of labor relations and the overall implicit Keynesian "social contract."

The debt crisis was construed by Western elites and their associates very much as the "oil crisis" of the 1970s was: as a pretext to increase accumulation on an unprecedented scale. The crisis justified belt-tightening, anti-labor and pro-business policies. The financial crisis was used to rationalize the imposition of massive structural-adjustment packages by whatever name in both the North and the South, not to mention the former East. What all of this adds up to is the breaking down of labor's share of the economic "pie," generalized unemployment, and a concomitant process of transnational accumulation of capital. It has also facilitated a major revamping and concentration of the global power structure.

The dismantling of the foundations of a yet unborn "new international economic order" – a more equitable trade regime based on price stabilization for basic commodities for producing countries – enhanced the historical trend of deteriorating terms of trade extant in traditional export economies (Todaro, 1989). According to Singer and Sakar (1992) the long run deterioration of terms of trade entangled the debt trap in a sort of mutual causation. When the terms of trade fall, the purchasing power of exports declines. This increases the need to borrow to continue importing. In turn a rise of debt creates pressures on export prices and on the overall terms of trade through devaluation and other measures to entice exports.

Poverty and unemployment

It has been estimated that the effects of deteriorating terms of trade accounted for about 357 billion USD of the debt in less developed countries in the mid-1980s. By the end of that decade, it had risen to about 500 billion USD. Singer and Sakar (1992) note that over 70 percent of this increase can be explained by deteriorating terms of trade in poorer countries. But this long-term and structurally conditioned tendency has in the long run also negatively affected increasing numbers of people elsewhere. Unstable commodity prices and unfavorable terms of trade in the LDCs not only have created depressed living standards for the majority there but also, most importantly, reduced the capacity to import. This has had a negative effect for manufactured exports in developed countries, resulting in job losses and marginalization at both ends.[5]

The transnationalization of production and the displacement of manufacturing to the semi-periphery, on account of the comparative advantages brought about by depressed economic circumstances and the low-wage economy, result in import dependency in the North. This import dependency does not imply that developed countries become dependent on LDCs for the satisfaction of their consumption needs. Because most international trade takes place among transnational corporations, all import dependency means is that First World conglomerates buy from their affiliates or from other transnationals relocated in peripheral territories. The bulk of the population at the center, therefore, becomes dependent on imports coming from core firms domiciled in investor-friendly host countries. Via plant closures and job losses, such globalism reproduces depressed conditions in the center similar to those in the periphery.

Manufacture evolves into a global *maquiladora*, operating in economies of scale and integrating its finances and distribution through major TNCs and franchises. Abundant and, above all, cheap labor and pro-business biases of host governments are fundamental conditions for the new type of productive system. Because many peripheral areas have easy access to inexpensive raw materials and have unrepresentative governments willing to go out of their way to please foreign investors, a decline of employment and wages at the center will not necessarily create incentives to invest or increase productivity. Nor would it increase real "competitiveness." Because production, distribution, and accumulation are now global, it would rather evolve into a situation of permanent unemployment, transforming the bulk of the blue-collar workers – the working class – into a non-working underclass. In the current global environment, production, distribution, consumption, and accumulation are not constrained by the tight compartments of the nation-state, national legislation, or responsible governments. On the contrary, regulation has become anathema. The implicit social contract articulated in the system of labor relations and collective bargaining in the industrialized countries has become invalidated by transnational business. The new correlation of forces is one in which blue-collar workers have lost, and lost big, while agricultural workers have remained permanently outside this franchise. Permanent unemployment has been increasing by leaps and bounds in the West as well as in the less "competitive" countries, as a proportion of total unemployment (OECD, 1991, 1992). This means endemic and inescapable poverty.

The global economic regime

The present world economic order is, by far, more centralized, concentric, and institutionalized at the top than it has ever been. Its fundamental components are trade, finance, and the protection of the proprietary rights of international business. Rules, actors, and mechanisms constitute a *de facto* functional system of global governance, with core elite interests in the center and the periphery increasingly intertwined. As the Bush Sr. administration was ostensibly vetoing a global environmental regime at the 1992 Rio Summit, its representatives, in conjunction with their counterparts in the Group of 7, were adding the final touches to an international trade and financial regime. This mechanism to replace the General Agreement on Tariffs and Trade would come into being a year later: through the World Trade Organization. Princes and merchants, to use Nerfin's terminology, can reign supreme, while citizens and the public at large are increasingly peripheralized.

The regulation of deregulation confers upon transnational elites the ability to exercise control by manipulating the rules of the game: what some analysts have referred to as "metapower." In this context, the management of development is displaced by that of globalization, with distinctively oligarchic features.

References

Almond, Gabriel and Sydney Verba (1989) *The Civic Culture: Political Attitudes and Democracy in Five Nations.* Newbury Park, CA: Sage, pp. 1–45.

Birdsall, Nancy (2002) "Asymmetric Globalization: Global Markets Require Good Global Politics," The Carter Center, Development Cooperation Forum Conference on Human Security and the Future of Development Cooperation, Center for Global Development, Working Paper No. 12 (October).

Brown, Lester (1993) "A New Era Unfolds," in L. Brown et al., *State of the World 1993: a Worldwatch Institute Report on Progress Towards a Sustainable Society.* New York: W. W. Norton.

Center for Global, Regional and International Studies (CGRIS) (2005) *UC Atlas of Global Inequality.* Santa Cruz: University of California at Santa Cruz, http://ucatlas.ucsc.edu/income/debate.html.

Chambers, R. and G. Conway (1991) *Sustainable Rural Livelihoods: Practical Concepts for the 21st Century.* IDS Discussion Paper, No. 296, Brighton.

Chronic Poverty Research Centre (CPRC) (2005) *The Chronic Poverty Report 2004–05.* Institute for Development Policy & Management, University of Manchester.

Dollar, David and Art Kraay (2002) "Spreading the Wealth," *Foreign Affairs*, 81, 1 (January–February).

Firebaugh, G. and B. Goesling (2004) "Accounting for the Recent Decline in Global Income Inequality," *American Journal of Sociology*, 110, 2 (September), pp. 283–312.

Garrett, Geoffrey (2004) "Globalization's Missing Middle," *Foreign Affairs*, 83, 6 (November–December), pp. 44–96.

Hogan, Jenny (2005) *New Scientist*, Print Edition, March 12, p. 1.

Huntington, Samuel (1993) "The Clash of Civilizations?" *Foreign Affairs*, 72, 3, pp. 22–49.

International Development Research Centre (IDRC) (1992) *The Global Cash Crunch: an Examination of Debt and Development.* Ottawa: IDRC.

Jimenez, Viviana (2005) "World Economic Growth Fastest in Nearly Three Decades," *Eco- Economic Indicators*. Earth Policy Institute.

Melchior, Arne, Kjetil Telle, and Henrik Wiig (2000) "Globalisation and Inequality: World Income Distribution and Living Standards, 1960–1998," *Studies on Foreign Policy Issues*, Report 6B. Oslo: Royal Norwegian Ministry of Foreign Affairs.

Michels, Robert (1968) *Political Parties.* New York: Macmillan Publishing Inc., The Free Press, first published in 1911.

Milanovic, B. (1999) "The Ricardian Vice: Why Sala-i-Marti's Calculations are Wrong," World Bank, Development Economics Research Group paper. www.ssrn.com.

Milanovic, B. (2003) "Can We Discern the Effect of Globalization on Income Inequalities?" World Bank, Development Economics Research Group paper. September 22.

Nef, J. (1999) *Human Security and Mutual Vulnerability: the Global Political Economy of Development and Underdevelopment.* Ottawa: IDRC, pp. 45–57.

Nef, J. and J. Vanderkop (1989) *Food Security and Insecurity in Latin America and the Caribbean: Politics, Ideology and Technology.* Center for Food Security Research Series No. 1, University of Guelph.

Organization for Economic Cooperation and Development (OECD) (1991) *Employment Outlook.* Paris: OECD, July.

Organization for Economic Cooperation and Development (OECD) (1992) *Employment Outlook.* Paris: OECD, July.

Patel, Surendra (1970) "The Economic Distance between Nations," in Gerald Meier (ed.), *Leading Issues in Economic Development: Studies in International Poverty.* Second edition. New York: Oxford University Press, pp. 13–20.

Sala-i-Martin, Xavier (2001) "The Disturbing 'Rise' of Global Income Inequality," http://www.columbia.edu/~xs23/papers/GlobalIncomeInequality.htm.

Seers, Dudley (1977) "The Meaning of Development," *International Development Review,* 2, pp. 2–7.

Sen, Amartya (1993) "The Economics of Life and Death," *Scientific American* (May), pp. 40–7.

Sen, Amartya (2002) "How to Judge Globalism," *The American Prospect,* 1: 1.02, http://www.prospect.org/print/V13/1/sen-a.html.

Sheppard, Mathew (1994) "US Domestic Interests in the Latin American Debt Crisis," in Richard Stubbs and Geoffrey Underhill (eds), *Political Economy and the Changing Global Order.* Toronto: McClelland & Stewart.

Singer, S. and P. Sakar (1992) "Debt Crisis, Commodity Prices, Transfer Burden and Debt Relief." Sussex: Institute of Development Studies.

Sklar, Holly (1981) "Trilateralism: Managing Dependency and Democracy: an Overview," in H. Sklar (ed.), *Trilateralism: the Trilateral Commission and Elite Planning for World Management.* Montreal: Black Rose, pp. 1–55.

Todaro, Michael (1989) *Economic Development in the Third World.* New York: Longman.

United Nations Department of Economic and Social Development (UNDESD) (1993) *Report on the World Social Situation.* New York: United Nations.

United Nations Development Program (UNDP) (1992) *Human Development Report 1992.* New York: Oxford University Press.

United Nations Development Program (UNDP) (1994) *Human Development Report 1994.* New York: Oxford University Press.

United Nations Development Program (UNDP) (1997) *Human Development Report 1997.* New York: Oxford University Press.

United Nations Development Program (UNDP) (2002) *Human Development Report 2002.* New York: Oxford University Press.

United Nations Environmental Program (UNEP) (1999) *GEO 2000. Global Environmental Outlook.* Nairobi, Kenya: UNEP.

Wade, Robert (2004) "Is Globalization Reducing Poverty and Inequality?" *World Development,* 32, 4.

Weller, Christian and Adam Hersh (2002) "Free Markets and Poverty," *The American Prospect,* 13, 1, pp. 1–5.

4
Marginalization and Exclusion

In general, marginalizing refers to the process of relegating, downgrading, or excluding people from the benefits of society. In the context of globalization, one can interpret marginalization to be the intended or unintended relegation of individuals, groups, or entire nations by limiting their access to the benefits of globalization. Limited accessibility could be based upon persisting historical or cultural reasons or on social, economic, and political choices made by those in control of the local, national, or global system. In either case, the end result is the same: exclusion due to inaccessibility and non-participation. The industrial revolution denied many people – the poor, the uneducated, the rural, the elderly, children, and women – equal access to participate in the benefits of modern life. Globalization, coupled with the technological revolution, promises to embrace these historically excluded people and offer them new channels of participation. For instance, rural people can theoretically access the virtual marketplace via the internet in the same manner as their urban counterparts. The same holds true for home-bound women and the elderly who face challenges of mobility. Irrespective of their capacity to pay the high cost of private tuition, children can find access to educational material via the internet. Villagers and farmers have the opportunity to join an organization to seek information and voice their opinion in any part of the world.

But technology is neither free nor readily accessible. In reality, poverty and education still determine a person's ability to participate in an information-rich society. Women, children, villagers, and the elderly rarely have the capacity to acquire the equipment and/or master the skills, let alone indulge in the time necessary to engage in the global economy. Traditionally marginalized sectors, such as women, continue to be further marginalized while new groups face marginalization for the first time, thus widening the scope of marginalization on a global scale. Shifts in production modes and skills needed to participate in the global economy are prompting the most recent wave of marginalization (Carr and Chen, 2004).

We can illustrate this by engaging in two case studies: one offering a glimpse of the marginalization of women, and the other examining the plight of people who experience challenges concerning technology. The first case illustrates new ways in which a traditionally marginalized sector becomes further relegated to the periphery, while the latter example provides an understanding of the ways in which a newly marginalized class emerges for the first time. It is interesting to note that irrespective of the historical basis of marginalization, the instruments of marginalization remain the same, which suggests that policy solutions for both must also bear commonality.

The double marginalization of women

Prior to 1970, women were generally ignored as agents of development. They were not only disqualified from any consideration, but were also excluded from the very development that was supposed to advance their lives. During the 1970s and the 1980s, serious work by a core group of feminist scholars brought women to the center of the intellectual discourse related to development. The United Nations also advanced the agenda by designating 1975 as the International Year of Women, which allowed women's issues to be accepted as genuine policy issues and permitted women and women's issues to take the center stage in public discourse. Scholars who were focusing on women *and* development exposed the exploitation of women through unpaid work, while those emphasizing the role of women *in* development offered strategies to empower women for the sake of development (Bhadra, 2001). By the late 1980s, when the stage was being set for the formal recognition and institutionalization of global economic integration, feminist scholars had already exposed the oppressive tendencies of the existing patriarchal superstructures defined by the social, political, and economic systems that were responsible for women's continued subordination and marginalization. The WTO came into existence during the time when the international agenda to empower women was already at its peak, owing to multiple international conventions (1992 in Rio; 1993 in Vienna; 1994 in Cairo and Copenhagen; and 1995 in Beijing). Yet, little attention was paid to recognize and mitigate the negative consequences of globalization for women. By the turn of the century, the impact of globalization on women had become an area of increased scrutiny by feminist and globalization scholars alike.

Proponents of global economic integration tout globalization as gender-neutral and sometimes even gender-positive. At the source of this argument are the statistical reports that indicate an increase in the participation of women in the workforce, an increased rate of female economic activity, a decreased rate of female illiteracy, and an increased rate of female life expectancy. According to the ILO (2004: 1), women comprise 39 percent of today's workforce – more than ever before. They have experienced improved access to formal employment near their homes, owing to the outsourcing of global manufacturing, as well as employment outside of their homes on account of the global service industry. A large number of women are benefiting from the opportunities offered by the fluidity of the global labor market and are crossing their national borders in search of better jobs. The narrowing gaps in education and healthcare provide testimony to the positive impact of globalization on women.

The other end of the scholarly spectrum is drawn by those who believe that globalization is far from being gender neutral. In fact, in most cases, they see it as not only gender-biased but even gender-averse (Aguilar and Lacsamana, 2004; Beneria, 2003; Channa, 2004; Chow, 2002; Kelly et al., 2001; Man, 2004). The apparent claim of neutrality, according to Joan Acker (2004: 19), hides the "implicit masculinization of macro-structural models." In discussions about the spread of capitalist globalizing processes, the lack of reference to women's unpaid work slants discussions and hinders the understanding of its true impact. While there are large numbers of women in the workforce, their claim to land ownership remains insignificant in comparison to men's. According to the United Nations Development Program (UNDP, 1995), women's work is undervalued by $11 trillion and women own less than 1 percent of land. While women in all countries and all classes are adversely affected by globalization, the impact is intensified for the poor women in poor countries. One may argue that women define the failure of globalization because they are the main producers of food and yet they are the poorest of the poor. Hawthorne sums it up quite simply: "Poor men in poor countries have even poorer wives and children" (Hawthorne, 2004: 246).

Despite their increasing numbers in the workforce, women are still marginalized. Their marginalization is defined by the type of economic role that they have and by the value that is attached to it. The feminization of the workforce often means a disproportionately large number of women in peripheral jobs that are less secure and lower paying, and women generally perform in substandard working conditions. Many women, because of social and family obligations, accept casual or temporary work with no benefits and security: "These jobs are normally characterized by very low pay, irregular income, little or no job or income security and a lack of social protection" (ILO, 2004: 11). Beneria finds that "Globalization has intensified trends of women workers in export-oriented, labor-intensive industries relying on low cost production for global markets" (2003: 77).

Women's labor is a necessary global commodity. Multinational companies need cheap labor in order to make the production profitable – and women with limited mobility, little education, and few skills fill this need (Acker, 2004). The growth of the female labor force is related to the growth of the service sector and low-cost manufacturing. Women in developing countries are viewed as inexpensive to employ, obedient, and able to withstand repetitive work. Aguilar and Lacsamana effectively sum up the situation: "Globalization has created an international division of labor, producing a female proletariat consigned to the lowest-paid and least secure jobs with the worst working conditions" (2004: 18). Mexican women in *maquiladoras*, textile workers in Malaysia, sex workers in the Philippines, Nicaraguan women in Free Trade Zones, and foreign brides in Taiwan all provide testimony to this international division of labor.

Observations drawn from quantitative reports on the female economic rate, the Gender Development Index (GDI), and the Gender Empowerment Measure (GEM) provide further evidence of women's marginalization. The female economic rate, which is defined as the share of females aged 15 and older in the population who supply or can supply labor to produce goods and services (UNDP, 2003), far exceeds that of men. And yet, the proportion of female-earned income is only a fraction of male-earned income. The UNDP reports the female economic rate to be 64.2 percent in the least developing countries, 55.8 percent in developing countries, and 51.5 percent in OECD countries (2004: 232). Data on the GEM and the GDI collected and analyzed by the UNDP demonstrate that women do not experience the same opportunities as men in any country; however, for poor countries, this disparity is particularly alarming (see Table 4.1). The data further suggest a close relationship between the Human Development Index (HDI) and the GDI, indicating that the overall development is not possible without gender development.

Table 4.1:   Gender development and empowerment measures for a select group of nations

Nation	GEM	GDI	GDI Rank	Ratio of estimated female to male earned income	Human dev. rank
Norway	.908	.955	1	.74	1
US	.769	.936	8	.62	8
Japan	.531	.932	12	.46	9
UK	.698	.934	9	.6	12
Singapore	.648	.884	28	.5	25
Slovakia	.607	.840	38	.65	42
Chile	.460	.830	40	.38	43
Saudi Arabia	.207	.739	72	.21	77
Peru	.524	.736	74	.27	85
Egypt	.266	.634	99	.38	120
Bangladesh	.218	.499	110	.56	138
Swaziland	.487	.505	109	.31	137
Yemen	.123	.436	126	.3	149

Source: Data from UNDP (2004: 217–25)
Notes:
1. Gender Empowerment Measure (GEM) evaluates gender inequality in three basic dimensions of empowerment: economic participation and decision-making, political participation and decision-making, and power over economic resources.
2. Gender Development Index (GDI) measures the average achievement in three basic dimensions captured in the human development index: a long and healthy life, knowledge, and a decent standard of living – adjusted to account for inequalities between men and women.

With rare exceptions, such as Japan, the two rankings are in the same descending order. The correlation between GEM and GDI is also striking, although there are some exceptions to this rule: Japan shows a more serious drop in GEM than in GDI and Peru shows a stronger number in GEM than GDI. Japan has fewer opportunities for women to develop than expected from its HDI, and it has even fewer opportunities for women to participate in decision-making than expected from its high level of human development rating. On the other hand, Peruvian women have a greater voice in political, social, and economic decision-making than their general development rating would suggest. Data in Table 4.1 are only for a randomly selected sample; nonetheless, it suggests a complex relationship between women and development. Globalization only increases the complexity of these relationships as societies find that they are less able to control the factors that help shape women's development.

In the global economy, women are less prepared for the formal job market as well. They are twice victims of poverty and illiteracy; first because they are disproportionately present in these groups, and second, because they have fewer means to escape from them. Out of 550 million working poor in the world, 66 percent are estimated to be women (ILO, 2004). Similarly, two-thirds of the world's women are illiterate. Their poverty and illiteracy marginalizes them from a society that is increasingly dependent on accessing information through technology.

The global economy has pushed a large number of women into the service industry, including hotels, cruise lines, and home cleaning. Their migration to rich countries, following the labor trends, brings challenges not just to their personal working conditions but also to their families and communities. Aguilar believes that "the most distinguishing mark of globalization is the unprecedented diaspora of migrant women workers from poor exploited nations to more affluent countries of the North" (2004: 17). These women fill the needs of the global economy; however, they are unable to advance themselves because of the nature of the skills that they acquired in their home country and the lack of opportunities available to them in their country of work (Carr and Chen, 2004: 143). Since 1987, millions of Chinese women have migrated to Canada; however, their fair assimilation is yet to occur. Guida Man reveals that educated women, who would have been highly qualified for jobs in China, are not even entered into the skilled worker category after entering Canada (Man, 2004). Women of color are the lowest paid of all workers in Canada. Scholars believe that the development of skills will be necessary for women to take advantage of future economic opportunities (Man, 2004; Heyzer and Sen, 1994).

The last two decades have witnessed a noticeable increase in informal employment and women comprise a large portion of this sector. Beneria's study of the Philippines, Thailand, India, Pakistan, and Sri Lanka reveals that the informal sector results in lower earnings, no consistency in work contracts, difficult work conditions, and long hours (Beneria, 2003: 116). Women are concentrated in informal, non-market activities and this work is not regarded as contributing to the national economy. Women's role as food producers is overlooked and undervalued as well (Hawthorne, 2004). Ironically, women are not viewed as the primary contributors to the economy, and yet they carry a heavier work burden than men. Data indicate that in comparison to their male counterparts, female workers put in an average of 107 percent more hours in the urban areas of Colombia, Indonesia, Kenya, Nepal, and

Venezuela, and 120 percent in the rural areas of Bangladesh, Guatemala, Kenya, Nepal, and the Philippines (UNDP 2004: 233). In India, Mongolia, and South Africa women are believed to put in 116 percent more hours than men (UNDP 2004: 233).

The distribution of time between market and non-market activities for women is skewed heavily towards non-market for women and towards the market for men (UNDP 2004: 233). On average, 60 percent of women are employed in the market sector and 40 percent in the non-market sector. However, in the urban areas of developing countries, women spend 69 percent in non-market activities and only 31 percent in market activities. In comparison, in developing countries men spend 79 percent of their time in market activities (UNDP 2004: 233).

In summary, women continue to be marginalized and remain economically disempowered, despite their increased participation in the national and global economy and their advancing literacy rate (Gunter and van der Hoeven, 2004: 25). They remain economically undervalued, politically silent, and socially stereotyped. The same factors that marginalized women in the industrial era and kept them excluded from their national capitalist economy are keeping them at the periphery of the global economy during the global era. Their lack of access to education coupled with their role as the primary caregiver forces them out of the formal economy, which in turn pushes them away from receiving a fair market valuation. Since the global economy relies heavily on education and technology, this exclusion only intensifies over time. The impersonal nature of the global economy, in which the production is far removed from the consumer, makes their fight for better wages and working conditions even more difficult. Women become victims twice over: they are victims of inadequate resources because of prevalent poverty and illiteracy; and they are victims of inaccessibility to the economy because of social and family obligations.

"Technologically challenged": the newly marginalized class

The global economy, coupled with technological transformation, is marginalizing a new group of people, the "technological have-nots." On the surface, the information-based global economy appears to be a panacea for human development as it allows countries to leapfrog into the new age of development without having to go through the intermediate and painful stages of infrastructural development. A good example of this is wireless communication technology, which gives countries the luxury of reaching the most remote areas of their territory without having to develop the intermediate infrastructure of roads, railways, and cables. But, the promise of wireless communication technology reaches beyond the economic sector to include nation-building through increased political participation. According to Norris (2001: 6):

> Digital networks have the potential to broaden and enhance access to information and communications for remote rural areas and poorer neighborhoods, to strengthen the process of democratization under transitional regimes and to ameliorate the endemic problems of poverty in the developing world.

However, a careful analysis reveals that the promise of technology in the global economy is, at best, conditional. Not all developing countries have the capacity to develop a technological edge and not all those countries that have the capacity to develop it have the infrastructure to take advantage of it. The same factors that kept developing countries at the periphery when the manufacturing sector dominated the world economy in the twentieth century – absence of an educated and skilled workforce as well as minimal fiscal resources – threaten to keep them out of real economic growth during the information economy in the twenty-first century.

According to the UNDP, internet inaccessibility is a major obstacle to the network age in developing countries (Hill and Kanwalroop, 2003). Because the internet is the underlying infrastructure propelling traffic on the global highways, internet accessibility is drawing the most defining line between the haves and the have-nots. There are 945 million internet users worldwide, growing at a rate of 150 million per year – a number as large as the population of the entire Russian Federal Republic. Industrialized Western countries account for 86 percent of internet connections, 97 percent of internet hosts, and 92 percent of hardware and software consumers (Hill and Kanwalroop, 2003: 1021). In 2001, developing countries, with more than two-thirds of the total world's population, accounted for less than one-third of new internet users worldwide. The annual penetration rates (the percentage of the new population with access to the internet) in Africa and Asia are 1.4 percent and 7 percent, respectively, compared to 69 and 30 percent respectively in North America and Europe (Internet World Statistics, 2004). The low user rates, coupled with even lower internet penetration rates, has set the stage for an even more unequal world in the future. Africa accounts for only 1 percent of internet users and even with the penetration rate of 1.4 percent, it would take decades before the field is leveled for it to participate in the global information economy.

The global digital divide is really the global economic divide for two main reasons: (a) most developing countries lack the infrastructure to develop information technology; and (b) people in these countries lack the capacity to develop these technical skills on their own. In Africa, there are only 3 computers per 100 households, compared to 85 per 100 households in North America. Technological literacy is extremely low even among African college graduates, only 5 percent of whom have information technology (IT) skills as opposed to 78 percent of North American graduates. The normal internet access charge for a US citizen is estimated to be 15 percent of the average monthly income; the comparable figures are 614 percent for Madagascar, 278 percent for Nepal, and 191 percent for Bangladesh (Hill and Kanwalroop, 2003: 1030). The Technology Achievement Index (TAI), which measures the ability of a country to participate in the network age, demonstrates this gap more clearly (UNDP, 2001):

.556   Average TAI of all countries

.272   Average TAI of developing countries

.182   Average TAI of South Asia

.150   Average TAI of sub-Saharan Africa

Scholars argue that information and communications technology (ICT) is at the basis of global trade and tourism and is thus essential for developing countries if they are to take advantage of their cheap labor and natural bounty. According to the Summit of the Americas (2004), ICT stimulates economic growth, creates wealth, and improves services for the poor. The World Bank (2000) identified three key factors in the fight against economic underdevelopment – opportunity, empowerment, and security – and claimed that ICT holds the promise to enhance all three. Information and communication technology presents new opportunities even where traditional infrastructure support systems, like roads, airports, and energy, are lacking. It affords global identity and connectivity to the people marginalized by the traditional patronage system and gives them the tools to combat social, political, and economic exclusion (Norris, 2001).

In contrast, some scholars argue that IT is a short-sighted strategy that marginalizes the vast majority of poor people and does not uplift the economy. According to the United Nations, the digital divide threatens to further marginalize the economies and people of many developing countries (Kenny, 2003). In an new era where knowledge is fast becoming the centerpiece of global prosperity and information is emerging as the new fluid capital in the global marketplace, the infrastructure-rich are likely to become even *richer*, marginalizing billions to an even greater extent.

In light of the uneven playing field, the panacea of technology as a tool to lift all of humankind remains an empty promise. According to Pal (2003), information technologies only benefit the underemployed and educated urban, leaving behind the urban poor and the rural in a state of constant decline. The stark reality is that 80 percent of the people in the world have never heard a dial tone, let alone sent an e-mail or downloaded information from the World Wide Web (Black, 1999). The future for these people in the information age is bleak unless their educational and economic capacities can be strengthened. Ironically, in the wake of the technological race, many developing countries have either already undermined or are in danger of undermining their investment in general human development areas. In this context, technological development becomes a distraction from the long-term progress of a society. The following case study of India's call centers offers a glimpse of the opportunities and challenges inherent as developing economies use their technological edge in the global marketplace.

India's call centers: a case study

In 2003, India controlled 80 percent of the global outsourcing market, offering 150000 jobs and earning more than US$4.1 billion in revenue. Leading international companies such as American Express, GE, Citibank, and British Airways established the first wave of call centers in India. While tough competition from other countries is inevitable in the future, the share of the growing pie will still allow India's revenue to grow to US$24 billion by 2008. India is an interesting model since it has only 22 phone lines and 0.72 personal computers per 1000 people, in comparison to 661 and 66, respectively, in the United States (Warschauer, 2003). Two-thirds of the call center jobs are concentrated in three cities – Bangalore, Delhi, and Bombay – although many other cities are luring this new market. Bangalore is planning for an influx of over 1 million technology service jobs over the next eight

years (Davis, 2003). The call center industry, according to some estimates, is expected to generate 2 million jobs by 2008 (Times News
Network, 2003). Forrester Research estimates that "3.3 million US
service-industry jobs and $136 billion in wages will move offshore to
countries like India, Russia, China, and the Philippines" (Campbell,
2003: 2).

Although India has one of the largest and most developed IT industries in the world, only a small fraction of its citizens enjoy the benefits
of this industry. In Bangalore, India's much touted high-tech city, 45
percent of the population is illiterate and 40 percent live on under US$1
per day. Only 0.5 percent of the population of the city uses the internet
(Warschauer, 2003). Manpower typically accounts for 55–60 percent of
the total costs in a call center and is available at a fraction of the cost
overseas. At *24X7 Customer,* one of India's fastest-growing call centers,
98 percent of the employees have college degrees and can usually solve
customers' technical problems much faster and more easily than their
counterparts in the United States, who often have only high school
education or less. Yet Indian employees make US$2000–$5000 a year –
about one-tenth what the workers in the United States earn (Davis,
2003).

Do call centers provide a boon to the Indian economy? Are they
advancing India's developmental and political agenda? Economically,
they are a great contribution to the economy, employing thousands of
disenchanted college graduates, reversing the brain drain, and opening
doors to the global market. However, one must examine them in the
social and political context in order to assess their true impact on
society. Indeed, because of relatively high wages for call center employment in comparison with other sectors in the country, fewer university
graduates are leaving the country for greener pastures abroad. However,
there are social costs: a call center worker is required to work odd hours,
learn the American accent, and have a pseudo-American name. If
working for an American clientele, they are given time off on American
holidays, such as July 4 and Thanksgiving, as opposed to traditional
Indian festivals and holidays (Seshu, 2003). While appearing benign
on the surface, these job requirements can have severe cultural impacts,
such as loss of identity in the aggregate. Young people feel alienated
from their communities because they work odd hours and are not available to build social or familial connections. India's social network,
albeit patriarchal, is also on the verge of collapse. With more young
women taking advantage of the opportunity provided by call centers,
the family dynamic is becoming more "nuclear" in structure and

women are asking for parity in familial arrangements. Fast food restaurants, carry-outs, Western-style wine-and-cheese parties, and night clubs in high-tech cities where call centers are also located, are some indicators of the changing social fabric. Studies also indicate that the rates of depression, as well as divorce, among the young IT professionals are rising fast in the high-tech areas.

Call center workers also report serious health-related side-effects. Continuous conversation in an artificially adopted accent is believed to cause physical damage to the voice box and can result in voice loss. Working at a desk under severely stressful situations results in numerous health problems. These personal hazards lead to a high attrition rate amounting to 30–40 percent in the call centers (Seshu, 2003). One might also argue that the call centers waste human capital because highly qualified and educated members of the workforce are taking up jobs which are generally done by workers with much more modest backgrounds in Western economies.

"[India] . . . although democratic politically and with a well-educated and highly prestigious civil service, still suffers from a severe lack of synergy; it has failed to lessen the divide between the modern haves and have-nots" (Warschauer, 2003: 172). Over the last two decades, India has increased its United Nations rankings in science and technology areas. However, its human development rankings continue to remain the same, indicating that the country has put a higher priority on technology than on improving the lives of millions. A disproportionate amount of spending on higher education as opposed to primary education is also disturbing, for it means that the haves will continue to have more and the have-nots will continue to be blocked at the very first step.

According to Konana and Balasubramanian (2001), there is little trickling down of the prosperity offered by call center operations, and the digital divide continues to widen. Projections indicate that a couple of million people will be employed in call centers at its height and even if we believe that this phenomenon will lead to a greater base of IT jobs in general, it will still be only a drop in the employment bucket in a nation with over a billion people. Until IT achieves the capability to advance the quality of life of the average person, its economic impact will only be limited. Call centers in particular, and IT in general, do not address the underlying social and economic problems; in order for India to thrive as a globally connected economy, it will have to develop its human capital by developing mass access to electricity, water, education, and healthcare instead.

Social and political marginalization: the hidden multiplier

Economic marginalization is necessarily linked to social and political marginalization, sometimes as a cause and other times as an effect. Women and technological have-nots, once marginalized for their labor, also lose their political voice and social standing. Hawthorne claims that "just as women's role in farming, fishing and forestry is frequently not regarded as work, is not counted as contributing to the national economy, so too women's knowledge is overlooked" (2004: 250). Studies reveal that women prefer to participate in non-governmental organizations (NGOs) because they find that arena to be more conducive to their belief system and lifestyle. Aubrey (2001) argues that the disproportionate large number of women in NGOs indicates that women are more interested in the domesticity of the private sphere. While NGOs fill a social need and perform an important policy function, albeit indirectly, they are not direct political participants and do not groom women for formal political leadership. Aubrey notes that in the mid-1990s, in only 9 percent of the countries, women constituted 15 percent or more of the legislative and executive government positions: "through cultures of politics that are highly patriarchal, the state has systematically and progressively sought to keep women out of the political world of men, while at the same time giving the false impression of being gender conscious and acting on that consciousness" (Aubrey 2001: 92). Ironically, NGOs form a significant voice in the global social arena, but their voice in the global political arena is yet to be heard.

Similarly, the social standing of women, while improving in some instances, remains a cause for serious concern worldwide. The news of a school teacher beheaded in Afghanistan because he taught young girls is a testimony to the atrocities caused by a male-dominated social structure. Can the global economy penetrate any of these areas and help empower women? The case study of India's call centers suggests that the effect of women's employment in the IT sector is showing cracks; nonetheless, the wall dividing millions of rural women from their urban counterparts remains strongly in place. The ripple effect of the new-found freedom of urban women is not seen in the lives of rural women. Nor is it breaking class or ethnic barriers. The same phenomenon is true of Malaysia, Indonesia, Nigeria, and Mexico.

In the case of the technological have-nots, the link between economic marginalization and sociopolitical marginalization is not as clearly established. They are socially disadvantaged in urban areas;

however, in rural areas, because the role of technology is minimal, there is little impact on their daily social life. In the political arena, their participation is not limited because their vote, assuming it is meaningful, is still a valuable asset and the vast majority of political leaders in poor countries are not among the technology "haves." In the near future, as the technological divide becomes more pervasive in day-to-day life, the social and political marginalization of the have-nots is bound to become more severe.

Suggested policy actions

It is clear that the benefits of globalization have thus far been unequally distributed. The global market, because of its competitive nature, tends to favor urban, educated, technologically skilled males in advanced countries at the cost of rural, uneducated, technologically challenged females in poor countries. The argument that the global economy lifts all boats by raising the level of the water falls short of explaining why women, the technologically challenged, and the poor feel more help-less today than they did two decades ago. Proponents of globalization neglect the reality that the rising level of global water may pose new challenges for those with smaller boats – or no boats at all.

Global forces will only continue to increase integration and may even increase the pace of integration. What does it mean for those who must bear the consequences? The likely scenario is that the negative effects will continue to increase to the point where the marginalized become engaged in destructive practices and eventually undermine the promise of the global economy. It is also likely that the marginalized will entirely give up and revolt against the system. Can the unintended consequences of globalization be mitigated in a way that negates these likely scenarios? Can the marginalized be empowered to join the core of the system? Of course, the biggest assumption in raising these ques-tions is that the global economy has the capacity to sustain its six billion-plus population at a higher level of development, prosperity, and generalized well-being. This assumption identifies the need to redefine "development" and address environmentally destructive pat-terns of modern living.

In this context, it would be useful to address some of the following issues:

• The feminization of the workforce ought to be viewed as a real outcome and not as an afterthought. Women's work must carry fair value, for their indirect contribution is worth several times more than their direct contribution to the formal economy.

- The technological dependency of the global economy must also be taken seriously. While the challenge of tackling technological illiteracy may seem frivolous in societies where general illiteracy is widespread, nonetheless, it must be realized that the absence of technological literacy could minimize the advances of general literacy if people are still left at the periphery of the economy.

- Policies to mitigate poverty and inequity must be made in a socially responsible manner (Little, 2003). The capitalist economy, whether national or global, does not recognize the existence of the public good; therefore, conscious policy programs and regulations will have to be adopted which encourage actors to elect the public good in areas where it may otherwise be ignored.

- Policies are also needed to prevent deliberate dualism in distributing the benefits of global proximity. The UNDP reported that "the network society is creating parallel communications systems: one for those with income, education, and literally connections, giving plentiful information at low cost and high speed; the other for those without connections, blocked by high barriers of time, cost and uncertainty and dependent upon outdated information" (UNDP, 1999: 63).

- Such preferences, even though inadvertently pursued, undermine the true integration of the system and continue to widen the gap between the haves and the have-nots. Therefore, these problems should be addressed both in the private and pubic arenas.

- Feminist scholars have long argued that the empowerment of women, by means of including them in decision-making at the local level, is critical. Such empowerment is essential for women and the poor, if the long-term sustainability of the global economy is to become a reality. Elizabeth King and Andrew Mason argue that legal, social, and economic institutions must be reformed to establish equal rights for men and women (2001: 1–2). These institutional reforms are necessary not just to reverse the suppressive tendencies of the system, but also to increase the efficacy of development policies.

- While the global political sphere lacks a formal institutional setting, actions at the global level through agencies such as the WTO, United Nations, World Bank, and the International Monetary Fund can be used to mitigate the undesired consequences of globalization. The realization of the unintended consequences is the first step in this journey.

• Finally, the yardsticks that measure development and/or progress must also be examined and changed. It is encouraging to see that the UNDP now offers measures such as the GDI and GEM. More such efforts within the context of globalization will be necessary. Sustainable, holistic, and human development should eventually shape the success of the global society.

Technology can become a tool to help a society reach its goals. However, the society itself must agree upon and define its goals. A marginalized sector is a drain on the society and a drag on its progress towards the future. The challenges of globalization are as vast as the opportunities offered by it. The global economy has the potential to exacerbate the marginalization of the traditional sector, as seen in the case of women, and to create new ones, as illustrated by the case of technological have-nots. Choices can be made now to reverse the process of exclusion and marginalization. A global consensus around the issues of exclusion and marginalization is the very first argument in this discourse.

References

Acker, Joan (2004) "Gender, Capitalism and Globalization," *Critical Sociology*, 30, 1, pp. 17–41.

Aguilar, Delia and Anne E. Lacsamana (eds) (2004) *Women and Globalization*. Amherst: Humanity Books.

Aubrey, Lisa (2001) "Gender, Development and Democratization in Africa," *Journal of Asian and African Studies*, 26, 1, pp. 87–103.

Beneria, Lourdes (2003) *Gender, Development and Globalization: Economics as if All People Mattered*. New York: Routledge.

Bhadra, Chandra (2001) "Gender and Development: Global Debate on Nepal's Development Agenda," *Nepalese Studies*, 28, 1, pp. 95–107.

Black, Jane (1999) "Losing Ground Bit by Bit," *BBC News Online*, November 1 (accessed August 9, 2004).

Campbell, Doug (2003) "Passage to India," *Business Journal*, 5, 51 (August 22).

Carr, Marilyn and Martha Chen (2004) "Globalization, Social Exclusion and Gender," *International Labour Review*, 143, 1–2, pp. 129–60.

Channa, Subhadra Mitra (2004) "Globalization and Modernity in India: a Gendered Critique," *Urban Anthropology*, 33, 1, pp. 37–71.

Chow, Esther Ngan-ling (2002) "Globalization, East Asian Development, and Gender: a Historical Overview," in *Transforming Gender and Development in East Asia*, ed. Esther Ngan-ling Chow. Routledge: New York.

Davis, Aaron (2003) "Millions of High-tech Jobs may Follow Hundreds of Thousands Already in India," *Knight Ridder/Tribune News Service*, November 14.

Gunter, Bernhard and Rolph van der Hoeven (2004) "The Social Dimension of Globalization: a Review of the Literature," *International Labour Review*, 143, 1–2, pp. 7–43.

Hawthorne, Susan (2004) "Wild Politics: Beyond Globalization," *Women's Studies International Forum*, 27, pp. 243–59.

Heyzer, Noeleen and Gita Sen (eds) (1994) *Gender, Economic Growth and Poverty: Market Growth and State Planning in Asia and the Pacific*. Utrecht: International Books.

Hill, Ronald Paul and Kathy Dhanda Kanwalroop (2003) "Technological Achievement and Human Development: a View from the United Nations Development Program," *Human Rights Quarterly*, 25, pp. 1020–34.

International Labour Office (ILO) (2004) *Global Employment Trends for Women 2004*. Geneva: International Labour Office, pp. 1–16.

International Labour Organization (2001) "Introduction: the Digital Divide: Employment and Development Implications," *International Labour Review*, 140, 2, pp. 113–17.

Internet World Statistics (2004) "Usage and Population Statistics: the Big Picture," July 31. http://www.internetworldstats.com/stats.htm (accessed August 5, 2004).

Kelly, Rita Mae, Jane H. Bayes, Mary Hawkesworth, and Brigitte Young (eds) (2001) *Gender, Globalization and Democratization*. Lanham: Rowman & Littlefield Publishers, Inc.

Kenny, Charles (2003) "Development's False Divide," *Foreign Policy*, 134, pp. 76–7.

King, Elizabeth and Andrew Mason (2001) *Engendering Development through Gender Equality in Rights, Resources and Voices: Summary*. World Bank.

Konana, P. and S. Balasubramanian (2001) "India as a Knowledge Economy: Aspirations versus Reality," McCombs School of Business, University of Texas, Austin.

Little, Daniel (2003) *The Paradox of Wealth and Poverty: Mapping the Ethical Dilemmas of Global Development*. Boulder: Westview Press.

Man, Guida (2004) "Gender, Work and Migration: Deskilling Chinese Immigrant Women in Canada," *Women's Studies International Forum*, 27, pp. 135–48.

Norris, Pippa (2001) *Digital Divide: Civic Engagement, Information Poverty and the Internet Worldwide*. Cambridge: Cambridge University Press.

Pal, Joyojeet (2003) "The Developmental Promise of Information and Communications Technology in India," *Contemporary South Asia*, 12, 1, pp. 103–19.

Seshu, Gita (2003) *Midnight Coolies in the Sunshine Sector*. Resource Center, http://www.indiaresource.org/issues/globalization/2003/midnightcoolies.html (accessed December 6, 2003).

Summit of the Americas, Florida International University (2004) "Trade & Integration," http://www.americasnet.net/trade/ (accessed June 2, 2004).

"The Female Poverty Trap; Educating Women; a Key to Development (Statistical Data Included)," *Economist Newspaper*, July 3, 2002.

Times News Network (2003) "Call Centres to be India's Biggest Job-maker," *The Economic Times Online*, December 18 (accessed August 12, 2004).

United Nations Development Program (1995) *Human Development Report 1995: Gender and Human Development*. New York: Oxford University Press.

United Nations Development Program (1999) *Human Development Report 1999: Globalization with a Human Face*. New York: Oxford University Press.

United Nations Development Program (2001) "Today's Technological Transformations: Creating the Network Age," *Human Development Report 2001: Making New Technologies Work for Human Development*. New York: Oxford University Press.

United Nations Development Program (2003) *Human Development Report 2003: Millennium Development Goals: a Compact among Nations to End Human Poverty*. New York: Oxford University Press.

United Nations Development Program (2004) *Human Development Report 2004: Cultural Liberty in Today's Diverse World*. New York: Human Development Report Office.

Warschauer, Mark (2003) *Technology and Social Inclusion: Rethinking the Digital Divide*. Cambridge, Massachusetts: MIT Press.

World Bank (2000) *World Development Report 2000/2001: Attacking Poverty*. New York: Oxford University Press.

5
Trade, Labor, and Human Rights in a Global Context

Perhaps the most significant feature of globalization is its reliance on trade. Fueled by technological advances, world trade is not only intensifying but is fast transforming the social and cultural fabric of even the remotest of nations. Each year, $7.3 trillion dollars worth of manufactured goods and $1.8 trillion dollars worth of commercial services are exported. In 2003, the real merchandise growth was 4.5 percent and in 2004, it is recorded as a solid 8.5 percent. Elites in countries with mutual trading interests have formed trade regimes as a way to facilitate growth and enhance their role in the global trade market. Table 5.1 indicates a significant increase in trade in 2003 in countries participating in major trade regimes.

With the advent of cross-border commercial transactions, the need for a common set of rules and regulations to manage trade is also emerging. Established in 1947, the General Agreement on Tariffs and Trade (GATT) provided this direction until 1994. In theory, GATT was supposed to have assisted developing countries in achieving a greater level of parity with developed countries. Scholars argue that in reality the GATT initiatives forced developing countries into a higher level of dependency. According to the 1992 *Human Development Report*, international trade during GATT's existence widened the gap between the rich and the poor and produced "underdevelopment" in poor countries. The following findings are offered as evidence of GATT's failed performance:

- Developing countries were denied at least $500 billion of economic opportunities in the global market every year.
- The poorest 20 percent countries received only 2.7 percent of global foreign private investment and 0.2 percent of the global commercial credit.

Table 5.1: Growth of trade in trade regimes

Trade regime (no. of countries)	Annual percentage change	
	1995–2000	*2003*
APEC (21)	6	13
EU (15)	2	18
NAFTA (3)	7	5
ASEAN (10)	6	11
CEFTA (8)	7	29
MERCOSUR (4)	4	19
ANDEAN (5)	8	5

Source: World Trade Organization (2004, *International Trade Statistics*).

- The ratio of the real income of the wealthiest 20 percent to that of the poorest 20 percent increased and became 150 to 1 in 1990.
- Sub-Saharan Africa lost more than $50 billion in export earnings between 1986 and 1990 due to depressed commodity prices.
- In the 1980s, the poor nations were transferring $50 billion a year to their rich counterparts due to capital market arrangements.

In 1986, GATT initiated roundtable discussions, which culminated in the signing of a new agreement in Uruguay on January 1, 1995 and the establishment of the World Trade Organization (WTO). With 148 member countries, a budget of 162 million Swiss Francs (US $83 million) and a staff of 600, the WTO is charged with shaping the global economy by providing unrestricted flow of goods and capital across national borders. It is expected to "provide the principal contractual obligations determining how governments frame and implement domestic trade legislation and regulations" by providing predictable and growing access to markets, promoting fair competition, and encouraging development and economic reform (WTO, 2004). More importantly, it is expected to steer world trade in a manner conducive to the economic growth of both developed and developing countries.

Sustainable development and development for all is the paradigmatic background under which the WTO functions and measures its success. Past experiences illustrate that the system of free trade has not been equally favorable to all countries. In 1992, the United Nations reported that the post-1980s international economy has been redistributing wealth from the poor to the well-off within and between countries (UNDP, 1992). That UNDP Report (1992: 1) proclaimed, "Where world trade is completely free and open – as in financial markets – it generally works to the benefit of the strongest. Developing countries enter the market as unequal partners and leave with unequal rewards." Developed countries not only expect but also demand to reap the benefits of the new economy. President Clinton expressed American expectations from the World Trade Organization in his 1994 report to the Congress by stating that:

> When fully implemented, the Uruguay Round Agreements will add $100–$200 billion to the US economy each year and create hundreds of thousands of new, well-paying American jobs. They provide for a reduction in worldwide tariffs of $744 billion, the largest global tax cut in history. The United States will be the biggest winner from the Uruguay Round Agreements. We are the world's largest trading nation with the world's most dynamic economy. In 1993, the United States exported $660 billion in goods and services, accounting for more than 10 percent of the US GDP. (US President, 1994)

Though the above statement makes it patently clear who the major beneficiary of this trade is, the World Trade Organization is expected to be more sensitive to developing country needs than its predecessor, GATT. Its Economic Research and Analysis Division has produced several working papers on the impact of trade liberalization and investment on developing economies and they show positive and promising results. The WTO claims that during the seven-year period of the Uruguay Round (1986–93), over 60 developing countries initiated economic liberalization programs. The WTO's annual report points out that the Uruguay Round succeeded in substantially cutting tariffs, sometimes to zero, while raising the overall level of "bound" tariffs significantly. Realizing the disadvantageous situation faced by developing countries, the WTO provided a transition period so that they can familiarize themselves with new practices and rules. Furthermore, the WTO established a Committee on Trade and Development and charged it to examine the impact of liberalized trade on developing countries and find ways to assist them in meeting their obligations. A subcommittee of the Committee on Trade and Development was also established to specifically deal with issues faced by developing countries.

The founding principles of the WTO are unique, for they assume that: (1) rule-based world trade is better than government intervention-based trade; (2) a wider process of international economic integration and competition exists; and (3) liberalization is desirable (Cable, 1996). These assumptions of formalism, harmonization, and liberalization together create a thought process that, for many countries, is full of contradictions and conflicts. The primary conflict, from the Asian point of view, is that rule-based free trade, as promoted by the WTO, ignores cultural histories and ethical concerns of member countries. All members are not at the same level of industrial development, do not embrace the "N-Achievement with Protestant ethics" values adopted by Western industrialized countries, and do not share the similar historical experiences produced by industrialism. Some countries, for instance, have hundreds of years of colonial history that cannot be wiped off by granting a symbolic equal membership to a club such as the WTO. For these reasons, it is not uncommon to see countries consciously rejecting Western principles of development, capitalism, and democracy. In their view, these principles are not compatible with their cultural and historical heritage.

The most severe criticism of world trade comes from social and environmental activists who are fearful of its adverse impact on human rights and natural resources of developing countries. They argue that unprotected competition unleashed by free trade leads countries to ignore their commitment to human rights and environmental obligations (Conference on Trade and Human Rights, 1996; ICHRDD, 1996). Proponents of world trade, on the other hand, claim that any correlation between free trade and human rights and/or environmental degradation is not only speculative but also unnecessary. The use of the term "free trade" is intentional. The WTO supports free trade with clearly established guidelines and common rules rather than free trade with no barriers. Developing countries, which supported the World Trade Organization, were clear about this distinction during the Uruguay Round.

Alarmed by the impersonal side of the emerging global economy, human rights activists have solidified their cause through international summits and treaties. Only eighteen months prior to the convening of the Uruguay Round, which led to the establishment of the WTO, the activists held a World Conference on Human Rights in Vienna. The Conference, attended by the representatives of 171 countries, followed the same "social" agenda as embraced by other conferences of the 1990s, including the ones held in Rio (Earth Summit in 1992), Cairo (United Nations Conference on Population and Development, 1994), Copenhagen (Conference on World Social Development, 1995), and Beijing (Fourth World Conference on Women, 1995). The "social" agenda set forth by these conferences is embedded in all WTO documents. The WTO Agreement consists of 29 individual texts, covering everything from agriculture to intellectual property, and 25 additional ministerial declarations, decisions, and understandings, which indicate three points of philosophical departure from its predecessor, GATT: (1) acknowledgement that developing countries have the right to develop and that this right must be respected and observed; (2) acceptance that economic and social rights are necessary if political stability and respect for civil rights are to be ensured; and finally (3) admission that the pursuit of democracy is necessary if developing countries are to achieve development.

Environmental concerns have also been influencing the philosophy of the World Trade Organization. In 1997, a team led by economist Robert Costanza brought environmental concerns to the forefront by declaring that the services provided by the earth's eco-system are worth $33 trillion per year, 1.2 times more than the combined GNP of all countries in the world (Costanza, 1997). The team noted that nature provides many eco-services including gas regulation (worth $1.3 trillion per year), disturbance regulation (worth $1.8 trillion annually), water regulation (worth $1.1 trillion annually), water supply (worth $1.7 trillion annually), nutrient cycling (worth $17.1 trillion annually), waste treatment (worth $2.3 trillion annually), and food production (worth $1.4 trillion annually) which are currently outside of the global market system but may be in danger if not valued properly. The WTO responded to these findings and resulting concerns by establishing a Committee on Trade and Environment to assess the environmental impact of world trade and suggest guidelines for the WTO to adopt. The Committee, since its inception, has met several times and has produced a set of guidelines. However, if demonstrations at the 1999 WTO meeting in Seattle are any indication, environmental issues are far from being resolved.

Global sustainable development is contingent upon two issues: (1) the congruity between unrestricted world trade on one side and human rights observance and environmental protection on the other; (2) the existence of international mechanisms adequate to harmonize trade, human rights, and environmental protection. In essence, this means exploring the ethical issues related to human rights and environmental protection in the context of world trade. We will begin with a discussion of human rights and environmental ethics; then the impact of world trade in these two areas will be examined. Finally we will offer a conceptual model that can allow the international community and national policy-makers to build congruity between world trade, human rights observance, and environmental obligations.

Human rights and world trade

According to a report presented at the World Conference on Human Rights (1993), at least half of the world's people suffer from some form of serious violation of their economic, social, cultural, civil, or political rights (World Conference on Human Rights, 1993). These include diverse problems such as forced deportations in Latvia (Emelyanenko, 1996); election incidents in Russia (Kovalev, 1996); political exclusion in Chile (Agosin, 1992); arbitrary imprisonments in Burma (Evans, 1994); the kidnapping of environmentalists in Indonesia (McBeth, 1996); economic dispossession of fishing communities in Lake Malawi (Derman and Ferguson, 1995); and slave labor of children in Myanmar (Pilger, 1996). They also include the ritually based massive violations such as female genital mutilation (Maher, 1996), and killing of female fetuses and infant girls in India and China.

What are human rights? Are they collective or individual? Are they universal or culture-specific? Should they mandate what a state must not do or should they mandate what a state must do? These and other similar questions present a lively debate on the definition and scope of human rights. The most fundamental definition of human rights is offered by Jack Donnelly who ascertains that "human rights are the rights one has simply by virtue of being a human being" (Donnelly, 1982: 575).

Human rights are both individualistic and collective. According to Michael Freeman (1995: 25):

> The doctrine of human rights affirms two fundamental principles of western liberalism. The first is that the human individual is the most fundamental moral unit. The second is that all human individuals are morally equal. These two principles express a commitment to egalitarian individualism. Yet, the doctrine belongs to an international discourse which also affirms two collective principles: The first is that states are the primary agents of international relations. The second is that states represent nations.

Human rights can be both positive (what a government must provide such as safety, health, work) and negative (what a government is prohibited from taking away such as freedom and liberty). The positive

ones are directives to the state and can be labeled as social and economic rights, while the negative ones are prohibitions and can be better
understood in the context of civil and political rights. Historically,
the West has interpreted human rights as negative rights (a.k.a., First
Generation Human Rights), while most of the world treats them as
positive (Second and Third Generation) rights. The positive interpretation claims that everyone ought to be guaranteed a basic means for
sustaining life, and that violation of such a guarantee should constitute
a violation of human rights.

Among the rights that are considered basic by this interpretation are
the rights to food, clothing, shelter, primary healthcare, clean water,
sanitation, and primary education. Even though these rights are basic,
the Western-dominated international forum continues to exclude them
from the formal human rights agenda for several reasons. First, they
do not satisfy the simple test of being "justiciable and implementable."
Who is to judge that economic and social rights have been violated and
who is to force a government to implement policies that guarantee the
basic means of survival? Second, it is believed that economic and social
rights are already covered under other charters and handled by other
organizations. Feelings prevail that including them in the WTO agenda
would only create redundancy and confusion. Finally, it is realized that
the fulfillment of social and economic rights requires redistribution of
wealth within and among nations, and this runs counter to the WTO's
philosophy. From a free market point of view many such rights (like
health, water, air, food, or sanitation) are "profitable commodities" in
the commons, subject to privatization and closure. This may be the
single most important impediment to their acceptance as human rights.
It is perhaps for this very reason that countries include vague terms
like "available resources" and "progressive implementation" while
writing international agreements.

It can be argued that social and economic rights, as handled in the
Covenant on Social and Economic Rights, suffer from duality mainly
because, on the one hand, these rights protect the social achievements
of the industrialized nations to be used as a standard for best practices,
and on the other, they prescribe a minimum for the rest of the world
(Beetham, 1995). Needless to say, this duality shelters advanced economies from their responsibility of wealth redistribution, which, according to the less advanced economies, is essential if they are to achieve
their own social and economic development.

Political and economic theorists view the relationship between
human rights observance and unrestricted world trade with mixed

feelings. The strongest case in favor of a harmonious relationship is made by economic development and growth theorists who argue that free trade results in economic development which, in turn, creates a civil society that, by its very nature, is inclusive of human rights. On the other side of the argument are socialists, dependency theorists, anarchists, and postmodernists who perceive a discordant relationship between human rights observance and the advancement of global trade. From the socialist perspective, trade at the global level removes workers from their workplace, dehumanizes their labor, and alienates them from their product. In an alienated culture, abuse of workers and violations of their rights naturally abound. Anarchists not only criticize the expropriatory nature of market relations but the oppressive role of political institutions as well. The dependency perspective shares this view and claims that global trade intensifies the already uneven relationship between the haves and the have-nots, leaving the have-nots in a more destitute situation than ever (Cardoso, 1972). Lastly, there is the postmodernist perspective that also views the relationship between free trade and human rights as incompatible. Its claim is that free trade creates a modern global society that is void of spirituality and morality and thus incapable of protecting individual rights.

In contrast, practitioners and technocrats hold a more optimistic view of the evolving relationship between human rights and free trade, although they too are unclear on the scope and nature of this relationship. In 1996, the Chr Michelsen Institute and the Hordaland Folkeakademi of Norway hosted a one-day conference inviting policy-makers and World Trade Organization officials to discuss the ways in which countries could engage in free trade while honoring their commitment to human rights. Speakers at the conference noted two ways in which countries could manage the conflict arising in this area: they could either engage in dialogue, cooperation and trade expansion or could use confrontation, trade restrictions and economic boycott (Conference on Trade and Human Rights, 1996). Most spoke in favor of adopting dialogue and cooperation.

Similarly, another conference sponsored by the International Center for Human Rights and Democratic Development (ICHRDD) and the Canada-based Business Council on National Issues (BCNI) took place in 1996 and raised the issues of morality and ethics in world trade. During the conference, Richard Eglin, Director of the Trade and Environment Division of the WTO Secretariat, conceded that human rights issues were important issues, however the best forum to settle them was not the WTO. Other speakers disagreed with this view and emphasized that countries had a moral obligation to protect a minimum set of human and social standards.

Statistical evidence of incongruity between free trade on one side and human rights observance (in terms of Second and First Generation Human Rights) and environmental obligations on the other is provided in Table 5.2. Trade variables are the volumes of import and export in 1983 and 1998. Human rights observance is measured by the human development ranking established by the World Bank in its *Human Development Report* and environmental indicators are quantified by the level of carbon dioxide emissions and availability of water, sanitation, and health. These variables are not exhaustive; nonetheless, they provide empirical support to the claims made by many scholars.

Based on Table 5.2, higher level of trade is correlated with lower level of human development ranking, higher level of carbon dioxide emissions, greater level of economic prosperity and greater percentage of population without safe drinking water, sanitation and health facilities (Charnovitz, 1987; Elwell, 1995; Leary, 1992; Weston, 1994). There are many reasons for the adverse relationship between human rights and world trade. First, free trade marginalizes the rural poor by concentrating new industrial activities in the cities and thus favoring the urban rich. Cities, because of their superior infrastructures, have become natural recipients of foreign investments and new set-ups. This trend forces rural people to migrate to cities that are already over-crowded and lack adequate infrastructure, and thus subjects them to social uprooting and subhuman living conditions. Second, the growing competition for internationally mobile jobs created by the global economy limits choices for those who are unable to or unwilling to relocate such as women, children, the illiterate, and the elderly. Their relative immobility forces them to accept substandard jobs with lower wages and poorer working conditions. In many trade areas, women and children are employed on 18-hour-work-day jobs for less than 20 cents a day. Third, the pressure to remain cost-effective in an internationally competitive economy forces companies to operate with minimum infrastructures offering unsafe and unhygienic working conditions (Ho et al., 1996). This also hurts the local people. In Mexico's *maquiladoras*, women complain of environmental contamination, intoxication, and reproductive health problems. They are suffering 19 times more menstrual problems and 2.5 times more miscarriages than their counterparts in other parts of the country. They have given birth to twice as many low birth weight babies and three times as many babies with congenital malformations as women outside of these zones (*Le Monde*,

Table 5.2: Bivariate correlation coefficient among environmental, economic, human rights, and trade variables

Indicator	Human develop. rank	CO_2 emission (1980)	CO_2 emission (1995)	Real GNP per capita	% pop without safe drinking water	% pop without health care	% pop without sanitation facilities
Imports (1983)	−.503 (N = 104)	.865 (N = 100)	.746 (N = 102)	.750 (N = 83)	.366 (N = 76)	.382 (N = 92)	.308 (N = 87)
Imports (1998)	−.473 (N = 125)	.902 (N = 105)	.778 (N = 123)	.695 (N = 98)	.360 (N = 80)	.325 (N = 109)	N/s
Exports (1983)	−.519 (N = 109)	.796 (N = 106)	.677 (N = 105)	.682 (N = 85)	.328 (N = 75)	.377 (N = 78)	.310 (N = 98)
Exports (1998)	−.510 (N = 130)	.822 (N = 110)	.708 (N = 127)	.660 (N = 101)	.323 (N = 80)	.308 (N = 112)	N/s

All relationships are valid at 0.01 significance level. Human Development Index ranks countries with best record as 1; therefore the relationship has a negative sign.

1995). Last, the global economy produces "guest" workers who work on less-than-minimum wages and enjoy no political and civil rights.

The ILO estimates that about 20 million people are perpetually on the move in search of work throughout the world. These workers cannot assert their rights because they are neither a part of their own country's work sector, nor are they considered members of their host country's labor force. A large number of computer programmers from India work in the United States as guest workers, earning wages that are higher by Indian standards but lower than what their counterparts receive in the United States. Just because they get better wages in the USA than in India does not make their employment a fair practice in the United States. The practice hurts both the Indians by exploiting their earning potential and the Americans by denying them a fair competition. The rules of the global economy allow multinationals to enjoy unrestricted freedom and create their own havens. They do so through three mechanisms: (a) housing their production units in a resource-rich country, (b) exporting their labor from labor-rich countries, and (c) selling their product in consumption-rich countries. In a seamless trade regime, the rights of labor do not hold much value. Economically, it makes sense but environmentally and socially, the practice is unsustainable and inhuman. For these and similar reasons, free trade is often viewed as disharmonious to human rights, including social and economic rights.

Another perspective on the issue of incompatibility between free trade and economic and social rights comes from those developing countries that reject the human rights agenda on the ground that it hurts them in their pursuit of competitiveness and parity in the world economy. Advanced countries, they argue, have two motives in promoting human rights and advancing environmental standards. One is that they want to establish Western labor practices as universal labor practices. The other is that they want to protect their own labor from international competition. Asian opposition to these standards in Vienna made it clear that the idea of human rights was not a universal one, but instead a "Western" one which the West was using to achieve global economic dominance (ICHRDD, 1996). Many other groups also reject the human rights agenda, albeit on political grounds. Some Arab groups, such as the National Islamic Front in Sudan and the Islamic Front for Salvation in Algeria, proclaim the human rights agenda to be a Western agenda full of Western interests.

Scholars, in general, agree that competitive capitalism, if not handled properly, has the potential to hurt workers in all countries but more so in developing countries. Others further believe that some kind of safety net may be necessary to protect developing countries from the side-effects of free trade, citing the post-NAFTA impact on the Mexican economy to support their case. Two years after the North American Free Trade Agreement, the Mexican currency dropped to 50 percent of its value, newly privatized state enterprises posted big losses, unemployment skyrocketed, businesses performed at the lowest capacity level ever, wages declined in real terms, and many labor rights were found to have been violated.

Environmental obligations and world trade

Environmental obligation is of particular interest to environmental ethicists who delve into the question of who is obligated to whom. Other ethical questions are more essential: Does the sphere of morality extend to only humans or does it include moral subjects such as animals and plants or even non-life forms such as rocks and rivers? How do we know what is ethical? Are ethical codes determined (a) by God, (b) by religion, (c) by the majority, (d) by the common will, (e) by scientific consensus or (f) simply by the value that individuals place on things? Three areas are of particular interest to ethicists: the source of ethical guidelines, the scope of the ethical sphere, and finally the manifestation of ethical behavior.

In 1962, Rachel Carson portrayed a town in *Silent Spring* where no birds sang, no butterflies hummed and no children laughed (Carson, 1962). The unrestricted use of pesticides had destroyed the regenerative capacities of the land to welcome spring. This skillfully created imagery brought together Carson's knowledge of toxicology, ecology, and epidemiology and reached to the hearts of the people, igniting a debate on the effects of modern-day technological innovations on the quality of daily life. Forty years later, springs are still full of humming, singing, and laughter; nonetheless, our minds are entangled in a lively debate over environmental ethics. Many people, following Carson's lead, predicted a doomsday in the 1960s and called for an immediate moratorium on growth, for they believed growth to be the root cause of environmental destruction (Meadows et al., 1972).

In the years that followed, while economists and political scientists searched for proofs, philosophers began a deeper search on the moral framework that drives the engine of human thinking and logic. Lynn White, an early entrant to this intellectual forum, set the tone of discussion by putting the blame on the Judeo-Christian idea that humanity is to dominate nature (White, 1967). By seeing nature as alien, by replacing nature as an object of scientific rather than artistic exploration and by substituting scientific empiricism for natural theology, he argued that we have created havoc on earth and are reaping the consequences now. Lynn White's beliefs matched those of Max Weber who believed that the driving forces behind modern growth were the Protestant ethics that assumed humans to be rational and self-conscious beings capable of creating and accumulating wealth.

Lynn White's arguments persuaded many scholars to examine religious belief systems and their impact on the man–nature relationship. In subsequent years, political scientists proved that even though non-Western countries subscribed to uniquely different belief systems, their treatment of nature was no more harmonious than the one found in countries under the Judeo-Christian philosophy. Entangled in the game of "catch-up with the West," non-Christian nations were undermining the man–nature relationship prescribed by their own religious belief systems. The overriding impact of science and technology had altered the man–nature relationship in every society, irrespective of their individual religious belief systems.

The debate on the scope of the ethical sphere is shaped by nature-objectivists (those who believe in nature having an intrinsic value) on one side and value-subjectivists (those who believe that all values demand an evaluator and thus nature's worth is only as much as humans consider it to be) on the other. Their interpretations range from bio-ethics to anthropocentric ethics. International treaties and agreements adhere to the value-subjective view and perceive the environment as having a value for human survival alone. They present a limited view of the ethical sphere, for they value the environment only when it is beneficial to humans.

Environmental ethicists encourage the idea of biocentric ethics that places the biotic community (life itself), rather than humans, at the center of all value judgement regarding the man–nature relationship. Aldo Leopold defines bio-ethics by proclaiming "A thing is right when it tends to preserve the integrity, stability and beauty of the biotic community. It is wrong when it tends otherwise" (Leopold, 1949). It is commonly believed among bio-ethicists that nature cannot be dehumanized just as humans cannot be denaturalized. Humans exist within and are part of nature, and any part of nature provides a conceivable relational context for the emergence of values.

Since the first roundtable meeting in Uruguay that brought the WTO into being, many scholars have formulated and tested hypotheses on the direct or indirect impact of free trade on domestic environments of countries, particularly developing countries. According to some (Esty, 1994), countries eager to participate in the world market often relax their environmental standards and engage in a race-to-the-bottom. Often, eager countries altogether ignore the implementation of environmental regulation, creating "regulatory chill" that eventually leads to long-term destruction of the environment. Many others (Barrett, 1994) argue that countries set their standards low to encourage industries to flee from environmentally stringent countries. This process promotes ecological dumping and forces specialization of dirty industry in developing countries. In a recent study, Coperland and Taylor showed that lower income levels are correlated with the creation of comparative advantage in dirty goods in developing countries (Coperland and Taylor, 1994). The relocation of automotive and pharmaceutical industries from the United States to Mexico and other Latin American countries falls under this category. Transportation of solid waste to poorer countries is also a blatant example of this practice. In order to prevent developing countries from turning into pollution havens where race-to-the-bottom and regulatory chills can easily invite ecological dumping, the World Trade Organization is being asked to adopt a uniform set of environmental standards on products traded in the world market.

Not all scholars, however, agree with the argument that free trade creates environmental damage. Dasgupta, for instance, believes that free trade leads to policy diffusion where trading partners learn from and adapt to each other's practices (Dasgupta et al., 1995). Perhaps the opening of an economy lowers the toxic intensity of manufacturing output. Furthermore, scholars argue that free trade allows a country's own economy to grow thus permitting it to invest in better pollution abatement technologies and more efficient processes. They argue that without an improved economy, such an investment in technology and pollution abatement would not be possible in developing countries.

Statistical evidence presented in Table 5.1 provides preliminary evidence that free trade impacts the environment of developing countries adversely. In the most direct way, developing countries harm their environment. They do so by (a) accepting pollution-intensive industries from other countries; (b) accepting environmental externalities, such as excessive emission of carbon dioxide or hazardous waste, created by developed countries; (c) encouraging production and trade of resource-intensive trade; and finally (d) using cheap technology and thus being wasteful in the use of precious natural resources. Here are some examples to consider. In 1988, Europe offered to pay Guinea-Bissau, then a country of 830000 people, $140 million per year (a sum larger than the Gross National Product of the country) in return for rights to dispose of its hazardous waste in its coastal land. A larger volume of oil than that spilled by the *Exxon Valdez* in an accident off the Alaskan shore is wasted each year by oil-producing countries because of inefficient production and distribution processes.

Beyond these direct impacts, free trade also generates many equally devastating indirect effects in developing countries such as population migration, environmental conflict, environmental scarcity, and environmental refugees. The impact of the global economy on population migration comes in two forms. Firstly, the global economy forces people to move in selective and often unsustainable patterns. The varying costs of labor and raw material from one country to another forces the global economy to remain on the move by constantly shifting industry and production to competitively advantageous areas. Population moves follow industry moves. The above-mentioned case of computer professionals from India (and also from China) who are flooding the American software production market following the increase in demand in the United States is illustrative. At the same time, pollution-intensive manufacturing industries from the US are moving out to Mexico, Malaysia, Indonesia and other countries in search of less stringent production environments.

Admittedly, the transfer of computer professionals to the US software industry satisfies the demands of the global economy but eventually it creates serious inequity problems that have the potential to turn into unresolved ethnic conflicts. These computer professionals migrate in search of better living conditions than they get when compared to their homelands but soon they realize that they are being undervalued and underpaid in relation to their counterparts in their adoptive land. When the early joy of migration to the land of opportunity wanes, these professionals become discontented within their host country's fabric of life.

Similarly, when a US manufacturing industry moves to another location overseas, it also creates a superficial feeling of betterment for local workers who find their wages double or triple under the shadow of the global economy. However, soon their bliss, too, fades away, as the cost of living corresponds to the rise in wages. Furthermore, these people find themselves faced with health and environmental risks previously unknown. This situation became painfully evident in the 1984 Bhopal tragedy involving the functioning of an American-based pharmaceutical company, Union Carbide, in India. The Union Carbide's plant in Bhopal leaked a large quantity of methane gas, killing 20000 people and disabling another 150000 according to unofficial reports. The post-leak investigation revealed that the plant was operating under safety standards that would not have been allowed in the United States. Working conditions of textile and garment industry laborers in Asian countries are also testimony to the fact that people in developing countries are put at a higher level of health and environmental risk than what would be typically allowed in developed countries.

A second kind of migration by environmentally sensitive populations occurs when shifting rain or wind patterns precipitated by environmental damage destroy the productivity of land areas on which local people are traditionally dependent for their survival. Faced with food shortage and high prices of basic goods, local people feel forced to leave their homelands and move out to other areas, creating new problems of urban sprawl and unsustainability. A good example of such migration is Nepal where native people from the highlands have been moving out to *tarai* areas that were pristine at one point but have since become overcrowded and environmentally unsustainable.

Evidence indicates that this migration to *tarai* areas is now leading to ethnic strife, as new emigrants demand their fare share of the economic and social pie. Similar destructive patterns are visible in Bangladesh where resettlement of flood victims in the government-designated Chittagong Hill Tracts has now made this region extremely vulnerable to social and environmental problems. Environmentally speaking, the land has become unsustainable due to overuse and overcrowding, and socially speaking, ethnic violence has become rampant following the militarization of the tribal people.

Biocentric ethics, heralded by environmentalists, are incongruent with the environment in which free trade takes place. Each nation, in the international arena, is a sovereign and "moral" entity claiming its sovereign rights over its citizens, plants, and natural resources. Each nation, in other words, assumes its identity as a system on its own and not as a part of any larger natural or bio-system. National decisions are based on what is narrowly defined as "right" for their own economy and not for the bio-system that often crosses over several national boundaries. National interests, not bio-interests, are paramount in the international arena. The decision by Iraq to ignite more than 730 Kuwaiti oil wells in the aftermath of the 1991 Gulf War was based on its desire to weaken the political foe without any regard to the region's bio system that was inclusive of its own natural system. The decision by Europe to buy disposal rights in Guinea-Bissau was based on its desire to protect its own land and water irrespective of the potential of damage to the small coastal country or the larger bio-system.

There are more than 900 international treaties on environmental issues, ranging from fish to forests and acid rain to transboundary waste, imposing restrictions on how nation-states may or may not behave. Few analysts speak of environmental values or consider nature to possess an intrinsic worth of its own. In most cases, nature is considered important but only for the protection and benefit of humans. Developed and developing countries show a sharp contrast in their understanding of environmental obligation. Industrialized countries blame non-industrialized countries, who also happen to be more populous, for growing too much and too rapidly. Poor countries blame rich countries for consuming too much and too quickly. Population control is an issue, according to industrialized countries, because each person adds stress to the limited resources of the earth. Considering that the global population is now 6 billion people and is projected to reach 10 billion by the year 2050, it becomes a moral obligation of non-industrialized countries to curb their populations.

Non-industrialized countries, however, argue that industrialized countries place a far heavier burden on the earth's carrying capacity by their frivolous consumption levels than their own populations. Considering that the United States feeds 78 percent of its grain to raise cattle for meat and that it takes 21 lbs of grain to produce 1 lb of beef, it becomes the moral obligation of the United States and other high consuming industrialized countries to curb their appetite for consumption. It has been further claimed that an American consumes as many resources in his or her lifetime as do 35 Indians or 50 Bangladeshis (Brown and Kane, 1994). The earth can carry, according to some projections, 10 billion people if every one was willing to live like Bangladeshis; however, its capacity reduces to fewer than 5 billion people if every one desires to live like Americans. Since the human population has already crossed the threshold of 5 billion, it is unreal to dream that everyone can reach the same level of material opulence and consumption as Americans. Some scholars argue that is imperative for the North to colonize the natural resources of the South in order to keep its standard of living stable.

This phenomenon is called ecological imperialism or green colonization (extension of domination by industrialized countries over the natural resources of non-industrialized countries). The new international order, marked by globalization, liberalization, democratization, and technological advances validates the expansionist tendencies of the North. In the industrial growth paradigm, industrialized countries were the "haves" and non-industrialized countries were the "have-nots"; however, in the natural resource-scarce era of today, non-industrialized countries with their abundant forests and pristine lands have become the "haves" and industrialized countries with either limited natural resources (such as Japan) or protected natural resources (such as the United States) have turned into the "have-nots." In order for the North's industrial growth to continue, its extension into the South, similar to the colonialism of the industrial era, is necessary.

Even in the unlikely event that economic benefits were to accrue for developing countries from free trade, the system created by the WTO is not conducive to biocentric ethics. On the one hand, countries with stricter environmental safeguards like the United States and Sweden are forced to accept products processed in other countries through environmentally unsustainable methods. On the other hand, labor-rich countries such as Thailand and Indonesia find it difficult to raise their own environmental standards from fear of losing their competitive edge and consequently losing jobs and businesses to other less ecologically minded countries. Thus, the congruity between free trade and environmental protection continues.

Institutional mechanisms to build congruity

Currently, the World Trade Organization administers and implements multilateral trade agreements, and acts as a forum for multilateral trade negotiation. It also seeks to resolve trade disputes, oversees national trade policies, and cooperates with other international institutions involved in global economic policy-making. With the Ministerial Conference as its apex body and the General Council as the highest administrative unit, the WTO functions from its headquarters in Geneva with a staff of 450 and a budget of US$83 million and is equipped to handle mediation, negotiation, and policy-making responsibilities. The General Council, which also convenes as the Dispute Settlement Body and the Trade Policy Review Body, delegates responsibility to three other bodies: the Council for Trade in Goods, the Council for Trade in Services, and the Council for Trade-Related Aspects of Intellectual Property Rights. There are four additional committees that support the Ministerial Conference: the Committee on Trade and Development, the Committee on Balance of Payments, the Committee on Budget, Finance and Administration, and the Committee on Trade and Environment. The WTO covers many issues originally covered by the GATT such as environmental standards, labor standards, fair competition, foreign investments, exchange rates, and government support for advances in technology; but it has also embarked upon several new areas including TRIPS (trade-related intellectual property rights) and TRIMS (trade-related investment measures, and trade in services).

Other international institutions, including the International Monetary Fund and the World Bank, also impact the domestic economies of developing countries. These institutions, in the past, have promoted structural adjustment policies (SAPs); however, these programs have largely failed to help the poor. In fact, there is significant evidence that these programs may have intensified the disparity between the rich and the poor (Oxfam, 1993). National governments are also critical of the global trading system; however, scholars argue that they cannot be trusted to play an aggressive role in determining the impact of free trade. Globalization has eroded the power of national governments by subjecting them on the one hand to the international epistemic community (professionals and academics) and transnational business, and to NGOs on the other. Most governments since the 1980s are not as sovereign as they used to be before the advent of global technology, conditionalities, and structural adjustments.

Despite the doubts and anxieties accompanying free trade, it is safe to assume that the need to manage trade at the global level will not only remain strong but also continue to grow in the future. Free trade will benefit countries by offering them better opportunities and greater market access. However, the proposition that we would like to put forward is that even if free trade benefits all, it will benefit some more than others. Two factors will determine the extent to which a country is able to benefit from the global economy: (1) the level and manner to which its own economy is tied to the world economy; (2) the level to which its own political system is adaptable to external fluctuations. The first relates to trade vulnerability or a country's trade ties within and outside of their trading regimes. The second entails regime capability or a country's ability to respond to internal and external crises. This ability resides in a country's legal, administrative, social, political, and cultural systems, being expressed through its handling of issues ranging from economics to ethics. Variance can be found not only between developed and developing countries but also within developing countries. Since developed countries are generally "stronger" than developing countries both in terms of external trade ties and internal regime capacities, they are more receptive to economic liberalization and political openness in the world system. On the other hand, developing countries remain skeptical of any goals that create uncertainty, including liberalization, because they fear losing control of their destiny. Due to their external vulnerability (emerging from their unequal share in the global marketplace) and internal instability (emerging from their weak political regimes and fragmented social systems) they favor a more predictable global system, a system in which national economies, rather than multinationals, control economic decision-making, and nation-states, rather than NGOs, determine policy choices. One of the challenges for the global economy will undoubtedly be to keep developing countries engaged in the process by catering to their needs and remaining sensitive to their concerns.

Can existing mechanisms such as the WTO fulfill this need or are other mechanisms necessary? Unless the ethical "software" that guides national behaviors changes, no new mechanism can escape the weaknesses of the World Trade Organization. Thus, the first and foremost need is to bring about a change in the existing paradigm by focusing on the creation of a global society and not a global economy.

In its present form, the WTO has only a limited scope to influence adverse labor and unsustainable environmental practices. Nonetheless, in regard to labor practices, the WTO will be continually asked to stretch its formal authority and enter into informal areas to create safety nets for workers. Daniel S. Ehrenberg believes that it is possible for the WTO to carve out to a broader agenda than currently allowed under the formal agreement. He argues, for instance, that even though neither the provisions of the GATT nor the mandate of the WTO protect workers' rights explicitly, it is possible for the WTO to use the provisions of unfair trade practices to vindicate certain labor rights (Ehrenberg, 1995). The World Trade Organization can argue that the use of forced and child labor artificially lowers production costs and thus violates the anti-dumping provisions of GATT/WTO. Karen Travis also makes the same observation and finds that the WTO has sufficient room to influence labor practices (Travis, 1992). Similar possibilities exist in the environmental realm where the WTO can include sustainable production practices in its scope of jurisdiction.

Table 5.3 provides a conceptual hypothetical model of the impact of free trade on human rights and environmental obligations based upon a country's position in the global trading system. Regime capacity is treated as an intervening variable, implying that it is impacted by trade positions but that it also impacts human rights observance and environmental protection. The table divides WTO members into three

Table 5.3: Expected effect of trade liberalization on core, peripheral, and sub-peripheral countries

Trading position in the global market	Economic impact	Political impact	Social impact	Level of human rights observance	Level of environment protection
Core countries	Modest yet stable growth	Internal competition. State serving as a partner	Multiculturalism	High due to social awareness and political pressure	High due to public pressure and increased awareness
Advanced peripheral countries	Rapid growth due to economic agility and adaptability	Political demands. State serving in "structuralist" mode	Social unrest	Medium. Will depend on how they are handled	Low
Sub-peripheral countries	Struggle for survival	State will serve as an instrument of the corporate class	Suppression of differences. Primary objective being stability	Low due to lack of choice	Low due to lack of choices

categories: core, advanced peripheral, and sub-peripheral. For core trading countries (or countries that are fully enmeshed in the global economy), the future agenda of free trade will offer many economic opportunities and ensure a relatively stable, albeit moderate, growth period.

The "state" in these countries will work in partnership with the corporate class to reap the benefits accruing from the global economy. This means facilitating global capitalism; nonetheless, the state could also serve as the protector of human rights and freedom. Socially, these core countries may need to embrace multiculturalism and sustainability, if not willingly then out of necessity. These societies can fare better than either advanced peripheral or sub-peripheral countries in fulfilling their commitment to human rights and environmental protection. The WTO can best serve these societies by collecting data and disseminating information. The role of the WTO in these societies will be that of information gathering and processing.

Advanced peripheral societies or societies with significant, although not total, involvement with the global economy are likely to experience the greatest benefit from free trade. Due to their advanced trading ties, coupled with strong yet non-assertive political systems, they will be in the best position to tune in their energies to the global economy. The state in these societies will likely be a structuralist one that will create institutions that unify the corporate class and assist it in directing the national economy. For these countries, the possibility of social unrest will be high because they will experience an increase in the number of political stakeholders and level of expectations. These countries will be economically capable of observing human rights and environmental obligations; however they will not possess the political will to do so. The role of the WTO in these societies will be two-fold: to monitor the impact of trade on human rights and the environment and to persuade countries to honor their human and environmental commitments.

For sub-peripheral countries (or countries whose economies may be tied to the world economy but only through another core or advanced peripheral country), free trade will produce the least benefit. These countries exert a minimal influence in the world economy, for their primary struggle is still survival, not expansion. Their economy stands to suffer the most from globalization because it globalizes their needs while keeping the abilities local. In these countries, the state, owing to outside pressures, will become an instrument of the corporate class. Should social divisions and rebellion become barriers in the country's survival, the state will be expected to suppress them. In a sub-peripheral country, human rights, particularly economic and social rights, will most likely be trampled over by the state and the corporate class. Their environments will also come under attack from the narrowly defined interests of the corporate class. Overall, while these countries are least likely to benefit from the trade-induced wealth, they are most likely to suffer from trade-induced mayhem. The WTO may have a role to play here but this role will have to be more than tutelary. Unfortunately, in the current manifesto of the WTO, such a role is not envisioned.

To conclude, free trade will undoubtedly impact human rights and environmental agendas, if in no other way than by bringing the issue of abusive and unsustainable practices to the forefront. The global economy will sooner or later have to find a way to harmonize them. Meanwhile, the responsibility of creating a harmonious relationship between free trade and human rights observance seems to lie not with the WTO but with consumers, NGOs, and individual governments.

References

Agosin, Marjorie (1992) "The Generation of Disenchantment," *Human Rights Quarterly*, 14, pp. 135–141.

Amin, Samir (1974) *Accumulation at a World Scale: a Critique of the Theory of Underdevelopment.* New York: Monthly Review Press.

Barrett, S. (1994) "Strategic Environmental Policy and International Trade," *Journal of Public Economics*, 54, 3, pp. 325–38.

Beetham, David (1995) *Politics and Human Rights.* Cambridge, Mass.: Blackwell Publishers.

Brown, Lester and Hal Kane (1994) *Full House: Reassessing the Earth's Population Carrying Capacity.* New York: W. W. Norton.

Cable, Vincent (1996) "The New Trade Agenda: Universal Rules Amid Cultural Diversity," *International Affairs*, 72, pp. 227–46.

Cardoso, Fernando (1972) "Dependency and Development in Latin America," *New Left Review*, 74, pp. 83–95.

Carson, Rachel (1962) *Silent Spring.* Boston: Houghton Mifflin.

Charnovitz, Steve (1987) "The Influence of International Labour Standards on the World Trading Regime: a Historical Overview," *International Labour Review*, 126.

Conference on Trade and Human Rights (1996) (http://www.cmi.no/conf0296.htm). Organized by Chr Michelsen Institute and Hordaland Folkeakademi on October 24.

Coperland, B. R. and M. S. Taylor (1994) "North-South Trade and the Environment," *Quarterly Journal of Economics*, August, pp. 755–87.

Costanza, R. et al. (1997) "The Value of the World's Ecosystem Services and Natural Capital," *Nature*, 387, pp. 254–6.

Dasgupta, S., A. Moody, S. Roy and D. Wheeler (1995) "Environmental Regulation and Development: a Cross Country Empirical Analysis," *Policy Research*

Working Paper, No. 1448. Policy Research Department. Washington, DC: World Bank.

Derman, Bill and Anne Ferguson (1995) "Human Rights, Environment, and Development: the Dispossession of Fishing Communities in Lake Malawi," *Human Ecology: an Interdisciplinary Journal*, 23, pp. 125–43.

Dollar, David (1992) "Outward-oriented Developing Economies Really do Grow More Rapidly: Evidence from 95 LDCs, 1976–1985," *Economic Development and Cultural Change*, 40, 3, pp. 523–44.

Donnelly, Jack (1982) "Human Rights and Foreign Policy," *World Politics*, 34, 4, pp. 575–95.

Ehrenberg, Daniels (1995) "The Labor Link: Applying the International Trading System to Enforce Violations of Forced and Child Labor," *Yale Journal of International Law*, 20, pp. 393–6.

Eide, Ashjorn (1994) *Economic, Social and Cultural Rights: a Textbook*. Dordrecht: Martinus Nijhoff.

Elwell, Christine (1995) "Human Rights, Labour Standards and the New World Trade Organization: Opportunities for a Linkage – a Canadian Perspective," a report published by the Montreal International Center for Human Rights and Democratic Development, Montreal, Canada.

Emelyanenko, Vladimir (1996) "Europe's Forgotten Nationality: 'Permanent Residents,'" transcript of a special correspondent published in *Moscow News*, February 22, p. 4.

Esty, Daniel C. (1994) "The Case for a Global Environmental Organization," in Peter B. Kenan (ed.), *Managing the World Economy: Fifty Years After Bretton Woods*. Washington, DC: Institute for International Economics, pp. 287–309.

Evans, George (1994) "Human Rights in Burma," *Contemporary Review*, 265, pp. 178–81.

Frank, Andre Gunder (1967) *Capitalism and Underdevelopment in Latin America: Historical Studies of Chile and Brazil*. New York: Monthly Review Press.

Freeman, Michael (1995) "Are There Collective Human Rights?" *Political Studies*, 43, 4, pp. 25–40.

Ho, Laura, Catherine Powell, and Leti Volpp (1996) "(Dis)Assembling Rights of Women Workers along the Global Assembly Line: Human Rights and the Garment Industry," *Harvard Civil Rights – Civil Liberties Law Review*, 31, pp. 383–414.

ICHRDD (1996) "Globalization, Trade and Human Rights: the Canadian Business Perspective," organized by ICHRDD and the Canada-based Business Council on National Issues on February 22, 1996 in Toronto, Canada (http://www.ddrd.ca/site/publications/index.php/lang=en&subsection= catalogue&id=1283).

Kovalev, Sergei (1996) "Human Rights Were a Big Loser in Russian Election," *New Perspectives Quarterly*, 13, pp. 39–41.

Leary, Virginia A. (1992) "Lessons from the Experience of the International Labor Organization," in Philip Alston (ed.), *The United Nations and Human Rights: a Critical Appraisal*. Oxford, Clarendon Press, pp. 580–619.

Le Monde du Travail Libre, March 1995.

Leopold, Aldo (1949) *A Sand County Almanac*. New York: Oxford University Press.

Maher, Robin M. (1996) "Female Genital Mutilation: the Struggle to Eradicate this Rite of Passage," *Human Rights*, 23, pp. 12–15.

McBeth, John (1996) "Company Under Siege: Mining Firm Freeport Indonesia Hits Back at Critics," *Far Eastern Economic Review*, 159, pp. 26–7.

Meadows, Donella H., Jorgen Randers, and Dennis Meadows (1972) *Limits to Growth: a Report for the Club of Rome's Project on the Predicament of Mankind.* New York: Universe Books.

Offe, Claus (1972) "Advanced Capitalism and the Welfare State," *Politics and Society*, 2, pp. 479–88.

Oxfam (1993) *Africa: Make or Break* (Report). New York: Oxford University Press.

Oxfam (1994) *Structural Adjustment and Inequality in Latin America* (Report). New York: Oxford University Press.

Pilger, John (1996) "Death Railway Revisited: Rebuilding with Slave Labor," *World Press Review*, 43, pp. 10–11.

Rauscher, M. (1994) "On Ecological Dumping," *Oxford Economic Papers.* 46, 5, pp. 822–40.

Selden, T. M. and D. Song (1994) "Environmental Quality and Development: Is There a Kuznets Curve for Air Pollution Emissions?" *Journal of Environmental Economics and Management*, 27, pp. 147–62.

Travis, Karen (1992) "Women in Global Production and Worker Rights Provisions in US Trade Laws," *Yale Journal of International Law*, 17.

UNDP (1992) *Human Development Report, 1992: Global Dimensions of Human Development.* New York, Oxford University Press.

US President (1994) "Message from the President of the United States," September 27. 103rd Congress, 2nd Session, House Document 103–316, Vol. 1.

Weston, Ann (1994) *Trade and Migration: Some Interconnections and Policy Implications.* Ottawa, Canada: North–South Institute.

White, Lynn Jr. (1967) "The Historical Roots of our Ecological Crisis," *Science*, 155, 10, pp. 1203–7.

World Conference on Human Rights (1993) *Status of International Human Rights Instruments as of May 30*, volume 2. Vienna: United Nations.

WTO (2004) Home page on the Internet (http://www.wto.org/wto/about_wpf.html).

Part II
Contemporary Paradigms

6
The Transition from Development Administration to New Public Management: an Interpretative Exploration

Introduction

The internationalization of the theory and practice of public administration is a phenomenon closely related to the creation and evolution of the modern world system. Its roots are found in the European colonial expansion into the New World and subsequently Asia and Africa. The overseas empires and administrative systems that evolved there corresponded to particular modalities of accumulation in different historical periods. In the earlier cases of seventeenth-century Spain and Portugal, the mold was mercantile, while in the cases of British, French, Dutch, or Belgian expansion in the eighteenth and nineteenth centuries, modern capitalism prevailed.

The disintegration of the imperial order after World War Two brought about a complex scenario in Africa, Asia, and the Middle East. It involved the coexistence of what Nkrumah referred to as neo-colonialism with nationalist aspirations, fueled by the expectations of the United Nations First Development Decade and development policies of multilateral and bilateral assistance. A Western-centered paradigm of government administration and social engineering emerged in the postcolonial and Cold War context: Development Administration (DA). This "orthodox" model posited that higher efficiency and effectiveness was a function of the entrenchment of the bureaucratic standards – often referred to as Scientific Management – present in the most advanced industrial societies. The transformation of the public service, from a traditional to a modern bureaucratic organization in underdeveloped countries, was seen mainly as the result of external inducements, the transfer of technology, and training by foreign experts. The ideas of planning and induced material/industrial expansion were central to DA, which was earlier tested in the industrial world as the New Deal and European reconstruction under the Marshall Plan. The early antecedents of current administrative reform efforts can be traced back to initiatives such as President Truman's Point Four program in the late 1940s, the Colombo Plan in the late 1950s, the UN First Development Decade, and the US-sponsored Alliance for Progress in the early 1960s.

In postcolonial settings, this managerial transformation involved the conversion of a colonial "law and order" form of organization and modus operandi into a "rational productivity bureaucracy" that would provide the institutional conditions for economic "takeoff." The trend towards an administrative state, in the context of the Cold War, was furthered by the need to institutionalize precarious and fragmented political systems and enable them to accomplish nation-building and economic growth to stifle insurgencies. The bureaucratic model behind this view of management and organization was based on the dichotomy between politics and administration. It was also based upon other "principles" such as hierarchy, vertical departmentalization, unity of command, political neutrality, relative autonomy, recruitment and promotion based on merit, public service accountability, objectivity, and probity. At the end of the UN Second Development Decade (1961–71), the assumptions of the prevailing paradigm began to crumble. Deep political, economic, social, and cultural-ideological crises spread throughout the West and its periphery, bringing the era of post-World War Two economic *dirigisme* to an end.

As the Keynesian "administrative state" fractured under the double pressure of the worldwide fiscal crisis of the late 1970s, accompanied by an accelerated transnationalization of capital, a "new orthodoxy" emerged. The paradigm to replace the development administration model involved a combination of neoliberal economics and "New Public Management." The slogan of a "leaner but meaner state," implied the belief that a small core of public servants everywhere could be simultaneously better trained, more professional, more globally minded, more ethical, more productive, more customer-oriented, and more responsive to the demands of business in general. The expectation, in the context of a triumphant hegemonic neoliberal and monetarist ideology, was that a smaller civil service would result in better efficiency and responsiveness thus eliminating the opportunity as well as enticement for corruption. Based on this premise, the public sector itself was to retreat, privatize, deregulate, downsize, outsource, and localize. Supposedly, the gap created by a shrinking government sphere was to be filled by a concomitant vitalization of civil society and the private sector. The expected outcome in the post-socialist and post-welfare state would be development and prosperity on a national and global scale.

Yet, as with the "old" orthodoxy, instead of democracy, probity, and prosperity, most developing nations faced growing poverty, civil strife, and a host of insoluble developmental, environmental, and human problems. By and large, a truly effective public management system never materialized. While the West was celebrating the "retreat of the state," deprivation expanded at an accelerated rate worldwide, corruption increased, and civil society as well as social capital deteriorated. The net effect of the structural adjustment policies derived from the new formula, as with its Keynesian predecessor, was that the practices, styles, and structural arrangements succeeded in reproducing the symbolism, but not the substance, of modern developed administrative systems. Furthermore, the above-mentioned problems have not been limited to the Third World. The former socialist Second World and ever growing segments of the population in the West live under precarious conditions and expanding insecurity. Meanwhile, a privileged minority in all of these "worlds" has accumulated wealth and power at an unprecedented rate. Confronted with widespread corruption, an ineffectual civil service, and largely immobile governing institutions, the standard solution has been to call for more of the same administrative reforms that created these problems. A vicious cycle ensues.

When looking at metropolitan influences upon the administrative systems of postcolonial countries it is useful to make a distinction between two historical patterns. One is that of the Latin American nations, where formal independence took place in the earlier part of the nineteenth century and subsequently evolved into the neo-colonial situation of today. The other historical pattern is present in a much larger group of countries in Asia, Africa, the Middle East, the Pacific, and the Caribbean, and whose emergence resulted from the disintegration of the British, French, Dutch, and Belgian empires following World War Two. In the first group, in addition to the Iberian and Romanesque administrative legacy, a string of early twentieth-century reforms – some externally induced but others "home-grown" – have shaped their administrative systems. Cases in point are the numerous experiences with the welfare and administrative states, import substitution industrialization (ISI), modernization of budgetary and accounting practices, the development of public corporations, and the efforts at creating professional administrative cadres. Although the newer "emerging" nations inherited more advanced colonial bureaucracies, many of these possessed the outward characteristics of modern civil services. Yet, these features favored a resilience of colonial administrative forms, practices, and personnel often at odds with local needs and realities. In some cases, like in the Indian subcontinent, colonial administrative innovations – such as a professional administrative class – preceded similar developments in Europe. Moreover, some of the features of the administrative states in this region (including planning practices and the very concept of development administration) became exportable benchmarks of administration for development elsewhere. Upon close scrutiny, Development Administration was a synthesis of pre-existing local doctrines and traditions in the South, enduring colonial modalities and essentially Western ideas connected to scientific management, the administrative state, and the reconstruction efforts under the Marshall Plan.

The purpose of this largely interpretative chapter is to examine the above-mentioned continuities, as well as discontinuities, in development thinking and administrative paradigms in both Development Administration and New Public Management (NPM). An important task in this regard is to explain why both, the "old" and the "new" models, have had very limited success, to put it mildly. Concurrently, the very notions of development and administration that underpin these paradigms will be explored from a critical standpoint. The focus of the analysis will be a general discussion of the most salient and common features in the relationship between public administration, public sector reform, and development strategies in the "South." We will approach the subject from both a historical and a systemic perspective. First, the crises and continuities leading to the present paradigm shift will be briefly analyzed. Subsequently, we will focus our attention on the current administrative practices (namely NPM) in lesser-developed countries, with special reference to the context, culture, structure, processes, and the broader developmental effects of these practices.

The historical legacy

As mentioned at the outset, postcolonial administrations were modernized long before independence and the "spirit of Bandung." For instance, the Bourbon reforms emanating from Spain and Portugal in the eighteenth century or the creation of the All-India Civil Service since the mid-nineteenth century, under British rule, were attempts to make colonial extraction more efficient. Similarly, administrative systems in sub-Saharan Africa (with the exception of Ethiopia, which has had traditional monarchic roots), especially in nations like Ghana, Guinea, Mali, Nigeria, Côte d'Ivoire, Sierra Leone, Tanzania, Kenya, Uganda, Malawi, Zambia, Cameroon, and Gabon, inherited the European-based colonial administrative process although with a different nomenclature among the colonies (Balogun and Mutahaba, 1999: 196). Subsequently, external inducements to reform came via bilateral and multilateral conditionalities attached to foreign aid, trade, and military instrumentalities. More often than not these efforts linked the interests of Western elites with local, *comprador* sectors. The aforementioned modernizations have entailed protracted phases of colonial assimilation, decolonization, nation-building, early institutionalization, indigenization, bureaucratization, authoritarian rule and, more recently, liberalization and transitions to limited democracy.

Development administration and bureaucratic authoritarianism

As mentioned, development administration and administrative development in the 1960s were clearly part of a conscious strategy relying on modernization as counter-insurgency (Nef and Dwivedi, 1981). Foreign aid, professionalization, and development planning were central in a broad effort at refurbishing the civil services of South and Southeast Asia, Africa, the Middle East, and Latin America. Under USAID and European sponsorship, increasing numbers of students and trainees from these regions were exposed to Western, and especially American, ways. Financial assistance poured in to carry out domestic programs of technical cooperation in educational, agrarian, and tax reforms, and also for the training and rationalization of the public sector.

Broadly speaking, the DA model presented a number of common characteristics: (a) the fundamental goals of the state were induced development and nation-building; (b) government planning was paramount in the attainment of these goals; (c) rational administration manifested itself in central agencies for program and budget planning, personnel management, standardized procedures, and decision-making; (d) the state was to undertake anti-cyclical, demand-side management to reactivate and direct the economy; (e) regulation and protectionism were used to attain import-substituting industrialization complemented state ownership and operations; (f) the state provided a social package in health, education, and welfare and managed labor relations; (g) the backbone of induced development was a career, professional civil service; (h) the public service constituted a large administrative apparatus departmentalized by major purpose and with a wide developmental mandate; and finally (i) to accomplish these tasks in a more effective manner, the administrative machinery included a complex body of autonomous agencies charged with strategic development tasks.

At least equally important to the Western vision was the modernization and retooling of the security apparatus along national security and counter-insurgency lines, as was the case in Iran, South Korea, Pakistan, and throughout Latin America (Barber and Ronning, 1966). In fact, in numerous countries, administrative and military reforms went hand in hand, and many saw their officers as Nasserite or Kemalist nation-builders. While the reforms of the civil service, though extensive, remained narrowly focused, "technical," and piecemeal, the thorough-going transformation of the security apparatus had a much deeper, long-term, and often dramatic impact. On the one hand, it generated institutional imbalances between the civilian and military cadres of the state. On the other, because military aid was perceived as the main external power leverage by core countries, the proclivity to create entangled North–South praetorian linkages in a Cold War environment became entrenched.

Democratic transitions and receiver states

The illusion of officers as disciplined and "altruistic" bearers of national development and nation-building vanished towards the end of the Cold War, as did the idea of bureaucratic authoritarianism as a "fourth way" to development. Military aid was costly, it was rarely related to developmental outcomes, and more often than not it had failed to constitute reliable leverage. Bureaucratic authoritarianism was certainly repressive, but also cumbersome and hardly developmental. Worse, the belief that the so-called National Security regimes would bring order and stability was exaggerated, as such regimes were on the whole neither secure, nor really national. Repression and the militarization of development were often the flipside of intrinsic weakness and illegitimacy on the part of client regimes. Instead, more often than not, this paved the way to popular rebellions. Most importantly, with the deflation of the socialist "Second World," there appeared to be no need for dictatorial regimes to protect Western security and economic concerns. As authoritarian bureaucracies and national security doctrines in the South became increasingly associated with gross human rights violations, sheer terror, incompetence, and wholesale corruption, the public service function, both military and civilian, also lost prestige.

With the inauguration of the Carter administration, a new economic and political development paradigm, combining a return to a restricted form of democracy with liberal, market-oriented reforms, began to take shape. This perspective, referred to as Trilateralism, offered a common ground for Western and Southern elites. The implicit transnational alliance of central and peripheral capital constituted a seemingly workable form of power sharing capable of reducing the North–South cleavage of previous decades. First World critics had begun to perceive repressive regimes – such as those of the Shah of Iran, Somoza, Pinochet, Marcos, Zia ul Haq, or Suharto – as a liability for the long-term survival of their economic and political interests. Carefully orchestrated transitions to limited forms of democracy, superintended by the United States and its allies within the Group of 7, ensued. This "transition" had strict limits and conditionalities. On the whole, and despite an appeal to human rights, they maintained the socioeconomic and political forces that had benefited from decades of Cold War authoritarian rule, while excluding radical and popular sectors in the new democracies. The retreating security establishment was to be the warrantor of the process, the central authoritarian enclave, and the insurance policy of the new institutional arrangement. This "low-intensity" democracy (Gil et al., 1993) also preserved the basic pro-business and pro-Western economic policies of the authoritarian era. Chief among the institutional legacies of the authoritarian regimes was a "receiver state," whose prime goal was to manage fiscal bankruptcy and facilitate IMF-inspired conservative economic reforms (Vilas, 1995). The administrative corollary of the new state was the "New Public Management" doctrine. The political formula prescribed a "subsidiary" state of which the main functions were similar to those of the pre-development administration, law-and-order system, except for two features. The first distinguishing feature of the subsidiary states was the truly global nature of the public policy context, inserted in a unipolar international order with limited national sovereignty. The second distinguishing feature was the profound transformation and transnationalization of the state, related to the aforementioned "receivership" role.

Latin America became a test-case scenario for the emerging strategy combining liberal economic reforms with constricted democracy. Although market-friendly reforms have been associated with the explicit unfolding of a Friedmanite neoliberal agenda in the 1990s, many national security regimes had forcefully attempted "monetarist" structural adjustments and "shock treatments" along similar lines at least a decade earlier. In fact, these efforts involved considerable privatization, denationalization, deregulation, and downsizing, while making the national economies more hospitable for foreign investment. The examples of Indonesia, Brazil, the apartheid regime in South Africa, Chile, and, to a qualified extent, the Asian "tigers" involved the coexistence of monetarist, pro-Western, and pro-business policies, alongside a large public sector and a repressive state. Of all these, only the Chilean and South African experiments effected a transition from import-substitution and protectionism to fully-fledged neoliberalism, while undergoing conditional democratization. These "experiments" soon evolved into a model for Asia, Africa, and, years later, the "transitional" post-communist societies of Eastern Europe and Central Asia. One perceptive observer made the following comments:

> [the] state reform agenda for . . . developing countries is based on the approaches of the World Bank and other multilateral financial organizations. At the beginning, the emphasis of reforms was put on a number of policies to shrink the state and transfer most intervention activities to the market. These recommendations were called the "Washington Consensus." They arose in the context of fiscal and financial problems resulting from the 1980s [debt] crisis. (Vilas, 2000: 25)

The emergence and consolidation of Thatcherism, "Reaganomics," and other right-wing regimes officialized a new hegemonic ideology at a time when the Cold War and international socialism appeared exhausted.

New Public Management and neoliberal reform

The neoliberal paradigm entrenched a "categorical imperative" type of discourse: Margaret Thatcher's now famous "there is no alternative" (TINA) principle. This dictum would soon become acceptable common sense in the development community. During the last two decades of the twentieth century, especially at the heels of the crumbling of the administrative state, neoliberal economic reforms replaced Development Administration in redefining the role of the state and its agencies everywhere. The prescriptive package contained a series of policy and administrative measures aimed at reducing constraints on the classical "invisible hand." This was in sharp contrast to the preceding tradition. These measures included: (a) downsizing the public sector; (b) privatizing government services and economic activities; (c) reducing the state's role in direct economic management and social programs; (d) deregulating government controls on the private sector; (e) reducing direct corporate taxes; (f) cutting expenses and balancing the budget; (g) drastically downscaling and even eliminating protectionism; (h) outsourcing services whenever possible; and (i) localizing government functions.

In addition to these tasks, the public sector has also faced a myriad of challenges emerging from a more complex and transnationalized political and economic context, encapsulated in the term globalization. Unlike the administrative state, where the notion of the public – or national – interest was considered an objective policy parameter defined by a "common good," policy objectives are determined by multiple transnational transactions geared to optimal macroeconomic balances, while realizing gains for those who control market forces.

Initially, the neoliberal formula was extremely successful as a political project in the developed world. Though its experimental origins were in the dictatorship of General Pinochet in Chile, under the intellectual mentorship of Friedrich von Hayek and Milton Friedman, it subsequently found legitimacy in the conservative electoral victories in the United States, the United Kingdom, and Canada, as well as in other OECD countries like Australia and New Zealand. From there it evolved into an article of faith in bilateral and pseudo-multilateral agencies such as the IMF, the World Bank, and the Inter-American Development Bank. It finally became the hegemonic discourse in most Western intellectual establishments. It was largely through the structural adjustment conditionalities attached to Third World debt relief by lending agencies that neoliberal policies were entrenched. But despite this early success, less than two decades later the outcome has been more successful for its pervasiveness than for its social effects.

The combination of incomplete democratic transition, restricted democracy, and the widespread existence of receiver states has had deleterious effects upon the administrative systems in peripheral countries. Privatization, budget cuts, downsizing, deregulation, and denationalization – especially in the developmental social, energy, agricultural, and industrial areas – have dramatically reduced the scope and functions of the state. Moreover, the continuity of the institutional and cultural features of repressive practices has stunted further democratization of both state and society in a way similar to the continuity of colonial administrations after independence. As profit and personal gain, on the one hand, and the national interest on the other, become blurred in the new ideological domain privileging private interests and greed, the notion of public service becomes increasingly empty.

Furthermore, with the status and income levels of civil servants declining, and with a thriving worldwide illegal economy in drugs, weapons (Lee, 1988), and human trafficking, systemic corruption increases, reaching the highest levels of government and the bureaucracy. Under these circumstances, externally induced efforts at making public administration more accountable, responsible, universalistic, effective, client-oriented, and less corrupt have been as formal and as ineffectual as the Development Administration prescriptions of the 1960s.

In a nutshell, this is and continues to be the crux of a "Catch 22"-type of dilemma for public administration in developing nations. On the one hand, the existing international "development" practices create conditions incompatible with any administrative reform to make such a system work. On the other hand, the administrative prescriptions, couched in technical lingo, tend to be either patchwork or simple rhetoric. Despite this, bureaucracy continues to be a favored organizational form in East and Southeast Asia. Yet, "its longevity varies considerably between countries, and there are differences in its operations across the region" (Turner and Halligan, 1999: 131).

A comparative perspective

The bulk of the literature on Comparative Administration has a distinctly universalistic flavor. It assumes the presence of culturally neutral traits and common traits in all forms of administration. However, the circumstances, outcomes, and effects of administrative change tend to be regionally and country-specific. Administrative systems are also conditioned by the current modality, as well the legacy, of state–society relations. They are not divorced from politics. On the contrary, management and organization are not "technical" but, rather, are eminently political issues. From this perspective, administrative changes have to be conceived as driven by political interests and having political implications for the relationship between state and society. The point of convergence between politics and administration is public policy, and this is especially the case with development policy. Outcomes related to growth and distribution result from actions, inactions, and interactions among various internal and external political actors, using resources, and possessing diverse development ideologies, that justify their interests.

Two aspects in the theory and the practice of administration seem to have remained constant throughout. One is that the source of conceptual innovation has continued to be distinctively Western and, more specifically, serving the interests of a powerful minority in the global core. The other is the reciprocal relationship and identity between administrative theory and the development model, one in which these elites' ideas have remained simultaneously dominant and hegemonic.

To build an "ideal type" that portrays the public administration system for the entirety of the underdeveloped world with any rigor and precision is a nearly impossible task. However, despite the great diversity and complexity among the countries making up the "Other World," there are sufficient structural commonalities that allow one to configure an identifiable set of economic, social, and political traits, especially in contrast to the developed states of the Group of 7 and OECD nations. In this sense, it is possible to sketch a general outline of the structural, functional, behavioral, and attitudinal traits present in the complex conglomerate of state agencies in underdeveloped and lesser sovereign regions. These agencies comprise a wide array of public organizations, including those within the central government to functionally decentralized entities and territorially decentralized units such as state and local governments.

An important premise of the current analysis is that in all societies the public and the private sectors, and their respective cultures, tend to intersect, especially at the level of the power elite (Mills, 1957). The same applies to the distinction between the civilian and military spheres of the state. Complex organizations, whether business or public, civilian or military, are not compartmentalized in complete isolation from each other and the broader political, social, or economic forces, both internal and external. Rather, they are woven into the fabric of societies, their problems, and culture, including historical memories, myths, and symbols, as well as past and present cleavages. They are also affected by the international, and especially the regional, environments in which these administrations operate.

Development administration, as a Western "soft technology" artefact to be applied in the periphery, assumed many entrenched Euro-American managerial values. These included the formal separation of politics from administration and the belief that First World-style progress was not only inherently good, but essential to stop revolution. "Rational" thinking, for example, presupposed that public sector management would be the purview of professional administrators, the latter ably assisted by "objective" economic plans formulated to achieve national goals. In this "factual" model there was no place for political considerations, let alone "ideological" preferences in development and its administration. However, as the post-1974 Vietnamese, or post-1979 Iranian, or Nicaraguan experiences proved, politics could not be kept separate from economic planning, management of resources, or administration of the public sector.

Either the administrative system responded to changing political contexts, or the indigenous political leadership simply bypassed the established administrative apparatus and created their own mechanisms to
accomplish their objectives. The same was true in a way for radically
conservative reforms as in the Asian NICs or in Latin America. The separation of politics from administration remained artificially embedded in
the parlance of the theories of development administration, while political factors dominated the practice of economic, social, and even managerial concerns. This conceptual schizophrenia is yet to be acknowledged
by many scholars, practitioners, and international aid personnel.

By their very nature, developmental issues are *political* because they
deal with the authoritative allocation of values in the context of limited
and sometimes rapidly diminishing resources. In developing countries,
therefore, public sector management cannot remain purely within the
domain of so-called value-free administration. Otherwise, irrespective
of the amount of international aid, history may repeat itself, as in the
failed experiment of America's massive involvements in Iran or Vietnam.
What is needed is a multidimensional new style of development administration and management, blending political, economic, administrative,
cultural, and spiritual forces to produce locally defined outcomes.

The context of New Public Management

It has become fashionable to talk about democratic transition in developing nations, especially by contrast to the "exceptional conditions"
existing in many such nations in the 1970s and 1980s. However, upon
close scrutiny this characterization is deceiving. The type of restricted
democracy to emerge in most countries bears little resemblance to
either Western democracy, or even the democratic practices existing in
some of these societies prior to the emergence of authoritarian rule.
The alleged democratizing trend is basically a formal and exclusionary
arrangement sustained by the pacts of elites, where the key function
of the state is to be a debt collector and administrator of structural
adjustment packages. Current modalities of administration for development, chiefly NPM, enhance these exclusionary practices. Lack of
democratic governance, more than the often repeated issue of "ungovernability," is at the center of the continuous crisis. Limited democratic
participation, while facilitating elite control of popular demands,
reduces the scope of legitimacy.

The key to understanding the current crisis is deinstitutionalization:
the extent to which the liberalization packages have failed to address

the question of legitimization. Illegitimate regimes are unsustainable, irrespective of the social engineering to keep their administrative machineries running. Administrative efficiency without public support is simply ineffectual. Both public disillusionment with government and the increasing meaninglessness of the restricted democracies are ubiquitous. If the state cannot maintain political and economic sovereignty, protect the life and well-being of its citizens, safeguard democratic rights and assure participation – in other words, provide for human security – its very reason for existence becomes problematic. Furthermore, as the prevailing neoliberal ideological policy agendas reduce the state role to merely protecting business interests, there is little the public sector can do, no matter how efficient or effective it seems. The New Public Management (NPM) formula, with its corollaries of privatization, downsizing, deregulating, localizing, and outsourcing, in the absence of a strong and legitimate political order and community, has potentially destabilizing effects. Moreover, without a pre-existing cohesive and vigorous civil society, administrative modernization is simply a futile means to a vacuous end.

The impact of NPM

The New Public Management movement was launched in the 1980s in the West to improve the financial problems that beset their governments. The various versions of the welfare – and the "warfare" – state had become too costly, and the Keynesian principles on which they were based were discredited because politicians had taken to running systematic deficits in order to finance government programs and satisfy special interests and constituencies. There were also instances of growing militancy on the part of public sector unions, numerous strikes, and the rigidities resulting from the combination of big government with collective bargaining. Furthermore, the 1980s were a revival of conservative ideologies, disguised as "tax revolts." The election of Margaret Thatcher in Britain and Ronald Reagan in the United States gave powerful support to a new "managerial" and business-like approach to public sector management. In reality, this trend had deep historical roots in the Wilsonian Administrative Reform Movement in the early twentieth century and its quest for business principles, efficiency, and de-politicization. The novelty of the approach was that it occurred at a time when the New Deal had become exhausted and national industrial capitalism had mutated into transnational global finance.

The NPM movement espoused a number operational "principles": (1) need for budget restraint, (2) reducing bureaucracy, (3) accent on results,

(4) service to the public, (5) decentralization and devolution, (6) contracting out, (7) performance pay, and (8) accountability. These principles translate to an emphasis on results more than on processes, both in planning and in the evaluation of programs and people, and service to the public. Quality is paramount, as the citizen is defined as a "client," or user, capable of demanding services. Delegation of authority is instrumental to these objectives; so are other businesslike incentives for motivating employees such as merit pay, mission statements, "strategic planning," and quality circles (Dwivedi and Gow, 1999: 130). This means bringing decisions as close as possible to the level of action and empowering employees to take initiative. There is greater attention to cost reduction through comprehensive auditing, contracting out, and introducing competitive external bids. The NPM has also introduced notions like corporate management, corporate culture, and bottom-line management, all part of the market-driven rhetoric.

This paradigm is based on the premise that by reducing the opportunities for incompetence and corruption through the narrowing of the scope of government activities, then efficient, transparent, effective, and accountable governance would appear. The expectation is that with fewer bureaucratic structures there would be fewer administrative problems. Once more, the heavy emphasis is placed on the business criteria of responsibility and accountability, with a blind faith in culture-bound practices, and thus little concern for subjective and intercultural dimensions.

Developing nations are being urged to move towards market-friendly governance and administration. Since the public sector is posited more as a problem than a solution, New Public Management in the garb of "development management" is recommended as a panacea. International aid is being made conditional upon accepting this prescription. Shrinking the bureaucracy, eliminating subsidies, tearing down protectionism, accepting currency devaluations and other changes in monetary and fiscal policy translate, in many instances, into leaving societies even more exposed to the ravages of the Western economic elites. In a broader sense, these adjustments mean the end of Keynesianism and the welfare state. Constrained by supply-side monetarist policies designed by economists and business administration experts, the role of public administrators appears to be to preside over their own demise (Dwivedi, 1994).

The limits of NPM

There is no doubt of the relevance of emphasizing result-based performance. There is, however, a danger of neglecting political, institutional, and cultural dimensions that represent deeply seated values. At the same time, faced with the complexities of day-to-day operations and the conflicting values that the system has thrust upon them, development administrators need some fundamental reference points to implement policies. In this respect, a public manager differs essentially from a private executive. While the latter is trained to regard the law as a costly constraint that must be obeyed only if it cannot be circumvented, the public manager must uphold it. To be sure, Public Management proponents usually say that they are aware that the state is not a business, but the values of public accountability and respect for the law tend to be eclipsed by bottom-line considerations. In practice, though very few public servants in the developed and underdeveloped worlds actually believe that government should be thought of as a corporation, the marching orders are to do precisely that. The greatest problems with managerialism in the public sphere are its reductionism, its deconstruction of the notion of public good, and its overall ethnocentrism. It tries to reduce a complex phenomenon to a single model drawn from business (Dwivedi and Gow 1999: 178).

A great paradox with NPM, when examined closely, is that it is a powerful ideology posing as "objective" technique (Manzer, 1984: 27). Public Management also appears to neglect the importance of law and legality in public administration. By introducing notions such as corporate management, corporate culture, and even that of management itself, it tends to obscure how relations between senior officials and politicians are legal-normative in nature. As John Rohr states, the constitution must serve as a source of regime values for administrators. At lower levels of administration, the law is a guarantor of due process: "Government by law is the most bureaucratic of all institutions because to a greater extent than other institutions it feels bound by its own rules" (Rohr, 1988: 171).

To us, the most appropriate normative image for the public administrator is that of the steward, not the entrepreneur. This leads to another NPM paradox. Astley and Van de Ven (1983) have observed that there are two versions of organization theory, one which is basically deterministic and the other which is proactive in its outlook. The deterministic school sees management as fine-tuning, adapting organizations to changes occurring in the environment, an objective situation that administrators cannot change. The proactive outlook takes a strategic view: the context and circumstances of administration are challenges to be acted upon. While the language of NPM is full of references to proactive stances, where strategic planning, innovation, change, and growth are promoted – as in an idealized business environment – its basic thrust is profoundly deterministic. There really are no choices (beginning with the nature of the economic model and policy) and structural economic conditions and world trade competition are *natural* forces to which governments all over the world must adhere. This obscures how governments in developed countries, in reality, do things very differently. For instance, continental European countries favor a more corporatist form of national bargaining with business and labor, while Britain, the United States, and Canada prefer a more liberal approach, where individualism is seen as supreme. It also masks the existence of still other policies and state models besides the market model (Dwivedi and Gow, 1999).

The dynamics of reform: processes and effects

Administrative change in the periphery has been, for the most part, either externally induced or heavily assisted by external actors. Colonial reforms, the desire of local elites to modernize, the presence of international missions and consultants, development administration, and today's New Public Management with SAPs are all cases in point (Dwivedi, 1994). The instances of indigenous administrative reform have been fewer, piecemeal, heavily localized, and mostly reactive to deep discontinuities. Whether internally or externally induced, there is a common denominator of all administrative reforms aimed at development. Despite the persistent use of technical and antiseptic rhetoric, they all have a political impact and intent. Such initiatives ultimately strengthen, weaken, consolidate, or challenge existing power relations. Furthermore, they all attempt to instrumentalize in organizational and managerial terms a broader political, social, and economic project.

Administrative modernization in the 1990s has occurred within very different domestic and international environments (and programmatic objectives) from those of the structural reforms of the 1960s. While the framework for international cooperation in the 1960s was distinctively Keynesian, the dominant prescription for at least since the 1980s has been neoliberal. Markets, rather than planning and government intervention, are central, though this policy switch has been and still is contingent upon strong state enforcement. Many developing countries came out of the Cold War and transitioned to a limited and not very transparent form of democracy brokered by external agents. The countries were also saddled with enormous and unmanageable debt burdens. The international financial community and its international bodies used debt-management to impose stringent conditionalities. The latter included a number of measures for attaining macroeconomic equilibrium via debt reduction, open market policies, and institutional reforms.

It is precisely in the context of these structural adjustment policies that the bulk of the prescriptions for current administrative reform have to be seen. The administrative corollary to the neoliberal package contained in the SAPs is fundamentally the New Public Management (NPM) paradigm. The latter is well known in the United States through the work of Osborne and Gaebler, particularly in *Reinventing Government* (Osborne and Gaebler, 1992). Yet, its lineage can be traced back to the conservative administrative reforms in the 1980s in England, New Zealand, Australia, and Canada, which materialized what was then called a "neo-conservative" agenda. Its administrative correlate has been a profound shift from civil service to public management. Downsizing government, making it publicly more accountable and transparent, turning it into a more efficient mechanism for delivering services on its own (or in partnership with private and/or voluntary organizations) are not purely isolated measures to secure "better" service. They are all manifestations of a broader ideological rationale that includes a number of articulated prescriptions: to re-establish the rule of the market over the "collectivist" idea of the "public good"; to reduce taxes and public expenditures; to deregulate the private sector; and to privatize the public sector (Nef and Robles, 2000). The role of the state under this model is mainly subsidiary; that is, its main directive is to protect the functioning of the market and private property. The basic "social contract" is post-Fordian in the sense that it reduces and fragments the role of workers in the system of labor relations, enhancing instead the uncontested hegemony of big business, both foreign and domestic. The notion of popular and national sovereignty is replaced by the sovereignty of capital. The liberal-democratic hybrid is thus displaced by a new type of state, a plutocracy with popular support and wide abstention. This state arrangement manifests itself in labor, taxation, and welfare policy. It also means a "postmodern" return to patrimonialism.

Over the last two decades, there has been a redefinition of the role of the state throughout most of the world, along the lines mentioned above. This has manifested itself in a transition between two models: the Keynesian "administrative state" whose central mission was the attainment of national development, and a "receiver" state whose principal role is the management of structural adjustment and whose subsidiary role is the implementation of palliative development. Such development refers mostly to targeted programs addressing the plight of those who fall off social safety nets as a result of orthodox economic policies, by means of micro-credit, capacity building schemes, limited poverty reduction, and the like. This transformation, as mentioned earlier, came on the heels of the bureaucratic authoritarian restructuring of the 1970s and was largely facilitated by it. It has been accomplished by closures, the privatization of many activities – especially in public utilities, health, social security, and education – and also by outsourcing in the private sector. A myriad of private entities have emerged to take on these downloaded public functions with captive clienteles and low competition.

The record of privatization has shown mixed results, ranging from improved quality and rationalization of service, to more effective costing and profitability, to situations of exclusion and a manifest decline in quality, coverage, and accessibility. In some cases, it has provided an impetus for modernization, improved standards, generated sources of new investment, and even cheaper and better products (as in telecommunications). However, privatization has, more frequently, spearheaded speculative appropriations at the public expense, and encouraged widespread fraud and large-scale corruption (as in the case of power utilities). Downsizing the civil service has led to a proliferation of personnel on limited service contracts, and to a large quantity of private consultants. It is not uncommon to see parallel structures to the officially downsized agencies, made up of contractual and external personnel. More often than not, this "temporary" structure evolves into a persistent clientele conditioned to the ups and downs of patronage politics.

Fiscal management has moved to the center stage of public administration. By and large, the financial base for public programs has been significantly reduced, while budgetary processes have been streamlined and expedited. Budget cuts have been geared towards attaining fiscal balance, improving efficiency in cost, and, above all, facilitating the entrenchment of structural adjustment policies. In addition to the macro issues of privatization and fiscal management, the administrative reform under NPM has had some remarkable achievements throughout the Other World, especially when it comes to the "micro" and efficiency-oriented aspects of administration. Of all the activities implemented, clearly the most successful have been the efforts to rationalize procedures and to de-bureaucratize and computerize services. The quality and timing of services rendered to customers has clearly improved in many lesser-developed countries. This applies especially to licenses, certificates, and the filing of income taxes. Certainly there has been a reduction of red tape. More substantial structural reforms have met with less success, ranging from limited accomplishments (e.g. localization), to mere cosmetic changes, to complete ineffectiveness, or worse. Basic issues, such as corruption, the inability to meet public needs and systemic breakdown, stand as the most nefarious outcomes of the new orthodoxy.

Conclusions

This interpretative exploration, though tentative, has allowed us to construct a basic outline of the relationships among administrative values, structures, and functions sketched above and the larger social and political order in which development takes place. It has also pointed to the dynamic relationship between such patterns and attempts at reform. As a general conclusion, nine propositions, with prescriptive implications, can be derived from the preceding analysis.

1. The administrative systems of the Third World reflect the distinctiveness and complexity of the various national realities, combined with common regional and global trends. The latter include persistent dependence, the perpetuation of rigid and particularistic social structures, chronic economic vulnerability, weak and unstable growth, social marginalization, low institutionalization, and acute social and political polarization. The above translates into high levels of ambiguity and uncertainty. Administrative life (and change) in these nations is conditioned more by these circumstances than by the declared goals of "technical" reform. Ostensibly, structural transformations have taken place; yet administrative culture and behavior have persisted, producing syncretistic adaptations rather than profound reorganizations. On the whole, the political economy of public administration in postcolonial societies has been conditioned by a bias for the maintenance of the domestic and regional status quo.
2. Generally, the administrative systems in most of the Other World have exhibited for quite some time the formal attributes of bureaucracy. Successive reforms have entrenched these traits. Yet, under the circumstances described here, the presence of "legal-rational" and "managerial" characteristics do not constitute substantive indicators, let alone predictors of responsiveness, effectiveness, or democratic accountability. Rather, the formality of the legal-rational

model often hides the reality of a "mock" bureaucracy, where complex procedures and technical trappings ultimately create a dysfunctional mixture of issue non-resolution and non-issue resolution. Public administration in these countries has been distinctively derivative. As a reflection of an entrenched center-periphery, regional, and global order, it has tended to follow trends and solutions manufactured in the developed societies. In this sense, it has been exogenous in its motivations, the identification of problems, and prescriptions. The tendency to define problems and questions from this static vantage point has provided for a rather mechanistic and uncritical approach. The scientific and technological institutions in the region have been more interested in reproducing the prevailing modes of social engineering than addressing larger contextual – and politically contentious – issues. Technical cooperation has not fared any better.

3. One emerging cultural pattern which has a deep impact on administration is cultural globalization. This trend towards one homogeneous managerial "monoculture" has its roots in Scientific Management and Development Administration. The ideas of efficiency, the automaticity of the market, and the myth of achievement, are all hallmarks of Western, specifically American, administrative culture. As the Soviet-led Marxist-Leninist strain of modernization fell into disrepute in Eastern Europe, its capitalist variety has become, by default, the dominant paradigm. There seems to be no alternative discourse at the present time – other than the reassertion of some indigenous model of development including Islamic revivalism – or the nostalgic critique offered by the postmodernism of Western intellectuals.

4. The above-mentioned global thrust, even under the guise of internationalization, often means technological dependence and continued reliance on the grafting of theories and methodologies of First World administrative modalities. This translates into the transplantation and replication of ideas, institutions, and "know-how" in postcolonial contexts. Under the language of "flexibility," the management style continues to be hierarchical, patrimonial, and centralized. Internationalization also requires that Western values and practices prevail everywhere, with standards of performance based on indicators developed in the core. An imitative and derivative system of public management emerges which favors downsized and streamlined government, the freeing of the business sector from overregulation and controls, and an efficient delivery of public goods

and services. Thus, it is no surprise that Western (or Western-trained) advisors recommend government restructuring, public service reforms, campaigns against corruption, and extensive training and education for public servants along the lines of NPM reforms undertaken in the United States, the United Kingdom, France, Germany, Australia, and Canada. For underdeveloped nations, there appears to be no choice but to accept the prevailing prescriptions. But the result of the therapy is often a hotchpotch of outdated colonial or neo-colonial administrative practices superimposed on ineffective bureaucracies being pulled in different directions. The world of the twenty-first century may be ready for fast food chains, blue jeans, and pop, but certainly not for the Western notion of "one size fits all" in the field of governance and administration.

5. During the last two decades of the twentieth century, there have been ostensible improvements in "de-bureaucratizing," "de-cluttering," reducing wait-times, and cutting down red tape. This has been accompanied by deregulation, a reduction in the size of the civil service, and a transfer of many public functions into private agencies. The failure of the democratizations of the 1980s and 1990s, debt crises, and structural adjustments have altered the content and instrumentalities of public policy (Nef, 1997). Peripheral administrative systems have been directly affected by current circumstances and challenges derived from a concerted effort at modernization along the lines of the prescriptions of First World governments and international agencies. However, this alteration has not resulted substantively in greater efficiency, let alone effectiveness, to "get things done" for the public; nor does it seem to effect a deep transformation of administrative practices and behavior.

6. The same applies to the question of administrative responsiveness to public demands. In a narrow technical sense, the transformation of the recipient into a "client" – as has been attempted in numerous reforms – does not alter substantially the intrinsic quality of the service. The irony is that, while there are increasing social demands on the public sector to tackle mounting problems and to provide more services, the state apparatus is shrinking. What is happening instead is a revolution of rising frustrations resulting from the inability of the political systems and their bureaucracies to tend to the most basic problems people face in their daily lives.

7. In this, the inability to control corruption is indicative of the incongruous logic of many current prescriptions. Such prescriptions are

not only flawed but also hypocritical. Administrative systems are immersed in a larger cultural matrix, containing values, practices, and orientations towards the physical environment, the economy, the social system, the polity, and culture itself. This matrix defines the parameters of both "public" and "private" spheres. Corruption in these cases is not only public; it is systemic (Caiden et al., 2001). A predatory attitude towards the environment and resource extraction, often fueled by foreign debt, possessive individualism, amoral familism and clientelism, a weak civic consciousness, and a tendency to imitate "the modern," configures a reactionary mind-set with ethical double standards. This also engenders irresponsibility and a lack of the capacity and the will to anticipate and make strategic policy shifts. Administrative reforms promoting privatization, a smaller role for the state, deregulation, downsizing, outsourcing, and formal decentralization have not addressed the fundamental issues of inequality, lack of democracy, and abuse that underpin administrative structures and practices. The existence of corruption and inefficiency is continually eating away the public trust in effective governance. Bureaucratic delays, ambiguous laws, widespread graft, and very slow redress by judicial mechanisms have all effectively produced collective misery and distress. Cynicism and apathy, but also frustration and rage, prevail. At the same time, ever growing numbers of people look at corruption and abuse as a normal way of life. The *mantra* for survival becomes "pay or suffer" – without the ability to pull strings in the corridors of power, nothing will get done. From erratic electric power and water supply, ill-maintained roads and street lights, illegal encroachments, open drains, and practically useless sewage disposal facilities, to tardy public transport – the list continues. At the same time, for those who can pay, everything is available. For most of humanity in the "other" world, but also for countless in "this" world, these challenges appear to be monumental. Yet, despite widespread corruption, there are pockets in the bureaucracy and the body politic devoid of the scourges of dishonesty and inefficiency. The picture is complex. For example, with respect to the South Asian nations, the World Bank report stated the following: "In South Asia . . . in many countries state inefficiency and corruption have co-existed with a relatively competent and efficient civil service, albeit one whose quality has suffered a noticeable decline" (World Bank, 1997: 165).

8. Historically, the administrative experience of the Other World has been moulded by numerous failed attempts at modernization and

recurrent crises. This results in a protracted condition of institutional underdevelopment. It has also contributed to perpetuating a self-fulfilling prophecy of immobility. Without real political and institutional development, addressing real issues such as poverty, unemployment, or lack of effective citizenship, administrative reforms – even when wrapped in the rhetoric of public sector modernization – are merely patchwork. The contribution of the current vogue towards real development and democracy remains marginal, as the protection of market forces, not development and democracy, is its prime directive. Despite the historical differences among the countries comprising the lesser developed component of the "Other World," their objective insertion into the international division of labor as export economies created a postcolonial order based upon commodities and rent. This characterization does not include the "transitional" societies of the former socialist world that became peripheralized in the 1990s. The dependent nature of such commodity states has continuously affected the basic functions of their administrative systems and the scope of possible reform. This may help to explain why the attempts at modernization via DA strategies in the 1960s, and NPM at present, merely reinforced the existing inequities and vulnerability, increasing social unrest, and political turmoil.

9. The fundamental issue is not so much management but governance. Perhaps the most comprehensive definition (as well as an ideal model) of "good governance" is offered by the United Nations Development Program (UNDP). For them, it entails among other things, government that is "participatory, transparent, and accountable. It is also effective and equitable. And it promotes the rule of law. Good governance ensures that political, social, and economic priorities are based on broad consensus in society and that the voices of the poorest and the vulnerable are heard in decision making over the allocation of development resources" (UNDP, 1998: 3). This definition evokes once again the concept of human security. From this definition, the basic characteristics of such governance can be spelled out: (a) One is public participation in decision-making. (b) Another is impartial enforcement of the rule of law. (c) The third is transparency in, and access to, governing process (including institutions and information sources). (d) A fourth is the responsiveness of institutions to the needs of all stakeholders. (e) Fifth is consensus among different and divergent interests in the society. (f) Sixth is the assurance of ethical behavior to all people, so that they may improve their well-being. (g) Seventh is effective and efficient responsibility and

accountability on the part of institutions – and this includes possessing the statecraft to serve the basic needs of all by using public resources with optimum accountability (Caiden and Dwivedi, 2001: 251–3). (h) Eighth is the need for strategic vision on the part of the leaders towards broad range, long-term perspectives on sustainable human development. (j) Finally, there is stewardship of governance where governing elites are dedicated to serve the public. Substantively, good governance and sustainable human development, especially in developing nations, also require conscientious attempts at eliminating poverty, enhancing and sustaining livelihoods, fulfilling basic needs, and offering a clean and open administrative system.

No country seems to be immune to the global ethical breakdown we have witnessed recently. Even the People's Republic of China, once hailed as a paragon of public virtue and morality by visitors and observers in the 1970s, has revealed a very different face. In many nations, a widespread sense of moral disarray, and decay, exists, and neither industrial nor developing countries are exempt. The need for probity is clearly an imperative. This is especially so in societies where traditional organizational and managerial values drawn from indigenous religious and secular sources were displaced in favour of the Western style of management, consumerism, and individualism. By casting out these fundamental beliefs, and with insufficient time and conditions for the "modern" values to take root, no specific standards were left against which the conduct of public officials (as well as business people) could be measured. Religious and other leaders with moral authority, particularly in non-Islamic nations, were told to keep out of state affairs, and the protective layer of public morality was left exposed to the onslaught of dishonesty, sleaziness, deception, and possessive individualism. That axiological protective layer in the body politic needs to be reaffirmed, for no nation or society, irrespective of its political, religious, or secular orientation, can sustain itself in a moral vacuum. The presence of "self-evident" articles of faith (drawn from the societal values, cultural traditions, and spiritual ideals) governing people's lives is, in this sense, not only an ethical but a practical necessity. Good governance is essentially moral governance (Dwivedi, 1987).

In hindsight, these generalized dismal results regarding the security of most people, contrary to the optimistic predictions derived from conventional modernization theory (both Keynesian and neoliberal), should have been predictable. So far, existing wisdom has tended to dismiss these failures as singular anomalies. However, when these cumulative discontinuities became too many to be treated as exceptionalities, the validity of existing models and trends ended up being largely irrelevant. We once used the expression "a fence around an empty lot." This was the case first with Development Administration in the 1970s and is happening now with New Public Management.

Any profound administrative transformation involves both structural and attitudinal changes (as well as much more profound value changes). Efforts at administrative restructuring, "modernization," and the like need to address, either directly or indirectly, the nature of administrative culture and the issue of democracy, or rather lack of democracy, throughout the globe. Administrative culture is something heterogeneous, and dynamic. Syncretism, continuities, and discontinuities are part and parcel of its fabric and texture. Lack of democracy or, put more directly, the contradiction between liberalism and democracy (Macpherson 1977), lie at the core of the current governance problem. From the era of bureaucratic authoritarianism to that of the new public managers, "governability," de-democratization and exclusion have been constants in the conventional political and administrative formula. The "problem" has been identified as "over-participation." The solution of choice has been to control, domesticate, or punish social demands. Administrative modernizations without real political democratic reform, beyond purely electoral and institutional facades, are fatally flawed and destined to fail. To paraphrase what John Stuart Mill articulated over a century and a half ago: small tinkering with big problems does not produce small solutions; it produces no solutions at all.

Acknowledgement

This chapter is a revised version of ideas first developed in the essay by O. P. Dwivedi and Jorge Nef (2004) "From Development Administration to New Public Management in Postcolonial Settings: Internal Problems, External Prescriptions," published in Gedeon M. Mudacumura and M. Shamsul Haque (eds), *Handbook of Development Studies*. New York: Marcel Dekker, pp. 153–75 (by permission of Routledge & Francis Group, LLC).

References

Astley, W. Graham and Andrew Van de Ven (1983) "Central Perspectives and Debates in Organization Theory," *Administrative Science Quarterly*, 28, pp. 245–73.

Balogun, M. Jide and Gelase Mutahaba (1999) "Redynamizing the African Civil Service for the Twent-first Century," in *Bureaucracy and the Alternatives in World Perspective*, Londom: Macmillan, pp. 190–216.

Barber, William and Ronning Neale (1966) *Internal Security and Military Power: Counterinsurgency and Civic Action in Latin America*. Columbus: Ohio State University Press, pp. 217–45.

Caiden, Gerald E. and O. P. Dwivedi (2001) "Official Ethics and Corruption," in Gerald E. Caiden, O. P. Dwivedi and Joseph G. Jabbra (eds), *Where Corruption Lives*. Bloomfield, Conn., USA: Kumarian Press, pp. 244–55.

Caiden, Gerald E., O. P. Dwivedi and Joseph G. Jabbra (eds) (2001) *Where Corruption Lives*. Bloomfield, Conn., USA: Kumarian Press.

Dwivedi, O. P. (1987) "Moral Dimensions of Statecraft: a Plea for an Administrative Theology," *Canadian Journal of Political Science*, 20, 4, pp. 699–709.

Dwivedi, O. P. (1994) *Development Administration: From Underdevelopment to Sustainable Development*. London, Macmillan.

Dwivedi, O. P. and James Iain Gow (1999) *From Bureaucracy to Public Management: the Administrative Culture of the Government of Canada*. Peterborough, Canada: Broadview Press.

Gil, Barry, Rocamora Joel, and Wilson, Richard (1993) *Low Intensity Democracy: Political Power in the New World Order*. London: Pluto Press.

Lee, Rensselaer W. (1988) "Dimensions of the South American Cocaine Industry," *Journal of Interamerican Studies*, 30, 3, pp. 87–104.

Macpherson, Crawford Brough (1977) *The Life and Times of Liberal Democracy*. Oxford: Oxford University Press.

Malloy, James (1977) "Authoritarianism and Corporatism in Latin America: the Modal Pattern," in James Malloy (ed.), *Authoritarianism and Corporatism in Latin America*. Pittsburgh: Pittsburgh University Press, pp. 3–19.

Manzer, R. (1984) "Policy Rationality and Policy Analysis: the Problem of the Choice of Criteria for Decisoion-making," in O. P. Dwivedi (ed.), *Policy and Administrative Studies*. Guelph, Canada: University of Guelph, pp. 27–40.

Mills, C. W. (1957) *The Power Elite*. New York: Oxford University Press.

Nef, Jorge (1982) "Empate político, inmobilismo e inflación: Algunas notas preliminares," *Revista Centroamericana de Administración Pública*, 2, 3 (July–December), pp. 141–55.

Nef, Jorge (1997) "Estado, poder y políticas sociales: una visión crítica," in Raúl Urzúa (ed.) *Cambios sociales y política públicas en América Latina*. Santiago: Andros, pp. 233–62.

Nef, J. and Dwivedi, O. P. (1981) "Development Theory and Administration: a Fence Around an Empty Lot?," *The Indian Journal of Public Administration*, 28, 1 (January–March), pp. 42–66.

Nef, J. and Robles, W. (2000) "Globalization, Neoliberalism and the State of Underdevelopment in the New Periphery" (with Wilder Robles), *Journal of Developing Societies*, 16, 1 (Leiden: Brill), pp. 27–48.

Osborne, David and Gaebler, Ted (1992) *Reinventing Government: How the Entrepreneurial Spirit is Transforming the Public Sector*. Reading, Mass.: Addison-Wesley Publishers.

Robin, Theobald (1995) "Globalization and the Resurgence of the Patrimonial State," *International Review of Administrative Sciences*, 61, 3 (September) pp. 423–32.

Robles, Wilder (2000) "Beyond the Politics of Protest: the Landless Rural Workers Movement of Brazil," *Canadian Journal of Development Studies*, 21, 3, pp. 657–91.

Rohr, John A. (1988) "Bureaucratic Morality in the United States," *International Political Science Review*, 9, 3, pp. 167–78.

Turner, M. and Halligan, J. (1999) "Bureaucracy and the Alternatives in East and Southeast Asia," in Keith M. Henderson and O. P. Dwivedi (eds), *Bureaucracy and the Alternatives in World Perspective*. Basingstoke: Macmillan, pp. 129–59.

UNDP (1998) *Good Governance and Sustainable Human Development*. New York: UNDP (UNDP/Docs/UN98-1.PDF).

Vilas, Carlos (1995) "Economic Restructuring, Neoliberal Reforms and the Working Class in Latin America," in S. Halebsky and R. Harris (eds), *Capital, Power and Inequality in Latin America*. Boulder, CO: Westview Press.

Vilas, Carlos (2000) "¿Más allá del Consenso de Washington? Un enfoque desde la política de algunas propuestas del Banco Mundial sobre reforma administrativa," *Revista del CLAD. Reforma y Democracia*, 18 (October), pp. 25–76.

World Bank (1997) *World Development Report 1997*. Washington, DC: World Bank.

7
The Challenges of Sustainable Development

Sustainable development is nothing new. Biological and historical evidence indicate that sustainability is built into the functioning of natural and man-made systems. Indeed, animals, plants, and humans have continually submitted to these rules by design, force, or by choice. Tribal communities still exhibit sustainability as a core principle in their daily lifestyles. What is new about the idea of sustainable development is its emergence as an explicit paradigm rather than a default system of adaptation or a last resort. The need for an explicit paradigm emerged from the loss of traditional livelihoods, once humans began to exercise their know-how to alter or control nature. As a consumption-intensive lifestyle began to overshadow the practice of sustainability, the need to find a paradigm that could reverse the course of events became necessary. In this chapter, we discuss the evolution of sustainable development as a paradigm, followed by a brief discussion of its various characteristics. We conclude by identifying the challenges we face in making sustainability a "way of life."

The Western roots of the environmental crisis

Humans are the ecologically dominant species in the ecosystem they inhabit. Although they have the same needs as all other species, such as heat, light, water, and food, humans possess attributes – and technological know-how – that give them dominance over other living species, and thus they can compete more successfully than all other living creatures. Furthermore, humans have been able to manipulate natural forces in ecosystems with an intensity unsurpassed by any other living beings. This manipulation has given rise to the breakdown of the natural self-protective and self-perpetuating mechanisms built into nature, a situation exacerbated by our belief that humans have the right to use the natural environment solely for their own designs and ends, without considering the systemic consequences of our actions. In Western civilization, this view has dominated the thinking regarding the environment (as natural resources). It has also provided justification for exploitative and predatory actions. It should be noted, however, that environmental crises are not limited to the West. The cases of the pre-Columbian Mayan civilization and that of the Rapa Nui of Eastern Island are telling examples of environmental exhaustion and, eventually, collapse.

Exploitation of nature justified

In early seventeenth-century England, Francis Bacon asserted that it was a duty of man to regain his rights over nature, assigned to him in the beginning by God, and to secure dominion over nature. His writings exerted a profound influence on the belief that the power of science and technology could improve the human condition. In his utopian work, *The New Atlantis* (published in 1624), he described a science-oriented community on an imaginary island where science and technology were pursued not so much as ends in themselves but in order to subdue and improve nature to meet human demands. In his view, articulated in his *Novum Organum* (1620), nature should not be left on its own because when nature is interfered with its secrets become more readily known than when left to its own course. Bacon was the first to stress the need for experimental science instead of purely intellectual philosophical deduction of natural phenomena. Bacon's dream was a science-based technology whereby applied scientists would replace craftsmen. In the spirit of the "Idea of Progress" – a philosophy which later became popular in the eighteenth century in the West – Bacon believed that through science, man could extend his power over the universe (Bacon, 1938). Consequently, Bacon advocated restoring man to his original God-given dominion over nature, and such a restoration would come through science. As such, Bacon was building on a tradition of dominion with a long Judeo-Christian (and also Islamic) lineage, going back to the Old Testament.

Two major developments took place in England as a result of Bacon's new science-based technological scheme. First, his teachings led to the formation of the Royal Society whose Fellows (members) set out to investigate not only nature but also followed a specified program of practical applications of science, and new patents. One example was the research for an engine to drain mines, which became one of the factors leading to the invention of a practical steam engine (Forbes, 1968: 20).

In addition, Bacon influenced many others who expanded his theme beyond the British Isles. The first was French philosopher and mathematician Descartes who emphasized the scientist-technologist approach to make use of nature freely, which was created not only to serve man but also to be potentially useful to all. In the Galilean and Copernican traditions, another scientist, Isaac Newton, also taking direction from Bacon, placed all of nature under the laws of mathematics; and it was from this focus that there emerged an anthropocentric and mechanical view of nature whose sole existence was to serve humanity. In keeping with the image of a machine, there also developed a system of dualism in the Western worldview by separating human beings from nature and placing them above it.

That dualism also created a paradigm of separating facts from values, objectivity from subjectivity, and detachment from emotions. By the seventeenth century, a radical view took over the scientific establishment: the world of nature was to be regarded as being essentially value-free, devoid of intrinsic worth, and to be used by human beings as they saw fit. The new scientific attitude, particularly from the eighteenth-century Enlightenment onward, was a de-essentialization and, hence, an "objectification" of nature (Merchant, 1995). As a consequence, nature came to be regarded as an object to be exploited by humans for their own purposes. Most importantly, the subjugation of nature – and "nature people" – along with the primary emphasis on the use of machines, became the credo of the industrial revolution and the motto of Western civilization aided by scientific discoveries and technological advances.

Positivism, pre-eminent amongst evolutionary theories, the enormous leaps in science and technology, and eventually the very origins of Taylorism, Fayolism, and Scientific Management reflected the triumph of the West in aggressive imperial expansion. Despite two world wars and a global depression, by the middle of the twentieth century, with the journey to the moon, hegemony over nature and the universe was complete and unquestioned. It was thought by many in the West that there was nothing science and technology could not solve. Pollution was seen, at least until the 1960s, as a manageable side-effect of material progress, which could be prevented much in the same manner as certain dreaded events, such as flooding, famines, and diseases like the plague and small-pox, had been brought under control. It wasn't until the 1970s that the impact of human activities which threatened the biosphere came to be properly appreciated, especially the myth of a "superabundance" of natural resources, and the idea of perpetual progress at the cost of continuous exploitation of nature and domination of the environment.

In summary, the subjugation of nature, along with the primary emphasis on the use of technology and machines, became the credo of the industrial revolution and the Age of Imperialism. It was also the motto of the Western world which was, in turn, aided constantly by many scientific discoveries and tremendous technological advances. Colonialism, in its search for ever-expanding sources of raw materials, extended the domain of this paradigm into the four corners of the world and, in so doing, it defined the non-Western world as commodity states to be used for material gain and for profit. In turn, Marxist socialism, while disputing the positive historical role of the bourgeoisie in ushering progress, hung on a very similar notion of the human subjugation of nature. When decolonization began in earnest at the end of World War Two, the mode of human–environmental interaction which developed during colonialism was firmly entrenched. This was the case even in cultures whose foundations were clearly different from the Western tradition, as in most of Asia and Africa.

This gives rise to a number of questions. Do people have an inherent right to continuously exploit nature in the name of economic development and material progress, even at the expense of the future? Can the belief in human superiority over nature and the myth that humans are endowed with abundant natural resources be singled out as a cultural cause of many environmental problems and even natural disasters? Seen in this perspective, the sustainable development paradigm must be interrogated in order to protect global survival.

Ethics of moderate consumption reinforcing sustainable development in non-Western traditions

An important question when considering sustainable development as it relates to exploitation would be "Is there an alternative approach?" Many non-Western cultures provide different living styles centered on the ethics of moderate consumption. It seems that "religious leaders and institutions in industrial nations have largely failed to address the consumerist engine that drives industrial economies" (Gardner, 2003: 168). Their consumption-intensive culture appears to have been driven by advertisers who deliberately confuse needs with desires and encourage acquisitiveness (Gardner, 2003). From this perspective it is impossible to revert back to a simpler lifestyle and roll back the consumerist tide. On the other hand, some developing nations in Asia and Africa are attempting, out of necessity, to create sustainable livelihoods which do not place too much demand on the environment. One good example is the Sarvodayan ethic of consumption, present in parts of Sri Lanka and India as well as in Southeast Asia. *Sarvodaya* means the uplifting or development of everyone together in a non-acquisitive manner through the sharing of available resources in the community. This ethic of moderate consumption requires people to follow a system of spiritual detachment from material goods so that needs rather than desires dominate their daily lives. The Sarvodayan ethic places limits on consumption and stigmatizes those who seek more than what is essential for a decent life as greedy. This ethic also demands a proper respect be shown for Mother Earth. The concept draws from the precept of *Satyagraha* as used by Mahatma Gandhi.

Satyagraha and treating Mother Earth with respect is another way of maintaining the balance between nature and human activities. Satyagraha literally means persistence and endurance for the truth. The term was initially coined in South Africa by Mahatma Gandhi to distinguish the non-violent resistance of the Indians of South Africa from the contemporary "passive resistance" of suffragettes and others. Non-violent resistance embodies four basic prescriptive elements, centered on the idea of "purity": (a) the first refers to purity of motive; (b) the second refers to the purity of means to be used; (c) the third element of purity is suitability of place and time; (d) and last, but not least, is the purity derived from the mental status of the doer or agent. Satyagraha entails holding on to the truth, or to the strength of truth. In his use of this concept, Mahatma Gandhi believed that the pursuit of truth does not involve inflicting violence on one's opponent, but convincing one's adversary of their error by patience and sympathy: "For what appears to be the truth to one may appear to be error to the other. And patience means self-suffering. So the doctrine came to mean vindication of the truth not by the infliction of suffering on the opponent but on one's self" (Gandhi, 1961: 6). He further emphasized that Satyagraha was not a mere experiment but a part of his life and for him "it is both a means and an end" (Gandhi quoted by Brown, 1977: 342). In recent years, a similar strategy, "Satyagraha for the environment," has been used by people in India against the construction of big dams such as on the Narmada river as well as to protect forests in the name of the Chipko movement.

The concept of Mother Earth

Stewardship of the environment requires one to consider the entire universe as one's extended family with all living beings in this universe as the members of the household. This concept, also known as *Vasudhaiv Kutumbakam*, is taken from the Hindu scripture Atharva Veda, and holds that all human beings as well as other creatures including inanimate objects on earth are the members of the same extended family of Mother Earth. This concept has been further explained by Dr. Karan Singh: "that the planet we inhabit and of which we are all citizens – Planet Earth – is a single, living, pulsating entity; that the human race, in the final analysis is an interlocking, extended family" (Singh, 1991: 123). We also know that members of the extended family do not wilfully endanger the lives and livelihood of others; instead, they think first in terms of caring for others before taking action. The welfare of all on our planet Earth could be realized through the thread of spiritual understanding and cooperation at the global level.

This means enhancing global as opposed to individual sustainabilities. Operationally, this means to affirm a sort of Earth Charter. There is a need of a holistic view of the basic ethical principles supported by broadly accepted tenets and practical guidelines that govern people's and nations' behaviors in their relationships with the earth and one another (Dwivedi and Khator, 2007). Such an approach attempts to lead to a new ethic of global sustainability and a global strategy for sustainable living. Only by considering the cosmos as a part of the extended human family can we (individually and collectively) develop the necessary maturity and respect for all other living beings. If nature is treated as sacred, and if we mould our perspective by using environmentally friendly ethics, development can be sustainable. This stand is not directly against the use of technology. Sustainable development requires the use of a combination of Western and non-Western approaches to construct a composite well-being of nations that includes both human and environmental well-being.

Sustainable development: evolution of the paradigm, 1972–2002

The year 1972 marked a watershed in the history of the international environmental discourse (Caldwell, 1984). Many world leaders gathered in Stockholm to discuss for the first time global environmental issues in a systematic and comprehensive manner. Until then, the world was seen as an unchanging backdrop to all kinds of unrestricted human activities. The Stockholm Conference raised several questions regarding the dichotomy between affluence and poverty and our capacity to address them within the international governance framework. The conference was divided between two blocs. One was the industrialized nations of the West together with the former socialist Second World of Eastern Europe. The other bloc was the poor countries in Asia, Africa, Latin America, and the Middle East. What has been often termed the "Third World" was led by India, the Philippines, Kenya, and China. Their delegates contested that each individual in the industrialized countries draws, on average, thirty times more heavily on the limited resources of the earth than their counterparts in the developing countries (Caldwell, 1984: 50). Despite all the controversy generated by the North–South split, the main achievement of the Stockholm Conference was heightening worldwide awareness of pollution problems and the legitimization of environmental issues as an object of national and international policy. It also impelled the national governments to start creating administrative mechanisms for environmental protection.

While preparations were being made for this first United Nations (UN) Conference on the Human Environment, the most heated debate in the history of environmental concern was intensified by the publication of *Silent Spring* (Carson, 1962) and the doomsday predictions by the Club of Rome. A subsequent publication, *The Limits to Growth* in 1972 by Meadows et al., expanded the debate and brought to the surface the question of sustainability in a world divided into rich and poor. With the help of computer system modeling, the book argued that there was an urgent need to control the present growth trends in world population, industrialization and pollution, food production, and resource depletion if the earth is to be spared a disaster of planetary proportions (Meadows et al., 1972). For the first time, scientifically based research seemed to contradict the old scientific view of progress.

The Stockholm Conference, while limited in scope, started a new wave of environmentally conscious international conventions and treaties such as the 1973 International Convention for the Prevention of Pollution from Ships (MARPOL) and the 1980 Convention on the Conservation of Antarctic Marine Living Resources. The UN General Assembly adopted the recommendations of the Conference on December 15, 1972, and it also established the UN Environment Program (UNEP), to serve as an environmental monitoring agency. Several years later, the Conference also led to the establishment of the World Commission on Environment and Development (WCED), known as the Brundtland

Commission. The WCED released its findings in a publication entitled *Our Common Future*, where the Commission offered explanations of how human–environmental interactions are collectively unsustainable and geared towards destroying the global ecosystem (WCED, 1987). It also stated that we cannot save the environment without development, but yet we cannot continue to develop unless we save the environment at the same time. The report's main recommendation was that without rearranging the existing institutions and legal mechanisms, the problems of fragmentation, overlapping jurisdictions, narrow mandates, and closed decision-making will persist. The report states, "the real world of interlocked economy and ecological systems will not change, the policies and institutions concerned must" (WCED, 1987: 310). The right questions had been raised and the right issue had been put on the agenda. Now, the world waited for a serious dialogue.

1992: developing a meaningful discourse

Twenty years after Stockholm, in 1992, the international community gathered again, this time in Rio de Janeiro, Brazil. The Rio Summit, formally known as the United Nations Conference on Environment and Development (UNCED) and popularly dubbed the "Earth Summit," was the second United Nations conference on the environment. The contrast between the 1972 and the 1992 Conference was remarkable: in comparison to 2 heads of state, 134 NGOs, and a handful of journalists who attended the 1972 Conference, the Earth Summit was attended by 116 heads of state, 7892 NGOs, and over 8000 journalists (Bryner, 1999: 157). The South's participation was markedly higher at Rio: one-third of the participants were from Southern countries as opposed to only one-tenth at the Stockholm Conference in 1972.

Much had changed in twenty years on the world scene. The Cold War had ended, the Soviet Union had broken apart and hence could not boycott the Earth Summit as it did in the 1972 Conference, globalization was rapidly expanding, scientific advances had emerged at an accelerated pace, shrinking the world itself, the internet was boosting the power of epistemic communities, and many environmental disasters had taken place with their effects spilling over national borders, proving that national boundaries had become meaningless with respect to environmental issues (Khator, 1995).

The Earth Summit emphasized that environmental protection could not continue to be a luxury; instead, economic and social issues must become part of the definition if the environment was to be protected in a sustainable manner. For a long time, developed countries had been reaping the benefits of their exploitative practices, and now it appeared that they had a moral and social obligation to assist developing countries in their march towards greater economic prosperity. The Summit adopted Agenda 21, which was essentially a plan for sustainable development, with consensus on goals of growth, equity, and environmental protection for future generations. The 800-page document outlined commitments from nations to internalize environmental costs, address poverty, change consumption patterns, include women and indigenous people in decision-making, undertake environmental assessments, build capacity in developing countries, strengthen scientific knowledge, and bridge the data gap (UNCED, 1992).

The Earth Summit also created a new agency, the United Nations Commission on Sustainable Development, to collect data on environmental and development activities and to monitor the individual and collective progress of nations towards achieving the goals set forth in Agenda 21. However, despite these ostensibly symbolic signs of progress, the underlying assumptions for development did not show any change. Many non-governmental and governmental delegates left the Summit viewing the glass as half empty rather than as half full when the Summit failed to deal with real issues. The US government, under George Bush (Sr.), basically sought to ignore most proposed instruments and protocols. The ultimate success of Agenda 21 was dependent upon the willingness of the North to provide funds and know-how to the South, but there were no mechanisms to ensure that such a partnership would indeed emerge. There was no doubt that by 1992, the issues of the South had gained legitimacy. Also, the necessity of participation of Southern scholars, activists, and members of non-governmental organizations in both the North and South in searching for solutions became more obvious.

2002: forming the agenda

Ten years later, the world once again came together in Johannesburg, South Africa for the 2002 World Summit on Sustainable Development (WSSD). By then, the term "sustainable" had become an integral part of public terminology even though no agreement existed on what it truly meant. Like any amorphous entity, sustainable development was left to take any form and shape depending on the boundaries and contexts in which it was to be used.

The discourse of the previous decade and the Summit itself left three concepts as the main pillars of the emerging paradigm: environmental protection, social development, and economic prosperity. The under-standing had emerged that the three were interrelated and could not be taken apart if the structure were to hold. It was also acknowledged that governments alone could not accomplish the goal of sustainability and thus partnerships with NGOs and the private sector had to be forged. Policy-makers also had to admit that lack of environmental quality and poverty were intimately linked and that developing coun-tries could not be blamed for polluting the environment and constantly put in the defendant's box as they were during the Earth Summit in Rio. It also became evident that the world was not meeting its goals of progress and that the world's environment remained in a very fragile state. Rich countries of the North had not fulfilled their promises and were as much at fault as their poor counterparts by pursuing reckless development practices.

The gap between the rich and the poor still persisted, and in many instances widened. As before, a tiny proportion of the world's popula-tion enjoyed wealthy and prosperous lives while a large proportion of the people lived in dire poverty. Initiatives by the World Bank and International Monetary Fund (IMF) had failed to make a dent in the wall of poverty and exclusion, and perhaps had made it worse. Efforts by various international conventions had also had a minimal impact, as people in the wealthiest countries continued their over-consumptive lifestyles, thus placing an extremely heavy burden on the environment.

The World Summit became the first real attempt to create balance between development and the environment. The Summit focused on five specific environmental areas: water and sanitation, energy, health, agricultural productivity, and biodiversity protection and ecosystem management. At the end of the Summit, two documents were adopted: the Plan of Implementation and the Johannesburg Declaration on Sus-tainable Development. The term "sustainable development" had thus become a new mission and a new hope.

Critics argue that even though it is too soon to gauge the success of the Johannesburg Summit, the Summit missed a major opportunity. It failed because once again it did not adequately address the marked dis-parity between the rich and poor countries. It also failed to take strong initiatives to halt the continuing assault on our ecological well-being. There were no commitments made by rich countries to sacrifice their positions of privilege to respond urgently to global environmental threats. Most importantly, the Summit failed to discourage multinational corporations from exploiting the resources of poor countries.

Sustainable development and well-being

Does a close relationship exist between sustainable development and environmental well-being? Since 1987, when sustainable development acquired the status of a paradigm, the term has been defined and elaborated differently. At one place, the WCED denotes sustainable development as "a process of change in which the exploitation of resources, the direction of investments, the orientation of technological development, and institutional change are made consistent with future as well as present needs" (WCED, 1987: 9). It is the historical continuity of that exploitation of natural resources that has been at the heart of the ecological crisis facing humanity; consequently, environmental well-being is closely linked with human well-being. In 2001, Robert Prescott-Allen published a report, *The Well-being of Nations: a Country-by-Country Index of Quality of Life and the Environment*, with the central argument that a society or a nation can be well and sustainable only when both its people and the ecosystem are healthy. His contention is that human well-being and the health of the ecosystem are closely linked because the ecosystem surrounds people much in the same manner "as the white of an egg surrounds and supports the yolk" (Prescott-Allen, 2001: 4). Based on this premise, he prepared a common framework of dimensions consisting of (a) human dimensions, including health and population, national and household wealth, education and culture, community and social capital, and equity; and (b) ecosystem dimensions, including land and forests, water quality and diversity, air quality, species and genetic diversity, and energy and resources use.

He defined (1) human well-being as "a condition in which all members of society are able to determine and meet their needs and have a large range of choices to meet their potential," and (2) ecosystem well-being as "a condition in which the ecosystem maintains its diversity and quality and its potential to adapt to change and provide a wide range of choices and opportunities for the future" (Prescott-Allen, 2001: 5). To measure the quality of life and environmental stress, he used a number of indicators to measure the well-being of nations including such factors as the UNDP Human Development Report, the Ecological Footprint, Environmental Sustainability Index, World Resources Report, the Environmental Pressure Index, etc.

He found that a society remains unwell and unsustainable if its people are poor and the ecosystem is degraded; that society is also unwell and unsustainable if either the ecosystem condition is bad or human quality of life is bad (Prescott-Allen, 2001: 5). From his analysis of 180 countries, his contention is that most of the developing nations of Asia and Africa suffer not only from environmental stress but also from a poor quality of life. On the other hand, the industrialized nations of North America, Western Europe, Japan, and Australia/New Zealand have better human well-being scores although they may suffer from a moderate ecosystem deficit. Sustainable development requires people and the ecosystem to function in unison, and the well-being of each sector should not be pursued singularly.

At the international level, well-being alliances have to be forged and partnerships built between the wealthy North and the poor South: "Wealthy countries have won much of their high human well-being at the cost of stress on the environments of other countries (via trade) or on the global ecosystem (notably impacts on the global atmosphere). Since they leave such a large ecological footprint, they should help [others]" (Prescott-Allen, 2001: 147).

Sustainable development as a policy paradigm

The Brundtland Commission defined sustainable development as "development that meets the needs of the present without compromising the ability of future generations to meet their own needs" (WCED, 1987: 43). This definition is an attempt to offer a set of principles; however, it fails to offer a clear set of operational guidelines to decision-makers with which to evaluate issues and form policies. The expectation was that countries and regions would come up with their own guidelines within this conceptual framework. Needless to say, hundreds of definitions and interpretations of the term have mushroomed over the last two decades.

Despite multiple attempts at defining sustainable development, the concept remains a most elusive term. It raises more questions than it answers: Whose needs are being met? Who decides if the needs are being met? What are the limitations imposed by technology? How will future generations perceive needs? Critics argue that the term is self-contradictory. Can any development really be sustainable in the long run? Development is inherently utilitarian in its approach and is aimed at overtaking nature, exploiting it, and reconstructing it to meet human needs and desires. Lele (1991) argues that sustainable development is "being packaged as the inevitable outcome of objective scientific analysis, virtually an historical necessity that does not contradict the deep-rooted normative notion of development as economic growth. In other words, sustainable development is an attempt 'to have one's cake and eat it too'" (Lele, 1991: 619).

Critics also claim that the term is deliberately misleading, making people believe that actions are being taken to protect and enhance the environment when, in reality, long-term damage is being done whose extent may not even be known today. The term has become a magnet for special interest groups who have attached themselves to this "fashionable notion only to subvert it for their own ends" (Victor, 2006: 92). Despite disagreements over the meaning of the term, sustainable development has become a powerful and emblematic idea and has also emerged as a central factor begging for further exploration and self-examination.

The Earth Summit offered a venue for heads of state, representatives from United Nations agencies, and NGOs to discuss this and similar challenges facing the meaningful implementation of sustainable development. After the Earth Summit, the United Nations Commission for Sustainable Development (CSD) was established to continually monitor the implementation and report on its progress. The CSD holds annual meetings to discuss the progress on Agenda 21. It is comprised of 53 members and operates as a functional commission of the United Nations Economic and Social Council. More than 50 ministers and 1000 NGOs participated in the CSD's work to ensure that sustainable development issues remain on the United Nations agenda.

Sustainable development, in theory, is a demanding concept because adhering to it implies restraining nations from activities that are the natural corollary of accumulated wealth. It can be especially challenging when we consider that we must refrain from these activities for the sake of future generations, and for all people in the world, whom we will never know. In other words, sustainable development demands that we accept the concept of group rights, rather than just individual rights (Weiss, 1993: 34).

Sustainable development implies change in the way we identify problems, conceptualize issues, conduct business, and formulate solutions. The relevance of sustainable development as a new paradigm for decision-making and its potential to challenge existing decision-making practices is hindered by the diminishing supply of resources that are necessary to implement the policies. We need to maintain flexibility consistent with the dynamism found within the reconceptualization of sustainable development if we are to understand the true needs and objectives of an interdependent, environmentally sound, sustainable future.

Sustainable development has dramatically changed the controversy over the environment and its relation to development. In theory, sustainable development challenges the entire traditional notion of economic development, negating economic growth as the core value of social and economic activities. Similarly, it does not accept environmental protection as a goal irrespective of its contextual relevance. In fact, it forces us to combine economic and environmental concerns into a plausible development strategy. According to the WCED, "We have in the past been concerned about the impacts of economic growth upon the environment. We are now forced to concern ourselves with the impacts of ecological stress . . . upon our economic prospects" (WCED, 1987: 5).

Sustainable development is more than just a directive to individuals and societies. It is an assurance that all peoples and their governments will commit to protect, conserve, preserve, and pass on a healthy environment and the legacy of human civilization to future generations and, thus, refrain from deliberate actions that may harm or threaten that heritage. This principle is based on the government understanding that long-term economic growth is only possible if a nation commits to sustaining its natural environment and cultural heritage, endorses an integrated approach to sustainable development, and acknowledges the interconnected nature of science, technology, society, culture, and the economy.

Sustainable development obliges humanity to use, develop, manage, and care for the environment and planetary resources in a manner that supports the stewardship of all creation (including all natural resources and the welfare of all living beings). It also involves the continuity of the cultural and spiritual heritage of each community, as well as the maintenance of harmony between people and nature for present and for future generations (Dwivedi, 1997: 28). It unites two key imperatives: the right to develop (economically, socially, politically, and culturally) and the need to sustain the environment. Future development must be carried out in a sustainable and equitable manner. It also implies a balance between sustainability and equitability. Further, it implies intra-generational equity between "haves" and "have-nots." At a fundamental level, sustainable development means the need to work towards a common, global goal for all people. A small percentage of the world's population continues to over-exploit our natural resources to maintain their over-consumptive and predatory lifestyles. The rest of the world's population is witnessing rapid population growth and continues to exploit its natural resources or allow others to exploit them in order to survive. For sustainable development to become meaningful, these two dramatically different, unsustainable patterns need to be altered through government regulation and personal commitments. Otherwise, the crisis will continue to spiral downward and human development will become increasingly difficult to sustain.

Sustainable development: challenges and prospects

Despite unprecedented progress made in advancing human capacity, wide disparities between the privileged and unprivileged have persisted and expanded. Human capacity building has not kept an even pace with economic and technological development. For example, the income gap between the richest and poorest people has risen – the World Bank estimates that the average income in the 20 richest countries was 37 times larger than the average income in the poorest 20 countries, and this gap has doubled in the past 20 years (World Bank, 2000: 3). One-quarter of the world's population does not receive their basic survival needs, such as adequate food, clean and adequate water, primary health, education, and shelter (Flavin, 2001). Trade barriers imposed by industrialized countries hinder poverty elimination. The United States gives $3 billion in subsidies to its 25000 cotton farmers, which consequently brings down world cotton prices. If these farm subsidies were eliminated, approximately 114 million people in developing countries could be brought out of poverty (Werlin, 2004: 1034).

The main distinction between the North and the South is primarily based on economic progress and material wealth. Geographical boundaries also play a role in dividing these two regions, as do trade barriers, economic prosperity, and political control. It must be understood that human development and economic growth must mutually reinforce one another: for development to be sustainable, both human development and economic growth must occur in tandem. This requires that people receive basic services and that they participate in the implementation and the design of developmental programs. We must acknowledge the need for greater cooperation between all facets of human development. We must be proactive in the global economy as globalization is currently disproportionately favoring people with expertise, power, and the ability to compete in the global market.

Although both the North and the South exploit the environment, they do so in different ways and for different reasons. That both take a toll on the environment should be the fundamental point of agreement on the need for cooperation to work towards a common goal. Certain environmental problems, such as ozone depletion, air pollution, the loss of biodiversity, and global climate change, are not contained within political borders, and hence addressing these issues requires international cooperation to protect the world's commons. Everyone must share the planet and its resources, and should divide up its finite and dwindling resources more equitably. Thus, population growth and poverty become the first testing ground for the applicability of sustainable development.

Population growth is considered to be one of the main factors in environmental deterioration, though population reduction is extremely difficult to achieve and is a complicated issue. Demographers state that even if we somehow manage to reduce world fertility rates to a level of simple replacement and then commit to stay at this level, the world's population would still continue to grow because of the current age distribution and expected increases in life-expectancy. It is likely that the population would continue to grow for about another 100 years before leveling off to about double the present size (Cabre, 1993: 2). In some developing countries, youth accounts for 40 percent of the population. The UN reports that over 100 countries have youth bulges in comparison to North America and Europe, where youth makes for approximately 20–25 percent of the total population (United Nations Population Division, 2003).

After the 1992 Earth Summit, the countries in the South hoped that the issue of poverty would be combined with global environmental issues. The economic crisis of the 1990s crushed this hope as industrialized countries focused their time and energies on attempting to get out of the recession. By 2002, it became clear that despite four decades of development, poverty and other urgent issues affecting developing nations had not been adequately addressed. The international aid programs and structural reform initiatives had brought mixed results. Sustainable development can only become an achievable goal for the world's poor when extreme poverty is eliminated and living conditions become tolerable. Shridath Ramphal, the former Secretary General of the Commonwealth of Nations and a member of the Brundtland Commission, stated, "If poverty is not tackled, it will be extremely difficult to achieve agreement on solutions to major environmental problems. Mass poverty, in itself unacceptable and unnecessary, both adds to and is made worse by environmental stress . . . That is why the global policy dialogue must integrate environment and development" (Ramphal, 1992: 17).

In 2000, the UN Millennium General Assembly established eight Millennium Development Goals (MDG): (1) to eradicate extreme poverty and hunger (supposed to be met by 2015); (2) to achieve universal primary education; (3) to promote gender equality and empower women; (4) to reduce child mortality; (5) to improve maternal health; (6) to combat HIV/AIDS, malaria, and other diseases; (7) to ensure environmental sustainability (supposed to be met by 2015); and (8) to develop global partnerships for development (UN, 2000). No one would argue against these goals, but can we really expect the Millennium Development Goals, especially goal number 7, to be achieved? Previous experience with UN developmental decades and other similar action plans have suggested that the results will be mixed, at best.

One of the clearest results of thinking in terms of sustainable development paradigms is that our old concept of economic development has been dramatically altered. While much has been accomplished at the theoretical and discursive level, even more needs to be done. We would like to offer the following concluding propositions for further discussion.

Human deprivation and environmental degradation

There are three main indicators of human deprivation: lack of access to proper healthcare facilities, lack of access to safe drinking water, and the proportion of malnourished children. By the end of the twentieth century, there were about 1.1 billion malnourished people worldwide encompassing as much as 40 percent of the population of some countries (such as Kenya, Zambia, and Zimbabwe) being malnourished (Flavin, 2001). Particularly with respect to children, the most depressing data come from South Asia where half of the world's malnourished children (about 84 million) are to be found in just three countries of South Asia: Bangladesh, Pakistan, and India (Haq, 1997: 30). Indeed the colossal example of human deprivation, according to the Human Development in South Asia Report (1997), occurs in South Asia where over 500 million people live in absolute poverty, with 260 million people lacking access to even rudimentary healthcare facilities, 337 million without safe drinking water, 830 million with no access to basic sanitation, and 360 million adults unable to read and write (Haq, 1997: 8). Many countries of Africa face the same fate. How is it possible to have sustainable development and thriving economic progress with so much human deprivation? The vision of the future for these nations entails not only a long-term economic growth with an improved and sustainable environment, but also the need to remedy past destruction of the environment while helping industries shift from waste management to pollution prevention, efficient resource use, and industrial ecology. Both the developing nations and their industries will have to use a forward-looking approach by helping their industries reduce or eliminate their waste and disposal costs by using sustainable technologies. To achieve this vision, these nations will need a regulatory system which stresses high environmental standards and, at the same time, encourages flexibility and creativity (but not ingenuity to bypass the system by corrupt methods) in meeting those standards. It will not be an easy task because the existing governmental regulatory system is not conducive to such a creative approach; it would have to be "reinvented" to carry out these new responsibilities. Government and industry will have to work to create an accountable and transparent industrial ecology. Together, these nations must transform their industrial, technological, and regulatory infrastructure to use less energy, to cause less environmental damage, and to serve the needs of their people. It will have to be a joint endeavor towards a sustainable future by balancing together human and environmental well-being.

International environmental crimes

Transboundary and global ecological threats have been increasing especially with respect to endangered species such as tigers, elephants, musk deer, and Caspian Sea sturgeon. The illegal trade of these wildlife species, however, originates in developing nations seeking to satisfy the demands of wealthy collectors and consumers of Europe, North America, and a few nations in the Middle East and Asia. For example, in 1999, the UK customs officials confiscated some "1600 live animals and birds, 1800 plants, 52000 parts and derivatives of endangered species, and 388000 grams of smuggled caviar" (French and Mastny, 2001: 172–3). It is a multi-billion dollar international criminal activity. In addition to the wildlife smuggling, marine resources are under threat not only from possible oil spills but also from sea dumping. Illicit waste dealers easily pass off their material in the name of recycled or reused material. Despite a number of international treaties such as the Basel Convention on the transboundary movement of hazardous wastes, MARPOL, the Convention on Biological Diversity (CBD), and even the Kyoto Protocol, the results are not very positive because of weak commitments and lax enforcement. The ecological integrity of our planet demands that international environmental crimes must be controlled if we wish to reverse the dangerous trend in environmental crises.

Each country needs to develop a government-wide sustainable development strategy

Environmental protection cannot be left in the hands of only one government department/ministry because of the interdisciplinary nature of sustainable development. Every department needs to coordinate its activities within a central framework. This approach requires the appointment of an inter-ministerial committee for sustainable development and environmental protection; a dependable monitoring mechanism; and the establishment of a central office to oversee operation of the strategy.

An integrative approach is needed to elicit support from all stakeholders

Bringing religious, cultural, traditional, and secular domains together is critical and will have a synergistic effect on development efforts. Different cultures have a different mix and influence in these domains; however, their synergy around sustainability is important to fully implement a paradigm of sustainability. In addition, there is a need to integrate economic strategies, environmental integrity, and social equality. This integration requires that we build the three pillars of sustainability simultaneously: "living within global biophysical carrying capacity; providing a decent standard of living for all people; [and] ensuring a reasonable measure of distributional fairness in access to resources and their economic benefits" (Sadler, 1996: 26).

Recognize contributions from the South and build bridges of collaboration between North and South

The North has dominated environmental discourse, but there must be conceptual linkages to the South's reality by building bridges with Southern intellectuals and researchers and integrating the perspectives of developing nations. A global agenda without sufficient Southern perspective and input is a doomed international effort. The North–South relationship would have to be more than merely commercial or trade based. Rather, it would have to be predicated on the developing nations recognizing that without the assistance from industrialized nations, the health of our entire planet is in danger. Wealthy nations must realize that they are primarily responsible for the current state of the planet. One of the biggest challenges for the twenty-first century is how to stabilize the current eco-health of the planet and ensure that future generations are left with a favorable legacy.

The state of the world

As we indicated at the beginning of this exploration, no single nation has a clean record of environmental protection, although most of the industrialized nations have better records compared to resource-rich developing countries. It is a challenge for all nations if they wish for sustainable development to become a reality. Towards this end, the United States and other industrialized nations should set an example of environmental stewardship and reverse its disappointing record on refusing to ratify key international environmental treaties and conventions. Other countries must follow the lead by putting their political differences aside in pursuit of a sustainable future. The Brundtland Commission sums up the challenges we face. We believe that the set of actions recommended above are a good starting point for us to overcome these challenges: "The Earth is one but the world is not. We all depend on one biosphere for sustaining our lives. Yet each community, each country strives for survival and prosperity with little regard for its impact on others" (WCED, 1987: 27).

Sustainable development does not mean zero growth or a society of despondency and stagnancy; nor is it one where the world's poor are bound to poverty permanently. Rather, it means a qualitative change in the logic of development; one in which people can aspire to social justice, freedom of action and choice, biodiversity in nature, cultural diversity, and a balance between non-material needs and material possessions. Sustainable development for this new century will have to include "the resurgence of life, the displacement of the mechanical by the organic, and the re-establishment of the person as the ultimate term of all human effort" (Meadows et al., 2004: 262). That is the vision and must be the hope for sustaining our world for the well-being of all.

References

Bacon, Sir Francis (1938) *The Advancement of Learning and New Atlantis*. London: Oxford University Press.

Brown, Judith M. (1977) *Gandhi and Civil Disobedience*. London: Cambridge University Press.

Bryner, Gary C. (1999) "Agenda 21: Myth or Reality," in Norman J. Vig and Regina S. Axelrod (eds), *The Global Environment*. Washington, DC: CQ Press, pp. 157–89.

Cabre, Anna (1993) "Population Growth and Environmental Degradation", *All of Us* (a UNESCO publication). Barcelona, Spain: Centre UNESCO de Catalunya, November.

Caldwell, Lynton K. (1984) *International Environmental Policy: Emergence and Dimensions.* Durham, NC: Duke University Press.

Carson, Rachel (1962) *Silent Spring.* Boston: Houghton Mifflin Company.

Doern, Bruce G. and Thomas Conway (1994) *The Greening of Canada.* Toronto, Canada: Toronto University Press.

Dwivedi, O. P. (1997) *India's Environmental Policies, Programmes and Stewardship.* Basingstoke: Macmillan.

Dwivedi, O. P. and Renu Khator (2007) "The Earth Charter: Towards a New Global Environmental Ethic," an essay prepared for the *Handbook of Globalization, Governance, and Public Administration,* ed. Ali Farazmand and Jack Pinkowski. New York: Marcel Dekker.

Flavin, Christopher (2001). "Rich Planet, Poor Planet," in Linda Starke (ed.), *State of the World – 2001* (a Worldwatch Institute Report). New York: W.W. Norton & Co, pp. 3–20.

Forbes, R. (1968) *The Conquest of Nature, Technology and Its Consequences.* New York: Praeger.

French, Hilary and Lisa Mastny (2001) "Controlling International Environmental Crime," in Linda Starke (ed.), *State of the World – 2001* (a Worldwatch Institute Report). New York: W.W. Norton & Co, pp. 166–88.

Gandhi, Mahatma M. K. (1961) *Non-Violent Resistance.* New York: Schocken Books.

Gandhi, Mrs. Indira (1972) *Address at the UN Conference on Human Environment,* Stockholm, Sweden, delivered on June 14, 1972, published by the Department of Science and Technology as Agenda Notes for NCEPC Meeting, July 28–29, 1972. New Delhi: Government of India, Department of Science and Technology.

Gardner, Gary (2003) "Engaging Religion in the Quest for a Sustainable World," in Linda Starke (ed.), *State of the World – 2003* (a Worldwatch Institute Report). New York: W.W. Norton & Company, pp. 152–75.

Haq, Mahbubul (1997) *Human Development in South Asia: the Challenge of Human Development* (Report). Karachi: Oxford University Press.

IENS (2003) *News Bulletin,* No. 43, May.

Khator, Renu (1995) "Managing the Environment in an Interdependent World," in Jean-Claude Garcia-Zamor and Renu Khator (eds), *Public Administration in the Global Village.* Westport, CT: Praeger, pp. 83–98.

Lele, S. (1991) "Sustainable Development: a Critical Review," *World Development,* 9, 6, pp. 607–21.

Meadows, D. H., D. L. Meadows, J. Randers, and W. W. Behren (1972) *The Limits to Growth: a Report for the Club of Rome's Project on the Predicament of Mankind.* New York: Universe Books.

Meadows, Donella, Jorgen Randers, and Dennis Meadows (2004) *Limits to Growth: the 30-Year Update.* White River Junction, VT: Chelsea Green Publishing Company.

Merchant, C. (1995) "Gaia: Ecofeminism and the Earth," *Earthcare: Women and the Environment.* New York: Routledge.

Prescott-Allen, Robert (2001) *The Well-being of Nations: a Country-by Country Index of Quality of Life and the Environment.* Washington, DC: Island Press.

Ramphal, Shridath (1992) *Our Country, the Planet.* Washington, DC: Island Press.

Sadler, B. (1996) "Sustainability Strategies and Green Planning: Recent Canadian and International Experience," in A. Dale and J. B. Robinson (eds), *Achieving Sustainable Development*. Vancouver, Canada: University of British Columbia Press, pp. 23–70.

Singh, Dr. Karan (1991) *Brief Sojourn*. Delhi: B. R. Publishing Corporation.

United Nations Conference on Environment & Development (UNCED) (1992) "AGENDA 21." Online at http://www.un.org/esa/sustdev/documents/ agenda21/english/Agenda21.pdf. [Agenda 21 for the Earth Summit/UNCED in Rio de Janeiro, Brazil, 3–14 June 1992.]

UNESCO (2002) "Enhancing Global Sustainability." Online at http://undesdoc. unesco.org/images/0012/001253/125351e.pdf [Report of the Preparatory Committee for the World Summit on Sustainable Development, New York, 25 March 2002].

United Nations (2000) "Millennium Development Goals (MDGs)." Online at http://www.un.org/millenniumgoals.

United Nations Population Division (2003) *World Population Prospects: the 2002 Revision*. New York: United Nations.

Victor, David G. (2006) "Recovering Sustainable Development," *Foreign Affairs*, 85, 1, pp. 91–103.

Weiss, Edith Brown (1993) "Intergenerational Equity: Towards an International Legal Framework," in N. Choucri (ed), *Global Accord: Environmental Challenges and International Responses*. Cambridge, MA: MIT Press, pp. 333–54.

Werlin, Herbert Z. (2004) "The Benefits of Globalization: Why More for South Korea than Mexico," *International Journal of Public Administration*, 27, 13 & 14, pp. 1031–59.

World Bank (2000) *World Development Report*. Washington, DC: World Bank.

World Commission on Environment and Development (WCED) (1987) *Our Common Future*. New York: Oxford University Press (also called the Brundtland Commission).

Part III
Issues and Challenges

8
Global Challenges and Managerial Culture

Anthropologists tend to define culture in broad terms. According to Singer (1968), the anthropological concept of culture covers all facets of humans in society: knowledge, behavior, beliefs, art, morals, law, customs, etc. Culture should also be seen not only as a material possession but also consisting of institutions, people, behaviors or emotions, a style of accomplishing things, and, specifically, how people perceive, relate, and interpret events both from within and without. Essentially, culture in this sense refers to the shared values and representations of the members of an organization, such as a governmental bureaucracy, or a territorial entity.

Despite some differences of emphasis, anthropologists agree that a culture is the way of life of a given society. This broad concept has some implications: (a) the concept is holistic because it involves the entire society; (b) it implies certain coherence among the elements of the culture; (c) finally, it reveals the fundamental values of a society, including its attributes, patterns (both explicit and implicit), and acquired behavior transmitted by symbols (Singer 1968: 528). Geert Hofstede defines societal culture as a collective mental programming of people who share a similar environment, shaping cultural values related to work and behavior in organizations (Hofstede, 1997). In general, a culture is a way of life of a group of people or a society, through which it views the world around it, gives meanings, attaches significance to it, and organizes itself to accomplish, preserve, and eventually pass on its legacy to future generations. Of course, a culture encompasses not only material or physical forms and means including arts and artefacts, but also the spiritual forms dealing with language and literature, customs, traditions, faith, and related symbols that underlie such objects. The study of culture attracts our attention to the world of symbols and meanings, the values and patterns of organizations and their behavior, which constitute particular ways of seeing, interpreting, and judging the world around and beyond. However, when it comes to the transmission of culture from one society to another, several actors participate (both consciously and unconsciously) in the process. Among these actors are the state apparatus, socioeconomic and political factors, as well as religious institutions.

Culture and socialization

Every society has institutions in place that transmit its key values, views, and practices from one generation to the next. The set of core values (axiology), aspirational views (teleology), and practices (deontology) constitutes respectively the main "layers" of a cultural matrix. The process of transmitting and inducing people to accept culture is referred to as socialization. This could be passive (when simple exposure and living together imprints attitudes), or active: based upon intentional training or indoctrination to affect cultural and behavioral change. The agencies of socialization include families, churches, the media, and formal organizations such as professional associations, unions, the educational system, bureaucracies, and the state itself. Cultural values and their attendant perceptions come from various sources: the physical setting, social mores, economic values, the prevailing patterns of political attitudes, as well as "winds of change" from the outside. In addition, organizations generate their own subcultures, by means of the division of labor and the creation of professional and institutional loyalties and standards.

When we talk about administrative culture we imply the above-mentioned values, views, and practices extant in complex organizations engaged in rational cooperative action, namely public and private bureaucracies. In order to understand an administrative culture, it is important to keep two things in mind. First, the government administration in all nations is larger and more complex than any single organization, as it is composed of many departments, agencies, corporations, and so on. Of course, there are some multinational corporations larger than some small countries, but for our purposes, we are talking about the state which is, in reality, "an organization of organizations" (Bergeron 1990: 181). Second, is through the state apparatus that policies and administrative decision get implemented, that financial and other resources get distributed, and thus the entire society is affected. The behavior of the state apparatus depends on the kind of administrative culture that prevails. As political, economic, and social values evolve, so does administrative culture. For in a cybernetic sense, culture is akin to the "software of an organization," from a primary group to a civilization. Changing the algorithms and chains of signification in people's mindsets – that is, learning – has profound effects in the way they function.

We can identify two main passive sources of administrative culture. One is external; it includes the "domestic" physical, social, economic, and political environment, as well as foreign influences. The other is the internal workplace that influences the prescribed behavior of employees in the form of controls exercised through rules and regulations, codes of conduct, and institutional constraints. Both sources penetrate the system of governance and administration primarily via the political, economic, and social context of organizations. Administrators do not leave their own idiosyncratic perceptions and values at the door when they enter their offices for work. Nor are these left behind upon return to private space. The culture of their workplace influences their behavior which in turn influences the practice of administration in their society. However, the main active source of cultural induction and change is intentional: policies of human resources development, and training. That is why the issue of training and learning in organizations is of primary importance in managing development, and for that matter managing any other public policy or human activity.

Lack of transparency and professionalism, as we have seen in several countries, are symptoms of a malaise existing in the administrative culture, well as in the broader culture of those societies. We should also note that no administrative culture is monolithic; instead, it is a part of the wider culture of a society. It includes attitudes, beliefs, and perceptions, as well as practices in the polity, the economy, and in the social, religious, corporate, and civil realms. Of all these constituent parts, it is the political culture that influences the administrative culture most. In fact, collective orientations towards authority shape the behavior of the state machinery and its employees. Finally, the administrative culture is sometimes supported and sometimes challenged by two other important subsets of cultural predispositions. First, there are the subcultures of each department or agency of government (or the enterprise), with their own traditions, prime directives, overriding commands, interests, client groups, and major occupational components. Secondly, there are also professional subcultures, such as those of accountants, lawyers, economists, engineers, diplomats, and scientists, that cut across organizational boundaries. A composite administrative culture reflects the values of all its constituent parts.

The theory and practice of public administration all over the world has been going through a period of flux and turmoil. The conceptual and operational paradigm of what public administration is and should do is reflective of numerous historical processes, particularly economic trends. After three decades of unprecedented growth from the end of World War Two until the mid-1970s, the industrialized countries began to experience severe financial difficulties. For many analysts the blame falls – among other things – on the cost and inefficiencies emanating from large bureaucracies, Keynesian demand-side economics, and the welfare state. Right-wing politicians and their constituent leaders in the business sector clamored for a "retreat from the state" couched in the formula of lower taxes. Such retrenchment was to be accomplished by the application of management practices from the business sector, which were seen once again – as it was with the Reform Movement two generation earlier – as the great cure for all of the ills of public sector management anywhere. The result of this drive to transform government services resulted in the emergence of the New Public Management movement (NPM), which we discussed in Chapter 6.

As industrialized nations took the lead, developing nations were impelled to accept the prescription: business-friendly policies and a "meaner and leaner" state. NPM became the instrument for implementing neoliberalism and structural adjustment policies. Tied by unmanageable debt burdens and the conditionalities imposed through the IMF, the World Bank and bilateral agencies, the global South had little choice but to acquiesce. The NPM movement, though a recent vogue in public administration, is but one example of an ongoing debate: whether or not the organization and management of administration are universal, or culturally specific; and more to the point, whether culture really matters.

In 1998 Gerald Caiden alerted us to this issue. However, he also said that despite the lure of Americanization (read "globalization"), people are interested in retaining their distinctive identity and culture (Caiden, 1998: 388). This appears to be true. For example, French people are keen to preserve not only their culture and language but also their administrative system. Similarly, other European nations have their distinctive administrative cultures and styles, though they do share some core administrative values. In this chapter, we are interested in developing a general framework for understanding administrative culture, as well as examining what approaches can be utilized to study and compare different administrative cultures.

Some traits of administrative culture

Administrative culture is understood here in its broadest sense as the modal pattern of values, beliefs, attitudes, and predispositions that characterize and identify any given administrative system. We recognize that the construction of a generally applicable model of the "administrative mindset" presents significant difficulties. Yet, we also recognize that it is possible to configure clusters of cultural matrixes that have important heuristic value in understanding the relationship among contexts, structures, behaviors, and effects. This understanding of administrative culture is not purely a "lofty" exercise. It is essential in order to configure strategies of cultural change to induce organizational and managerial changes away from ostensibly dysfunctional practices, like corruption, incompetence, and abuse of power. Most important, a serious and critical analysis could assist in breaking away from the prevailing "prescription without diagnosis" mold that has characterized much of the ongoing recipes and fads. We suggest eight general propositions that researchers may explore, in their specific ways:

1. The administrative culture of any discrete country, place, or entity reflects the distinctiveness and complexity of the various regional, national, and local realities; their unique historical experiences; their forms of insertion (subordination or domination) into the system of regional and global relations; and their levels of development and fragmentation.
2. Cultures are historical products, where past experiences, myths, and traditions have shaped modal psychological orientations.
3. Any administrative culture is also conditioned by existing structural and conjunctural circumstances and challenges. Even perceptions of the past are mediated by current experience.
4. The administrative culture is part of a larger attitudinal matrix, containing values, practices, and orientations towards the physical environment, the economy, the social system, the polity, and culture itself.
5. Administrative cultures, like all cultures, are dynamic and subject to change. Syncretism, continuities, and discontinuities are part and parcel of their fabric and texture.

6. An administrative culture is the result of a process of immersion, acculturation, and socialization, whose structural drivers are implicit as well as induced and explicit.
7. Most attempts at administrative reform and "modernization" address, either directly or indirectly, the question of administrative culture. Any profound administrative reform entails significant attitudinal and value changes.
8. Administrative cultures are influenced by global and regional trends. In the lesser-developed regions of the world they are particularly derivative, reflecting a center–periphery mode of international political economy (Dwivedi and Nef, 1998: 6–7).

The global challenges

The most important challenge to conventional views of administration and administrative culture, historically bound to the notion of the territorial nation-state, is the process of globalization. Irrespective of the definition used for "globality," the context, the structure, the processes, and the effects of administration are decisively influenced by it. The circumstances of administration are increasingly defined by parameters outside the confines of the nation-state. So are goals, resources (human, material, and "semiotic"), communications, and performance. The same is the case with the impact of policy decisions, non-decisions, actions, and inactions upon the context of administration, for the latter encompasses interwoven domestic and extraterritorial dimensions. In an era of growing interdependence, but also of mutual vulnerability (Nef, 1999), domestic and international micro and macro security are interconnected. At the center of this global–local interface, there is also an emerging global consciousness (Dwivedi and Nef, 1998: 6). Globalization during the twenty-first century is somewhat different from old-fashioned, seventeenth-century colonialism (First Wave globalization) and nineteenth-century imperialism (Second Wave globalization). Essentially, what makes this type of globalization stronger and more insidious is its political power supported by technology, economic wealth, and a solid demographic base. Globalization is not only about trade and economics, important as these are, but mainly about culture.

Americanization as a dominant world culture

"Third Wave" globalization has been associated with the Americanization of the "global village." This is happening through chains of franchises such as McDonald's, Burger King, Hollywood films, Much Music,

Levi jeans, corporate America, information technology, militarization, and dominant scientific research and discoveries. All these either originate from, or are managed by, the United States. However, despite such overwhelming presence, people in other sociopolitical contexts are trying to preserve and strengthen the diversity of ideas, languages and customs, values and beliefs, and ways of doing things. It should be noted that cultural homogeneity, unlike economic integration, is not an automatic thing. Cultural diffusion is often countervailed by cultural resistance. When people lose their culture, they lose their identity and heritage.

Historically, we already know that the Second Globalization (British colonialism during the nineteenth century and the earlier part of the twentieth century) produced a massive increase in world inequality. For example, during the nineteenth century, the increased wealth of Western Europe coincided with growing poverty and deprivation in the non-white colonies, Asia in particular. Poverty and concomitant famines in British India were the result of imperial taxation, natural resource exploitation, and trade policies. The challenge for the United States and for the Third Wave globalization is the expectation that the inequities of the past may be repeated.

New Public Management, with its reinvention of government, was intrinsically a sort of administrative "cultural revolution," or revolt by Western elites to solve the financial problems that beset their governments and in so doing increase their rate of accumulation. The various versions of the welfare state seemed too expensive. The Keynesian economic model on which they were based had become discredited because governments and politicians had taken to running systematic deficits in order to finance government programs and comply with the implicit social contract. There were also reactions by wealthy taxpayers and their associated classes to public sector unions, strikes, and the rigid bureaucracy that came from combining big government with collective agreements. But there were also some new policy parameters. For instance, the end of the Cold War and the demise of communism made it less necessary to buy out support from labor to prevent "socialism." Finally, the 1980s were a time when conservative ideologies, in the guise of neoliberalism, experienced a revival. The election of Margaret Thatcher in Britain and Ronald Reagan in the United States gave powerful support to the New Public Management movement with its accent on results, greater attention to cost, and the use of private sector approaches to motivate employees (Dwivedi and Gow, 1999: 130).

This worldview is based on the premise that by reducing the opportunities for incompetence and corruption, and narrowing the scope of government activities, efficient, transparent, effective, and accountable governance would appear. Freeing taxpayers' money would result in increased investment, leading to economic growth, more employment, ultimately leading to generalized well-being through the automaticity of market mechanisms. The rationale of NPM as an administrative ideology is that with less bureaucratic structures there would be fewer bureaucratic problems. Once more, the heavy emphasis is being placed on the objective criteria of responsibility and accountability with a blind faith in structures, processes, and procedures but with total disregard for the moral (or subjective) dimension. Most developing nations were being urged to have market-friendly governance and administration as a new phase of the "orthodox" notion of development administration. International aid has been made conditional upon accepting this prescription. Some of the instrumental recommendations in the formula included the shrinkage of the bureaucracy, the restructuring of the central banking system away from national controls, deregulation, privatization, the elimination of subsidies and protectionism, the acceptance of currency devaluation, and other changes in monetary and fiscal policy (Dwivedi, 1994).

One important aspect of socialization and learning is that often the core values of a culture – those that inform both the desired states or outcomes and the prescribed behaviors – are acquired and imbedded through the practices themselves. There is no doubt that the emphasis on result-based management is of value, but the danger of neglecting political, legal, and cultural dimensions and other subjective criteria of responsibility is quite real. At the same time, faced with the complexities of day-to-day administration and the conflicting values that the system has thrust upon them, new and old public managers need some fundamental reference point to which they may turn in case of doubt. In this respect a public manager differs from a private one, since while the latter may regard the law as a constraint, something he must obey, the public manager must also uphold it. To be sure, New Public Management proponents usually say that they are aware that the state is not a business and that the classic values of accountability and respect for the law tend to be eclipsed by it.

In practice, very few analysts actually believe that government should be thought of as a corporation. Indeed, "the greatest charge against managerialism is its reductionism and its lack of imagination. It tries to reduce a complex phenomenon to a single model drawn from business" (Dwivedi and Gow, 1999: 178). Together with the emphasis on good governance, the neo-managerial framework privileges new cooperative public–private modalities of management (where the notion of administration as public service almost vanishes) bringing together managed development concerns with an invigorated private sector. Even the semantics change: "customer" substitutes for "public," "servant" becomes "provider" and "service" is a "product." The assumption here is that such management occurs in the context of a well-functioning civil society with developed voluntary organizations and vigorous NGOs. From this perspective, the role of development management would be that of providing an enabling environment, security, infrastructure, and minimal regulations unencumbered by red tape. The private sector would do the rest. However, the reform package, as was generally the case with development administration, failed to materialize in terms of effectiveness and probity. In some notable instances, however, it was able to improve efficiency and reduce red tape. The problem remains that the pretended universalistic reforms have remained essentially a closed system in outlook. As such, they focus on structure and process, and sometimes outputs as technical (deontological) practices, but fail to account for context, culture, and consequences.

From a practical point of view, the NPM model remains strong in a number of developing countries, chiefly in Latin America. It is increasingly less so in the Group of 7 and the rest of the West, including the United States. Some Asian nations are still trying hard to implement the NPM philosophy although the movement has already lost its momentum. For example, in China, when trying to reconcile communist ideology with capitalist production, downsizing was one of the main aims of the 1998 public sector reforms. Administrative positions were cut; special retraining programs were introduced for a number of cadres, and there was a regrouping of some ministries and state corporations. India provides another example. While the federal and state governments have initiated a number of privatization plans for their public sector industrial units, labor unrest and the use of public interest litigation have forced governments to take a step backwards. Thus, privatization is not moving as fast as the government wants. The report of India's Fifth Pay Commission in the late 1990s recommended a streamlining of pay scales. The streamlining, oddly enough, meant pay increases, but these increases, it was argued, should be accompanied by a reduction in the number of positions and employees, and a revamped system of accountability. While the pay increases (including the two-year increase in the age of retirement) were immediately and retroactively implemented, no downsizing has taken place. It seems that the dismantling of structures and reducing bureaucracy is still a most difficult challenge, although the positive aspects of NPM in streamlining procedures and computerization are easily recognized.

The globalization of public sector practices

Development administration as an academic field has been the handmaiden of Western comparative public administration. It has not yet succeeded in breaking loose from its old moorings because it still presses for Northern, universalistic designs tied to a single, competitive, and capitalistic world economy. For example, the details of administrative structures, procedural and financial accountability, human-resources management, central–local relationships, organization of ministries or departments, the role of parastatals, linkages with civil society and grassroots groups, and recruitment/socialization mechanisms are all based on a system and culture developed in the North. It is now acknowledged even in the West that such an imitative system has not worked well. Sometimes, a few voices in the development community call for feasible change from the bottom up, and suggest that it would be desirable if the North would use many ideas from different sources in the South to enrich its own knowledge of development and administration.

Yet, for many years Western scholars have been unable to include non-Western contributions in developmental studies. There is little appreciation of indigenous culture, traditions, and styles of governance reflecting the distinctiveness and complexity of their identities and diversities. It is also difficult for an essentially deontological discipline, such as public administration to reflect upon itself and engage in critical analysis and research before moving into self-centered prescription. These factors must be taken into consideration when public service reforms and aid-related conditionalities are being imposed. For example, we know that in Asian and other developing nations, the nature of public expectations from their governments is basically different from those prevailing in the West. Despite the fact that demands on the public sector to provide more services are growing, the state apparatus in these nations is being forced to shrink and retreat. Thus, it is counterproductive to compel these nations to follow the costly fads prevailing in the industrialized nations.

We also know that the outer layer of these nations' style of governance is directly affected by current circumstances and global challenges. Any profound administrative reform entails significant attitudinal and value changes in local culture and traditions. Thus, efforts at administrative restructuring, "modernization," and bringing other types of reforms in the South need to address first, either directly or indirectly, the question of the existing indigenous style and values in governance. If we take the premise that a country's culture and style of governance is the key to the understanding of what makes a country function, it is imperative that any public sector reform also draws on local customs and traditions. Many countries, especially in Asia, may be "new" but their cultural traditions are longer and deeper than those of Western civilization, and draw on centuries of administrative and cultural heritage.

When local culture and traditions are discarded in favor of Western-style management practices, and with little time to reflect, experiment, and evaluate to see if such transplantation has already taken root, or functions in the body politic, cognitive and attitudinal confusion is likely to emerge. A hotchpotch of conflicting value systems start operating simultaneously. There is no one specific standard left against which the effectiveness of the existing administrative system, as well as the conduct of public officials, can be measured. As in Fred Riggs' transitional "sala" model suggested four decades ago, administrative distemper is likely to emerge. This problem points towards the need to develop an inclusive and multicultural mixture of alternate perspectives rather than always depending on the purely mono-cultural indicators of prescription and performance measurement (Dwivedi, 2002a).

Disrupting influences on indigenous administrative culture

There is also a need to examine the disruptive impacts of frequent public service reorganizations and reforms, as well as periodic paradigm shifts brought on by Western experts, with their own timetables, time-limits, and agendas. We already know that it is tougher to implement reforms than to design them. We also know that the work is not finished with implementation alone; the possibility of backsliding is always present. Without continuous nurturing, critical assessments, and follow up, reforms generally fade away. Thus it may be helpful to take pause from the apparent frenzy for reforms so that public service institutions may be able to have some breathing space to solidify gains made, and to strengthen and develop their organizational culture. After a time of reflection, test and analysis, further reforms and changes can be attempted. It is equally important that when international development agencies and their advisers contemplate new reforms, they consider alternatives available at the local level so that improvements are based on local circumstances, history, and culture. This needs studying and also a profound attitudinal and cultural change of the experts themselves. In addition, developing nations should undertake regular (periodic) assessments of progress made. Progress ought to be regularly and consistently assessed.

Cultural diversity in the theory and practice of administration

Throughout the twentieth century, scholars and practitioners of public administration carried out their work as if all public administration and governance values emanating from the West were akin to general scientific principles of nature. Certainly, under the influence of Logical Positivism, Scientific Management, and the concept of "social engineering" they were often seen as universally applicable. As mentioned earlier, in such a normative equation, local context or culture did not matter. The vestiges of a one-dimensional rationalism are now slowly giving way to a fuller recognition and understanding of the impact and consequences of people's values. However, this thought has not quite penetrated current epistemologies and professional canons. It is also clear that through globalization, a certain dependence and continued reliance on a "dominant-strain" Western theory and methodology of administration is being emphasized.

It would certainly be a pitiful situation if everywhere on the globe, governments and lifestyles became a mirror image of Western values and practices. Bad imitation is a source of caricature. Developing countries must overcome many challenges but so, too, must the West. One thing is clear: the current crisis of development and administration is precisely a consequence of the inability of the West to incorporate the substance of other non-Western developmental experiences into the prevailing conceptual mold and mindset. It is also worth acknowledging that alternatives to Western-led reforms might have value for other nations, just as alternative medicine has finally received acceptance in the West. The success of these alternatives requires new approaches to North–South relations. The essence of this plea is the identification of the "unity in diversity principle," so that alternatives (based in the South or elsewhere) do not get discarded simply because they are not well argued according to Western protocols. This does not mean advocating non-involvement or a total detachment of development administration from NPM, and from public (and comparative) administration. There are some core values (such as the rule of law and due process, efficiency, economy, accountability, impartiality, integrity, fairness, protecting and serving the common good, etc.) of public administration that are widely applicable and are relevant everywhere irrespective of local traditions, culture, and context. Thus, there is a need to consider a holistic approach to public administration inclusive of alternatives coming from "outside the box."

Unless conventional modes of thinking and action change, the diversity in administrative, social, and political culture may face the same fate as is happening with the decline of bio-diversity in the planet. Ethnocentrism and ignorance have continued to overshadow the need to appreciate the cultural diversity of local traditions and ways of doing things. For the world as a whole, diversity is a condition of survivability and resilience. True globalization – not imperial hegemony – means the ability to decide with an open mind, to understand and to incorporate different and alternative cultural traditions into a common matrix, and to respect diversity all around.

Inclusive and multicultural administration

"Globalism" of the type described above is the latest manifestation on a continuum of military, political, economic, administrative, intellectual, religious, and cultural encounters between the West and the so-called periphery in Africa, Asia, the Middle East, and Latin America. These encounters have allowed both sides to learn from each other. But they have also created areas of tension as the universalizing elements springing from one side ran into resistance from the other's local and indigenous cultures. Before the Enlightenment, which was followed by the industrial revolution, the West learned a great deal from the now despised Islamic civilization in the areas of medicine, mathematics, astrology, and the craft of running an empire. The great civilization that was created in Spain by Muslims had a cardinal influence on the indigenous Spanish culture, and in the rest of Europe, in the areas of literature, architecture, and government. Moreover, Greek philosophy and the notion of democracy were passed to the West through Arab and Muslim scholars. The Ottoman Empire, which succeeded the Muslim Arab Empire, also had significant cultural, political, administrative, religious, and military encounters with the West. This had long-lasting effects throughout the Balkans. The collapse of Yugoslavia was a clear illustration of how deeply rooted the influence of the Ottoman Empire was on Eastern Europe. We also know how important French and British influence was regarding the manner in which Istanbul governed the outlying provinces of the empire. The involvement of France and Great Britain in dictating to the Ottoman Sublime Porte as to how Mount Lebanon was to be governed is an example of the constant interfacing between the West and the region of the Middle East.

A similar situation obtained with regards to the longest surviving civilization, that of China. Until the Communist Revolution of 1949 China was plundered and despised by the West as a "backward" society characterized by poverty, despair, and chaos. It is interesting to notice that European attitudes towards the "Empire of the Center" were quite different until the seventeenth and eighteenth centuries. Until then, China was considered a rich market, producing exports for the West. In a way, with its emergence as a world superpower in recent years, China is once again in the cultural and economic center-stage. This pattern of conquest, exclusion, and later reinclusion is also beginning to emerge in the case of India.

The transformation of the world order in the post-World War Two years saw a waning of European influence and a pitched competition between the US and the former USSR for establishing hegemony in the region. Finally, the collapse of communism and the unprecedented expansion of a transnational capitalist economy set the stage for a "clash of civilizations" between Islam and the West, whose global repercussions we are witnessing today. Cultural misunderstandings and Western arrogance combined with Islamic paranoia are at the core of this paradigmatic encounter.

The global cultural challenge

The circumstances of the earlier twentieth century impelled national governments to regulate markets and commercial interests, to take care of the poor, unemployed, and socially disadvantaged sections of the society, and to provide healthcare and social security. These public functions were reflective of a shift in core values from laissez-faire to planning and interventionism. The Third Wave globalization will probably need intervention at the international level to offset the adverse effects of unregulated international business practices (including managerial failings of some mega commercial concerns). The behavior of rogue states and a myriad of global criminal activities will need to be controlled. Governments will have to monitor unprincipled NGOs, ensure the implementation of international treaties and conventions, prevent regional wars and conflicts, maintain peace, prosecute the perpetration of crimes against humanity, advance economic stability and sustainable development by building national capabilities, minimize religious persecution and racial prejudice, enforce human rights, guarantee food and water supply for all, improve public health and sanitation, ensure public safety and crime prevention both within the national borders and beyond, safeguard the victims of natural and man-made disasters, and so on.

In essence, there is going to be a very large role for a global Leviathan. Whether the countries are ready or not, the emergent international order necessitates a very clear role for the European Union, the OECD, China, India, and the single remaining superpower, the United States, in a borderless world. It also needs a reconfiguration of both the UN as well as the numerous regional, functional and neo-functional organizations. This structure of global governance will require a radical redefinition of sovereignty. Most importantly, the new Leviathan will need the trust of most if not all nations. It must act as a virtuous hegemon motivated by good thoughts and judgement in a multicultural, complex, and diverse world. This new global context cannot be ruled by neo-imperialism; the latter is a recipe for collective suicide.

Good governance and sustainable human development go hand-in-hand. The global South also requires conscientious attempts at eliminating poverty, sustaining livelihoods, fulfilling basic needs, and a political and administrative system that is clean, accountable, and moral. In an interdependent world there is a high degree of mutual vulnerability. Dysfunctions in one component, no matter how remote and small, may have catastrophic repercussions upon the whole system, including seemingly strong and secure actors. For these reasons poor nations need to set their houses in order. For them, the most fundamental challenge is to create conditions for effective and democratic governance. We also know that good governance depends on the performance of their leaders and public servants, in being open and transparent, and in advancing opportunities for sustainable development so that their people can live in dignity and peace. Unless such basic conditions are met, and until leaders and public servants are able to demonstrate their social conscience, good governance will not be attained.

There is a need for a comprehensive and multidimensional approach to human development worldwide. We know now that the developmental paradigm of the twentieth century was based on a single, all-purpose remedy; an approach that reveals the thinking of the various international agencies including the IMF and the World Bank. Instead, a comprehensive and multifaceted approach is needed to address a multitude of complex and interconnected issues that can be grouped under the rubric of "human security." A narrowly focused approach, such as liberalization of markets without complementary expansion of social opportunities (such as education, social security, healthcare, law and order, and transparent governance) will not be very effective; instead, it might retard the progress of a developing country and its social opportunities.

What is needed is a concerted effort on all fronts – environmental, economic, social, political, and cultural. This would require the strengthening of political institutions, sequencing and timing of reforms that are country-specific, applying conditionality judiciously, and avoiding any inconsistency of objectives (between and among various international development aid agencies and institutions). This implies a global "Marshall Plan" and organizational network to implement the Millennium Goals.

Globalization and administrative culture

We propose as analytical postulates, two empirical generalizations about administrative reform. The first is that the choice of objectives depends in part on the means available. That is, in public policy and administration, most choices are not moral absolutes, but depend on implicit calculations of costs and benefits and feasibility, not only to the public, but also to politicians and public servants. The second is that administrative reforms can have both intended and unintended consequences.

If we apply these generalizations to the last four decades of administrative development, especially the current NPM phase, we can make a number of observations. (1) Administrative reforms – both development administration and NPM – have been predicated on the worldwide ascendancy of liberal-democratic and capitalist values. (2) The metaphorical language of business management has become part the discourse of public administration: terms such as "corporate culture," "corporate management," or "management by results." There is also a rich ambiguity in expressions like "value for money" or "excellence." (3) The application of the technical reform package and doctrine requires the suspension of disbelief. In Dunsire's words such doctrines make things "plain, but in the manner of 'revealed truth' rather than the tentative hypothesizing of theory: it shows what must be done but as if it were from necessity rather than the mere instrumentalism of policy" (Dunsire, 1973: 39). (5) A fifth observation refers to selectivity in argument. The validity of the doctrine is present by the recourse to examples, "best practices," and anecdotal evidence without considering contrary evidence. (6) Last, but not least, is the issue of ideological inversion: a doctrine based on private interest is said to meet the requirements of the public good. These reform packages are predicated as technical and apolitical solutions. Yet, they rationalize and justify in antiseptic and instrumental terms a mode or agenda of private accumulation.

If politics is about the art of the possible, or what is acceptable in a society, and if it is also about the major value choices of that society – the values of "authenticity" and "justice" – then management has forgotten politics (Manzer, 1984: 27). Moreover, the "new" culture of management also appears to neglect the importance of law in public administration. This can be seen at two levels. At the top, introducing notions like corporate management, corporate culture, and even that of management itself, this cultural software tends to obscure the fact that those relations between senior officials and ministers are constitutional in nature. In turn, at the lower level, the constitution serves as a source of regime values for administrators. At that level, as stated by John Rohr, the law is a guarantor of democratic government: "Government by law is the most bureaucratic of all institutions because to a greater extent than other institutions it feels bound by its own rules" (Rohr, 1988: 171). For the public manager the law is something to be upheld at all times.

The paradox is that while the prevailing language of reform is full of references to a proactive stance, where strategic planning, innovation, change, growth, and freedom are promoted, its theory and practice are profoundly deterministic. The message is that there really are no choices, that deficits, structural economic change, and world trade competition are forcing the governments of all countries to adopt the same policies. This obscures the fact that these same governments do things very differently. For instance, European countries tend to accept a more corporatist form of national bargaining with business and labor, while Britain, the United States, and Canada in varying degrees are influenced by more liberal values, where individualism reigns supreme. Also obscured is the fact that economic "laws" are not laws of nature and that even deregulation and free market decisions are *political* decisions. Their "reality" is a socially constructed reality behind which there are concrete interests. This right-wing economic determinism also masks that there are other models of politics, management, and development than merely the market model. What is deontologically feasible informs what is teleologically desirable. But if feasibility is the only criterion for the desirable, public choice becomes a non-choice.

It is here where teleological and spiritual approaches become relevant. In this context, these two approaches acquire a holistic tone. In the end, public servants exist for the public they are employed to serve. It is this aspect that needs to be revitalized in the public service. Even with the current emphasis on downsizing, one should not abdicate the notion that public management serves the collective interests of its society. As such, it expresses above all a concern for the general welfare of the population. This commitment to a collective vision is one of the cardinal virtues of public servants; it is derived from the concept of public service as a "vocation," a kind of higher "calling." If the profession of public service is not a calling, then it is merely a job. And, in that case, loyalty to a specific job will depend largely on what material benefits and satisfaction that job may provide. To abandon the idea of commitment to serve the public as a vocation and to turn towards the adoption of market-based management practices would be a form of goal displacement. Any predisposition to reject duty and commitment to vocation among public servants is not going to serve a society well. Indeed, duty-based teleological approaches have disadvantages apart from the fact that not all agree on their contents. In public administration, difficulties often arise because two or more values are in conflict, such as the sense of patriotism and the obligation to do one's legal and constitutional duty. Ethics, as we will see in Chapter 10, is not simply about making the morally "correct" decision. It is primarily about substance and procedure; being able to address ethical dilemmas with a critical, open, and informed mind, devoid of hypocrisy, cynicism, and double standards.

Signposts for the twenty-first century

The culture and style of governance are the keys to understanding what makes a country function. Any transplantation of administrative practices from one nation to another always encounters challenges from the local customs, culture, and traditions. For the West as well as for the rest of the world, a key to a just and sustainable society requires diversity in thought and action rather than one universal style of governance. This prescription runs counter to the pre-1989 Manichean vision held by those positing Marxist-Leninism and claiming "really-existing" socialism as the only scientific way to go (Dwivedi et al., 1985). The logical fallacy behind this dualistic form of thinking is the conclusion that with socialism gone, the world has reached the End of History. That is why we argue that not only administrative and other forms of culture differ, but such a difference should be respected, encouraged, and celebrated. True globalization means a global consciousness: the ability to decide with an open mind, to understand and to incorporate different and alternative cultural traditions into a common matrix, and to respect diversity all around (Dwivedi, 2005: 34).

References

Astley, W. Graham and Andrew Van de Ven (1983) "Central Perspectives and Debates in Organization Theory," *Administrative Science Quarterly*, 28, pp. 245–73.

Bergeron, G. (1990) *Petit traite de L'Etat*. Paris: Presses Universitaires de France.

Bruce, Willa and John Novinson (1999) "Spirituality in Public Service: a Dialogue," *Public Administration Review*, 59, 2 (March/April), pp. 163–9.

Caiden, Gerald E. (1998) "Are Administrative Cultures that Different?" in O. P. Dwivedi, R. B. Jain, and Dhirendra K. Vajpeyi (eds), *Governing India: Issues Concerning Public Policy, Institutions and Administration*. Delhi: B. R. Publishing, pp. 377–93.

Drewry, Gavin and Che-po Chan (2001) "Civil Service Reform in the People's Republic of China: Another Mirage of the New Global Paradigm of Public Administration?" *International Review of Administrative Sciences*, 67, 3, pp. 461–78.

Dunsire, Andrew (1973) "Administrative Doctrine and Administrative Change," *Public Administration Bulletin*, 13, pp. 39–56.

Dunsire, Andrew (1988) "Bureaucratic Morality in the United Kingdom," *International Review of Political Science*, 3, 3, pp. 179–91.

Dwivedi, O. P. (1985) "Ethics and Values of Public Responsibility and Accountability," *International Review of Administrative Sciences*, 51, pp. 61–6.

Dwivedi, O. P. (1994) *Development Administration: From Underdevelopment to Sustainable Development*. Basingstoke: Macmillan.

Dwivedi, O. P. (2002a) "The Challenges of Cultural Diversity for Good Governance," *Indian Journal of Public Administration*, 48, 1, pp. 14–28.

Dwivedi, O. P. (2002b) "On Common Good and Good Governance: an Alternative Approach," in Dele Olowu and Soumana Sako (eds), *Better Governance and Public Policy: Capacity Building and Democratic Renewal in Africa*. Bloomfield, CT: Kumarian Press, pp. 35–51.

Dwivedi, O. P. (2005) "Administrative Culture and Values: Approaches," in Joseph G. Jabbra and O. P. Dwivedi (eds), *Administrative Culture in a Global Context*. Toronto: De Sitter Publications, pp. 19–36.

Dwivedi, O. P. and James Iain Gow (1999) *From Bureaucracy to Public Management: the Administrative Culture of the Government of Canada*. Peterborough, Canada: Broadview Press. [A joint publication with the Institute of Public Administration of Canada, Toronto.]

Dwivedi, O. P., William Graf, and J. Nef (1985a) "Marxism and Bureaucracy," *Pragya* (BHU, India), 30, 2, pp. 27–42.

Dwivedi, O. P., William Graf, and J. Nef (1985b) "Marxist Contributions to the Theory of the Administrative State", *Indian Journal of Political Science*, 46, 1 (January–March), pp. 1–17.

Dwivedi, O. P., William Graf, and J. Nef (1987) "Moral Dimensions of Statecraft: a Plea for Administrative Theology," *Canadian Journal of Political Science*, 20, 4, pp. 699–706.

Dwivedi, O. P. and J. Nef (1998) "Administrative Culture: a Global Perspective," *Africanus*, 28, 2, pp. 5–7.

Hofstede, Geert (1981) "Culture and Organizations," *International Studies of Man and Organizations*, 10, 4, pp. 15–41.

Hofstede, Geert (1997) *Culture in Organizations: Software of Mind*. London: McGraw-Hill.

Kiggundu, Moses N. (2002) *Managing Globalization in Developing Countries and Transition Economies*. Westport, CT: Praeger.

Manzer, R. (1984) "A Policy Rationality and Policy Analysis: the Problem of the Choice of Criteria for Decision-making," in O. P. Dwivedi (ed.), *Policy and Administrative Studies*. Guelph, Canada: University of Guelph, pp. 27–40.

Nef, Jorge (1998) "Administrative Culture in Latin America: Historical and Structural Outline," *Africanus*, 28, 2, pp. 19–32.

Nef, Jorge (1999) *Human Security and Mutual Vulnerability: the Political Economy of Global Relations*. Ottawa: IDRC Books.

Rohr, John A. (1988) "A Bureaucratic Morality in the United States," *International Political Science Review*, 9, 3, pp. 167–78.

Schaeffer, Robert K. (2003) *Understanding Globalization: the Social Consequences of Political, Economic, and Environmental Change*. New York: Rowman & Littlefield Publishers.

Sen, Amartya (1999) *Development as Freedom*. New York: Alfred A. Knopf.

Singer, Milton (1968) "The Concept of Culture," in *International Encyclopedia of the Social Sciences*. New York: Macmillan Press, pp. 527–43.

9
Democracy, Governability, and Governance

The term "government" has a long historical lineage, dating back to the origins of civilization. Etymologically it is derived from the Greek word *kyvernites*, meaning steersman, pilot, or rudder. The word also conveys the notion of power (as in *kratos*), and is also the root of the modern term "cybernetics." In essence it means the structures of decision-making and the procedures by which such decisions are implemented (or not implemented). Aristotle (384–322 BC) in his *Politics* was concerned with what makes government virtuous or venal; in other words what is good government.

In contrast, the word "governance" is of much more recent origin. It became commonly used by political scientists in the 1970s and 1980s around the debate on the crisis of democracy and the discussion on "governability" and "ungovernability." In a way, it stood against the authoritarian and elitist proposition that democracy was ungovernable because of too much participation. Governance offered a less ideologically loaded and more inclusive idiom. It is generally understood as the autonomous capacity of both rulers and the ruled for self-government, empowerment, and problem-solving. It involves citizens' participation in the handling of their own affairs, with respect for life and the recognition of human dignity. Governance goes back to the Aristotelian ideal of good government.

Human dignity is a cardinal concept underlying the idea of governance and its purpose. It encompasses a number of interwoven dimensions, under the general label of security: environmental, economic, social, political, and cultural. Environmental security means the rights of individuals and communities to live in safe biophysical surroundings. It also means reasonable access to resources on a sustainable basis, and effectively protected from the depletion of the commons.

Economic security involves accessibility to employment to satisfy needs for goods and services. This supply function is combined with real possibilities for improving collective and individual material quality of life, and the prevention of poverty. The social dimension comprises the ability of citizens to associate, organize, and take part in community life. In addition, it means building safety and support networks to secure education and shelter for them and their family members, and to escape from discriminatory and other exclusionary practices. The political dimension of security entails the ability to manage and resolve conflict; in other words, the capacity to govern. This involves the exercise of the right to representation, fundamental freedoms, and participation in the governing process; to seek change among those who govern, being able to express dissent without the fear of being harassed, and enjoying legal-juridical security. Finally, the cultural dimension relates to the access to knowledge and learning, identity, the practice of individual beliefs, and to the maintenance of values and traditions.

Of all these five dimensions, the political is the most crucial. Without it, other dimensions or rights cannot be realized. Politics involves a continuous process of conflict-management and problem-solving among individuals and groups within a given space for the fulfillment of their expectations and enhancing their capabilities to secure results for themselves or a larger collective. We will examine the relations between governance, democracy, and development management.

The ethical foundations of democratic governance

Democratic governance is based on a number of intertwined basic premises. (a) The first is fundamental freedoms for all, which means that human beings are the ultimate measure of all human values. (b) The second is equality of all, so that everyone receives the same recognition from others, without discrimination, but especially from the state. (c) The third basis premise is universal participation in the governing process. These principles are the foundations of a style of governance which draws upon three implicit virtues: equality, empathy, and tolerance. These three constitute the requisite conditions for a humane and open society. Further, not only the substance but the process (or means) by which these conditions are met are equally important; as is the commitment of the state in furthering them. As

Emmette S. Redford noted, "democratic morality will be meaningful only if processes exist through which each person, with tolerance of the same opportunity for others, has opportunity for meaningful participation" (Redford, 1969: 8). At the same time, the ethics of democracy raises many perplexing questions about public policy and its management.

Democratic governance basically allows individuals and groups to pursue their own ends of life without harming others' right to do the same. This requires that individuals and groups seek accommodation with others through the political process. One may differentiate between "democratic governance" and "good governance." While democratic governance relates to the political context for permitting people to participate in the process of governance, good governance requires the state and its public officials to demonstrate, by deeds, the highest standards of honesty and integrity. These include fairness, impartiality, equity, efficiency, probity, and prudence. Only when democratic governance exhibits a moral dimension, is it possible for the manifold variety of socioeconomic groups, voluntary organizations, media, creeds, cultures, and faiths to live with dignity and flourish.

The fundamental goal of democratic governance is the provision of appropriate conditions guaranteed by the state for the realization of individual (and group) potentialities. That is why the "ideals of democratic government, that is, government controlled by the people for their purposes, must be widely accepted and believed by the people or they cannot, by definition, be democratic" (Corry and Hodgetts, 1959: 25). One way to encouraging mutual respect and cooperation among various groups is to foster the convergence of such democratic ideals as respect for individuals, basic freedoms, equality, justice, the rule of law, and constitutionalism. So long as our definition of the state is an association for achieving common purpose, and so long as one of those "common purposes" happens to be individual freedom and equality in treatment, then no group of citizens would be left out of the process of participation in governance.

Of course, there are some who feel that democratic governance which encourages pluralism is a divisive force. However, we also know that the history of civilization attests to the fact that attempts by various rulers, dictators, conquerors to subdue or bring everyone into one fold, one creed, or one culture and opinion, have failed over time. Instead, diversity of thought, action, belief, and worship resulting in respect and goodwill for others, is a condition for social peace. Democracy, with its faith in tolerance and freedom, provides the opportunity to make choices and direct the pursuit of life either individually or in harmony with others.

The practice of "democratic governance" requires the involvement of both the elected and appointed officials who are competent and ethical in the art of statecraft. In this context, the first and foremost condition of the public official's role would be to recognize the governing process as a moral endeavor. Secondly, their belief would have to be sustained by a resolve to serve and care for *all* citizens. Thirdly, they ought to consider their role as protectors of the rights of not only human beings but also the environment in which humans dwell, and to guard the natural legacy for future generations. And finally, protecting and enhancing democratic ideals requires vision and probity. The latter, being an essential condition for serving the public, cannot be sacrificed in the name of administrative rationality or mere political expediency. This requires a professional ethos that sees the process of governing as a moral undertaking.

The goals of a democratic state are generally reflected through governmental policy pronouncements as well as by legal instruments. Public policies in a modern state do not just happen; on the contrary, they are intentional and goal-oriented. A public policy is based on legal norms, is authoritative, affects a large area of people's lives, and its effects are profound. In a democracy citizens participate, however indirectly, in the process of public policy-making. They are responsible for putting elected officials in power, who in turn initiate many policy decisions. Therefore these citizens are also partly responsible for its actions. Furthermore, because the government is supposed to represent all of the people, in that sense it represents their constituency's values and way of life.

Thus, any governmental action, or governmental policy, whatever its intent reflects, directly or indirectly, moral concerns. Since all governmental deeds are "purposive" courses of action, we tend to judge those who are in charge of performing such actions (i.e. elected politicians and public servants) as if they were our agents. Public officials are expected to work on people's behalf. They do have a moral obligation to conduct public policies with the single-minded purpose of optimizing the public interests and values, and not yielding to their personal or any single group's interest. Their prime directive is the common good. Thus, besides the better understood legal dimension of government, there is an ethical dimension as well.

Placing emphasis on the public ethos is a way of articulating a concern for the improvement of the quality of governmental output and the conduct of public servants. On the other hand, when we use the term "ethics or values in government" it indicates the means by which this improvement is to be achieved. Of course, such terms as "good governance," "morality," or "ethics/values in government," are ambiguous; but such ambiguity should not and cannot detract from the importance of the terms. Governmental conduct includes not only that of elected and appointed public officials, it also includes those instruments of governance which officials utilize in order to achieve certain policy objectives. Thus, lying behind the conduct of officials and the instruments of policy they wield is something that might be called the "form and spirit" of a nation. These are the shared core values which are derived from explicit constitutional documents and conventions, and from less explicit, but none the less real, societal belief-systems that permeate the sociopolitical order and the citizens' expectations of those who govern.

Governance: good and otherwise

As mentioned earlier in this chapter, the concept of governance as a process is of recent origin which goes beyond the classical functions of rule-making, rule execution, and rule adjudicating. Different schools of thought derive different meanings from the term "governance," depending upon the role of process versus activity, and control versus rules (Hyden and Court, 2002). In this chapter, we use a broad concept of governance involving all such measures in the public sphere that guide, steer, control, or manage society. In essence, the term "government," as an institution, refers to a set of instruments through which people living in a state, believe in and share a common core of values, and direct themselves by means of laws, rules, and regulations enforced by the state apparatus (Dwivedi, 2001). The term "governance" includes a range of activities involving all cultural communities and various stakeholders in the polity. This refers to all government institutions (legislative, executive, administrative, judicial, and para-statal bodies), political parties and interest groups, non-governmental organizations in the civil society, the private sector, and the public at large (Frederickson, 1997: 86). The concept is also viewed as the exercise of political power to manage a nation's affairs (World Bank, 1992), as well as "the manner in which power is exercised in the management of a country's economic and social development" (World Bank, 1994: vii).

As indicated in Chapter 6, motivated by the developments in modern-day management principles and private business enterprise, Western public administration theorists and practitioners came up with the New Public Management (NPM) paradigm, as a replacement of the "orthodox" notion of development administration. More than an analysis, it was a compelling prescription summarized under the slogan of a "leaner and meaner state." This model challenged the classical Weberian notions present in the "old" development administration mold, with its accent on anonymity, stable procedures, and a pyramidal meritocracy. The new concept emphasized training, professionalism, customer-orientation, ethics, productivity, responsiveness to the changing demands of business, and global-mindedness. A goal was to reduce dependency on the government and enhance entrepreneurship and innovation. While the West celebrated the "retreat of the state," the developing nations faced deprivation, corruption, and retardation in social capital formation. However, the symbols of Western managerialism often failed to connect with the local culture and traditions and therefore did not bear the expected developmental fruits. Administrative reforms, in the last analysis, are carried out in the local context and cannot be effectively imposed or imported from outside. Unlike the laws of physics, norms in the domain of public administration are culture-bound and do not, usually, have universal applicability.

"Good governance" has thus become an often vacuous catchphrase being used widely by various international agencies such as the UN, the World Bank, and the IMF. It means essentially a practice of "governing well," i.e. clean governance to achieve the anticipated goals and objectives of the public and the government. In essence, the concept incorporates the same core values present in democratic governance: pluralism, legitimacy, consensus, participation, the rule of law, responsiveness, efficient and effective accountability, transparency, morality, and strategic vision (Dwivedi, 2002; UNESCAP (2004) Website). As mentioned, good governance refers not only to the government but also to all the unofficial players involved in the governmental process. Good governance goes beyond the idea of democratic governance. It encompasses it, but it also adds notions of honesty and transparency, as well as more instrumental values such as efficiency and effectiveness. Thus, in addition to representativeness, openness, respect for human rights and other democratic attributes, it includes accountability, public probity, and "doing things well."

Corruption and governance

Corruption means influencing the due process from inside or outside the system for expediting, modifying, or winning a favorable outcome or depriving the deserving party for personal gain by those who are in or have access to those in positions of power to take decisions. In a corrupt governing system, the rule of law is substituted by unscrupulous performance, personal whims, fancy or gratification serving the private ends of individuals. Caiden has defined corruption as a behavior which deviates from the formal duties of a public role because of private-regarding (personal, close family, private clique) pecuniary or status gains; or violates rules against the exercise of certain types of private influence (Caiden, 2001: 20). This includes bribery, nepotism, patronage, cronyism, influence peddling, and misappropriation; all of which have an element of intentional deviation from the rule of law for personal gain.

Symptoms of corruption

Corruption in public life manifests in different forms at different levels. Major kickbacks in government deals for purchase of items from within or outside the country, *hawala* (informal money transfers) transactions, money laundering, institutionalized percentage cuts in contracts, seeking free hospitality or accepting valuable gifts or cash as bribes, institutionalized payoffs in lieu of services being rendered as a part of government duty, gratifications by different gatekeepers of the institutions, e.g. customs or excise clearances, financial considerations for tax exemptions/reduction etc. are quite common. In many developing countries, academic institutions, hospitals, other basic services in the government and elsewhere are no exceptions – corruption has impacted all walks of life in many societies to a greater or lesser degree. Recruitments, transfers, postings, promotions, and other human resource management matters in government service have become major sources of corruption. Even the judiciary has not escaped from being tainted. The media and the civil society organizations, including business (large and small, national and transnational) have their own share of corruption as well.

Corruption at the daily cutting edge level (or "retail" corruption) is most ostensible for the common public. Their day-to-day activities like seeking basic services or amenities are adversely affected. There is often an underhand deal between officials who have the authority to do a job and the touts who take a service charge from ordinary men and women to get their job done. This has become a way of life, often unquestioned. Whether dealing with development authorities, transport offices, passport offices, police departments or banks, it is the same story for the ordinary citizens, unless they have so-called influence or "contacts" in the right places. False billing or depriving the government of revenue by collusive sharing of the dues is also common practice. Blackmailing and harassment of the guilty, and sometimes even the innocent by the media or press is another form of corruption. Like a contagious disease, corruption tends to spread all over the body.

Controlling corruption

The literature in public administration offers some indication that corruption can be reduced and contained through appropriate counter-measures. It also indicates that as long as the underlying causes persist, corruption is unlikely to be eliminated altogether. Indeed as long as human beings are imperfect corruption will persist (Caiden, 2001: 19). Many strategies have been attempted and recorded in the literature with varying degrees of success. Because of human greed, corruption cannot be routed out altogether yet it can be contained to a great extent so that it neither retards growth and development of the country nor pinches the citizens in their daily life. Government policy can control the risks and benefits of corruption. Anti-corruption policies can reduce and eradicate opportunities of corrupt behavior, increase the rewards for honesty, while increasing the probability of detection as well as the cost of corruption. They can also provide safety to whistle-blowers, enhance the speed of punishing the guilty, and make heavy punishments and penalties for deviant behavior. Policies like those outlined above rest upon a number of operational conditions (Dwivedi and Mishra, 2007).

(1) *Political will*: In a democratic system of governance, political will from the highest level is absolutely critical for the success of anti-corruption campaigns. Cleansing the top political playing field adds moral strength to efforts to deal with corruption lower down the ladder. This can also break pre-existing politico-administrative collusions to plunder the state with relative low risk. Morality-based politics, like those espoused by a national hero (like Mahatma Gandhi), could be a motivator if they are emphasized at all levels of training for the bureaucrats.

(2) *Judicial activism*: Even when the lower level of the judiciary is tainted by corruption, higher-level and constitutionally protected judicial institutions (such as supreme courts) can set in motion processes to deal with corruption. A free and independent judiciary, by reviewing the decisions of legislatures and executives, can be instrumental in bringing probity in public life of all organs of governance including their own.

(3) *Simplification of bureaucratic rules and procedures*: Too many laws, complicated procedures, multiple levels of clearances, multi-level approvals and no set time limit and accountability provide enough scope to harass and extract private gains from the public. The greater the rigidity, the bigger the proclivity to generate illegal rules of exceptionality. Under ongoing administrative reforms many things have been simplified and information technology has been utilized to bring transparency into the system. Yet this is only a beginning and a long journey has to be covered to ensure full transparency in all government dealings with the public. Computerization of the Railway Reservation System is a major success story in India. Competitiveness has been improved by incorporating a web-based tendering system with open procedures and availability of status online. Good practices can be documented and shared widely.

(4) *Accountability of senior officials*: Strengthening institutional checks and balances, improving vigilance enforcement measures, reforming procedures with emphasis on codes of ethics, recognizing integrity and honesty as assessment criteria, and enhancing compensations to reward and retain honest personnel may bring accountability at all levels. Also, speedy disposal of disciplinary proceedings and severity of punishment may induce fear among defaulters. This "carrot and stick" approach may imbed a sense of vocation and service in the culture. Government is a public trust and working for the government is public service that demands the highest level of integrity and behavior that exhibits such virtues as honesty, impartiality, sincerity, and justice. In this context the conduct of public administrators is expected to be beyond reproach, and also conditioned by role expectations of loyalty, efficiency, and effectiveness.

(5) *The role of media*: The media can play a double-edged role. On the one hand, it can expose the corrupt bureaucrats and politicians, and on the other it may get involved in yellow journalism and help corruption prosper through collusive blackmailing. A professionalized

journalism and a vigilant judicial system may check excesses and provide for an ethical synergy.

(6) *The role of social activists/CSOs*: In combination with the above, social activists and civil society organizations (CSOs) may play an important role in educating the public of their rights and legal status on different matters so that the public may demand the services with authority rather than with fear or servility. Such individuals/organizations may expose the corrupt and create public pressure or initiate judicial action against the guilty.

(7) *Demystification of the state*: In many developing nations, the government is still viewed as a great Leviathan to be feared and to be obeyed. The public hesitates to approach government officials; and when they do so, it is with awe and unquestioning reverence. These attitudes are then exploited by lower-level government officials. The result is often the public paying *baksheesh*, *mordida*, or *ghoosh* (gratuity, a kind of service charge) for rendering the service which an official was supposed to do it as a part of his or her government duty. Alternatively, the work is not done, or is delayed. Opening of the system to bring transparency in procedure and improving public awareness is crucial for arresting corruption. Holding government agencies accountable to the public is to some extent a matter of institutional design and internal checks and balances. Ultimately, it is the people whom government supposedly serves who are responsible for monitoring its performance and demanding responsive behavior (Fukuyama, 2004: 30). The introduction of Citizen's Charters to help change the mindset of both officials and the public could set practical benchmarks, transforming the relationship from someone with power over the public to someone with a care of duty towards them (Centre for Good Governance, 2003). Information communication technology (ICT) based transparent provision of services may also help in limiting corrupt practices.

Educating public servants to serve

Keeping functionaries serving the public rather than helping special interests – or themselves – the cultural "software" of the civil service must reflect an algorithm of values and principles essential to democratic governance. These values are constant points of reference along one basic prime directive: to serve the public interest. Such a directive rests on the operational principle that moral, legitimate, and effective government is built upon public trust. In turn, trust is based on the belief that the state is a moral entity whose actions and policies are, and should be, liable to ethical and moral judgement. Government being a public trust, public service is a noble calling for persons who should know how to behave morally. This assertion has certain implications: (a) Public officials need to be aware of the ethical consequences of the power they exercise, as well as of the courses of action they choose in the exercise of their responsibilities. (b) Public policies should explicitly represent, enforce and re-enforce prescribed public service values. (c) There must be enough control from outside the individual functionary to discourage those inclinations towards indulgence of self-interest. (d) Conversely, there should be enough internal control to encourage the most socially constructive idealistic, altruistic, and creative impulses to flourish. (e) The balance of controls is essential for the fully responsible conduct of the public sector (Dwivedi, 1988b: 237).

From a pedagogical point of view it is not easy to define a simple and a priori module or cluster of ethical issues for training sessions, or classroom instruction. Rather, it is essential to spend considerable time working on it in a variety of ways before asking participants to develop the full range of critical steps leading to a final resolution of the issues under scrutiny. A course on public service ethics needs be approached from three dimensions: classical, legal, and contextual. The classical approach emphasizes drawing from the philosophical and cultural traditions of a nation. The legal approach focuses on laws, rules, and regulations, and constraints on individuals to regulate their administrative power and authority. The contextual approach aims as sensitizing public servants to the need to act as guardians of the state situated in a concrete setting. In addition, the approach drawing from the administrative culture and bureaucratic morality of a nation needs to focus on case studies and actual problem-solving (Dwivedi, 1988a: 124–5).

Training the public sector officials in ethics is the first step. However, one must keep in mind that moral ambiguities are going to remain because no one can formulate policies that are morally justified under all circumstances. It is important, therefore, that those formulating, implementing, and evaluating policies be made aware of these ambiguities and be ethically sensitive so as to act in a responsible manner. Although ambiguity does not diminish the importance of the issue; the moral dimension of governance represents a concern for the quality of public service and governmental conduct.

Ethical mindsets and spirituality

Morality in the public service does not only mean that governments should develop lists of negative obligations about doing no harm, or keeping officials out of trouble. The notion of governmental ethics suggests that administrators proactively undertake acts that are socially just. If they are to serve the present and future generations well, all governments must act within (and be measured against) some higher law. That law cannot be purely formal, because it is framed by people in their limited instrumental capacities and therefore limited in vision. The law has to be, perforce, based on the principles of higher spiritual and philosophical foundations to give a base to a moral and responsible statecraft. Connectivity between the "outer" and "inner" self of functionaries is essential to give norms meaning and to facilitate their implementation.

Spirituality can lead to mastery over baser impulses in the ego, such as greed, exploitation, abuse of power, and mistreatment of people. Spiritually based moral consciousness constitutes a sort of super-ego controlling those impulses. Holding public office responsibly and ethically requires self-discipline, humility, and above all, the absence of arrogance. The virtuous public service role requires that people center their values on the notion that there is a larger good which must be maintained. Spirituality serves both as a model and operative strategy for the transformation of human character by strengthening the genuine, substantive will to serve the common people. A spiritually oriented public official will be fulfilling two duties: one to the self, whereby one seeks inner strength through spiritual action; and the other to the community-at-large, whereby one works for the common good. As such, personal spirituality and character regulate human conduct and cast individuals into a character mold built upon substantial and not purely instrumental moral virtues. The latter strengthen the ethos that holds the social and moral fabric of a society together, maintaining order and coherence, building individual and group character, and facilitating harmony and understanding (Dwivedi 2002b: 48).

Spiritual reflection and self-examination may allow organizations charged with keeping the ethical boundaries in society, such as the judiciary, to play a vital role in cleaning up the political as well as the administrative system – and also to keep an ethical eye on the other two organs of government. Mass media, civil society, and a network of civic groups championing ethical reform can play a major role in developing public awareness and controlling corruption. Political parties too may shed their opportunistic differences and make a conscious decision to launch a national campaign to eradicate corruption from public life. The current level of public indifference to government is ostensibly rooted in long-term fatigue and any change would be welcome. Fed up with bad governance and the nuisance of corruption, the public at large may be willing to join or support any realistic movement against it led by worthy leaders (Dwivedi and Mishra, 2007). Needless to say, there are always dangers in messianism and self-righteousness: whether moral revivalism will lead to a democratic scenario remains a wide open question.

Democratic versus bureaucratic values

Democratic values such as equality, law, justice, rights, and freedoms have moral connotations, and in theory at least demand an unwavering commitment from those who govern. Public servants are duty-bound to uphold these values, which are often enshrined in a nation's constitution or considered as self-evident truths. Elected and appointed officials have a primary obligation to serve and protect the rights and freedoms granted to all. This is *the* basic premise upon which depend the normal functioning and survival of democratic governance.

Bureaucracies embody hierarchical and operational values such as obedience, integrity, anonymity, political neutrality, chain of command, fairness, professionalism, and a vocation of public service. In addition to these "classical" bureaucratic values bequeathed by the former colonial regimes, other values and missions have been added. These entail second- and third- generation human rights, like employment equity, language rights, trade union rights, and legal rights with respect to their employment and working conditions. Thus, these layers of values get superimposed upon the above-mentioned democratic and bureaucratic values. A common outcome is axiological and operational confusion leading to either paralysis or an ethical vacuum.

For the sake of simplicity and systematization, we can sketch the values and ethical standards that affect public servants' behavior in postcolonial settings into several categories. (a) One is *personal standards of ethics and morality*. These relate to self-image and the role of an individual in upholding the public interest as a morally accepted legitimate concern. (b) Another is professional *standards*: employing a code of conduct and related professional values which members of a profession are supposed to uphold. (c) A third set of standards is the belief in *core values of the country and society*: believing in fundamental freedoms, human rights, and other related values. (d) A fourth standard is *administrative heritage*: for instance, serving people with honesty and integrity, political neutrality, impartiality and fairness, prudence and efficiency, applying the merit principle, anonymity, and loyalty to the duly elected government (Jain and Dwivedi, 1990). (e) A fifth set is *political values*: these may include obedience to elected representatives, and the doctrine of ministerial responsibility. (f) Finally, there is a standard of respect for *the rule of law*. These ethical values and principles relate to the "ethics of consciousness." We will explain these in some detail below.

Louis C. Gawthrop draws a distinction between two ethical models. One is the *ethics of civility* which is mechanical, procedural, pragmatic, quantitative, and ultimately reductionist. The other is the *ethics of consciousness* which requires all administrators to become aware of the larger context of societal needs and a sense of purpose in an individual's life (Gawthrop, 1984: 141). The sense of purpose in a public servant is based on the service concept (in a sense treating their jobs as a vocation), the noblest of all virtues needed in a public servant. The ethos of any public service organization in a democracy is based on the idea that public officials genuinely care and show responsibility for their fellow citizens. That "genuine care," in turn, enables public servants to act as "equitable administrators." According to John Rohr, an equitable administrator is one "[who] actively intervenes to enhance the political power and economic well-being of disadvantaged minorities in order to address the neglect suffered by such minorities at the hands of customary procedures of representative democracy" (Rohr, 1978: 55).

The profession of an equitable administrator, to be sure, includes such values as "objectivity, effectiveness, impartiality, integrity and probity in the conduct of public affairs within the context of maintaining a professional public service dedicated to achieving a high standard of efficiency and competence" (Dwivedi and Engelbert, 1981: 144). These traditional values overlap considerably with other values such as: (a) loyalty to superiors, (b) support of legitimately established governmental policies and programs, (c) utilization of public resources in the most effective and efficient manner, (d) being responsive to the needs and demands of the public, (e) accountability to the public through elected leaders, and (f) obedience to and observance of established rules and procedures of the public service.

The above list should also include other ideals of public service like a spirit of self-sacrifice, serving the public and the community, undivided allegiance to the state, and avoiding conflicts of interest. These expected, and perceived, ideals mean that a public servant is expected not only to act within legal bounds but also to act within a moral context. It should be realized that public servants are a mirror of societal conscience, prevailing morals, and ethical standards. While they may be expected to maintain the highest standards of performance in the conduct of public business, they are also impelled to lead the nation in exhibiting a higher form of morality as part of the social fabric of the nation.

Ethical behavior in the public service is considered as a blend of moral qualities and mental attitudes. Such a mixture strengthens the basis of legitimate and effective government which is founded on public trust and confidence. That confidence is predicated on two sets of ideals. The first set is based on the above-mentioned belief that to serve others is the highest calling. This belief holds that government is a public trust and public service is a vocation for persons who should know how to behave morally. The second set of ideals holds that recruitment and promotion in the government service should be based on merit alone and that public servants should observe political neutrality in order to render objective service under any political party in power.

Such ideals, however, often come into conflict with the narrower and protective outlook characteristic of unions and employee associations. The latter have emphasized the view that public service is merely a job. They would rather not accept the traditional role of public servants wherein duty, serving the community at all times, and even sacrificing one's personal life for the higher cause, were considered more important than the union approach to work ethics. Thus, modern public administration faces an inherent conflict between the traditional expectation of those officials who serve the state, and the alternative expectation of government employees who perceive that their obligations to serve are restricted to only those duties that are part of their job classification, and for which they can be held legally but not necessarily morally responsible.

They also fall to the axe of conditionalities, structural adjustment and the voracity of receiver states. In this case externally induced administrative recipes and reforms are more part of the problem than the solution. It is not surprising, then, to see many public servants and elected officials viewing their domain as one where ethical issues do not enter into what is, for all intent and purposes, a functional rationality. But, ethical dilemmas never disappear – they continue to crowd the public servant's vision. One of these is the conflict between privately held convictions and publicly required obligations. Another dilemma is individual interpretation of government policies according to a personal sense of right and wrong: the obligation to "only follow orders." A third dilemma refers to the obligation to report inefficiency, incompetence, extravagant and unreasonable expenditures of public funds, and nepotism in the workplace. Last, but not least is the extent to which public servants subordinate or abdicate their claims to private life, property, and personal values.

These dilemmas simply will not disappear. Instead they are going to remain in the public domain because no one can formulate policies and programs which are morally justified under all circumstances. Moreover, the existence of a dilemma or ambiguity does not diminish the importance of realizing the ethical ideals of service to the public, because the moral dimension of governance represents a concern for the quality of public service and governmental conduct. Without an ethical direction or a commitment to quality of service, citizens cannot trust that their affairs are fairly managed. They will remain persistently suspicious that they have surrendered their rights and freedoms to an irresponsible and amoral, if not immoral, state.

Deficit democracy and the state

It is a paradox of history that the empire-builders of Europe who started their business in Asian and African nations with naked corruption ended up handing over a relatively clean administration to the leaders of those independent colonies. There is no doubt that during the British, French, Dutch, or Belgian rule, there was massive and obscene corruption. It was also brutal, racist, and tyrannical. For all its sanctimonious preaching, the Western world was not above imposing dictatorship on the peoples it exploited. Whether under direct or indirect rule, the very thought of freedom, equality, and majority rule was inconceivable and subversive under colonialism. However, in many former colonies, some of these corrupt and authoritarian practices continue. It is also another paradox that although the leaders of those newly independent nations started off with the highest standards of probity and accountability, they often find themselves in the cesspool of corruption (Narain, 1996). The major difference between corruption in the industrialized nations and the developing world is that in the former the office does not sanctify the office-holder.

The office of the president of the US could not protect Richard Nixon at the end and he had to resign; on the other hand, the office of president or the prime minister of several developing nations protects its holders against prosecution and being held accountable while in power. This said, one should not commit the easy mistake of assuming that only underdeveloped countries are corrupt or inherently undemocratic.

Underdeveloped countries have underdeveloped, highly visible, and annoying forms of corruption, both at national and local levels. Developed countries have more sophisticated and subtle forms of it. This type of corruption is by all accounts massive, largely invisible, and often legalized.

Oligarchic proclivities

In many developing nations, there is a general belief among elites that common people are ineffective and to some extent incapable of governing themselves. Many developed countries seem to share this view and have done precious little to develop popular, participatory democracy, let alone an equitable socioeconomic order. On the contrary, neo-colonial intervention and the unseating of popular governments at odds with Western economic or military interests have been common. Despite much rhetoric, the prevailing view among Southern and Northern elites is that only the higher echelons of society are able to bring about change towards "good governance" and a higher standard of morality in public life. On the other hand, it seems common people have lost their faith in the ability of present-day politicians and political parties to give good governance to their countries. This loss of credibility is largely due to rampant abuse of power and privilege, blatant selfishness, and corruption in politics and administration. Despite the claims of a new democratic wave moving across the world there seems to be a growing democratic deficit (Nye et al., 2003) affecting not only the global South, but also the North and the emerging institutions of global governance. At close scrutiny, the quantitative expansion of democratic practices is often confined to formal elections and market reforms, but the qualitative dimension of democracy trails behind. The above-mentioned term "democratic deficit" is often used to refer to this incongruity.

In some countries like India and Pakistan, all shades of the political spectrum have received opportunities to form governments but none of them have escaped blameless after being in power for some time. It is no surprise that people are looking for alternatives which can provide honest, decent, truthful, truly democratic, and competent government. But normally it is difficult for most people to see a credible and viable alternative. Moreover, it is also hard for most of the population to believe that an alternative leadership or mode of governance will be responsive, responsible, and honest. For an alternative or plan to become successful, the first requisite is that the public's confidence and trust will have to be restored. This requires grassroots action to shake up public apathy and helplessness, and to build public self-confidence and courage to fight corruption, authoritarianism, and even outright criminality. The same way as one could identify "good governance" (or "good practices") we are suggesting that "bad governance" or "bad practices" should be equally identified.

Fighting "bad practices"

The first phase in a possible scenario to tackle "bad governance" could be civic mobilization at the local government level. Due to smallness and greater familiarity, it may be easier for the public to find out how much funds are collected and where the money has been spent. At this micro level it can be equally possible to identify oligarchy, nepotism, and other bad practices. Also, it will not be too difficult to monitor corruption and the deficit in democracy. Once some success is gained at the micro level, the civic organizations which exposed such corrupt practices would then be able to expand their radius of operation and their public campaigns. But first, a good organizational set-up is needed to aid the struggle for government transparency, accountability, and democracy. Cooptation and cooperation of honest officers, whistle-blowers, and leaders will have to be cultivated, and should be welcomed in whatever manner it comes.

Grassroots organizations advocating transparency and democracy in government to be effective need to transcend a purely local or regional level. They need to evolve into a mass movement against corruption, bad governance, and lack of democracy: something akin to a second struggle for independence. While the first movement in Third World nations was against colonial rule, with its sequels of exploitation and tyranny, the second rising could be directed against its own corrupt leaders and public officials and their international cronies. In this struggle, help from all quarters, but chiefly from a growing alliance of actors in the global, citizen-centered Third System (Nef, 2006) is a strategic necessity. This would entail NGOs, honest public officials, educators, media, religious organizations, even business groups, but most importantly social movements and ordinary citizens. It is essential to understand, however, that corruption and deficit democracy are not just bad traits of government officials. Whenever there is a corrupt public sector or a violation of due process of human rights, and authoritarian tendencies there is also an equally "shadowy" private sector and social groups able to generate the inducements to cross the probity and non-democratic line. Most important, it generally rests on public apathy, fear, or both.

Breaking public apathy

A generalized public perception is that corruption, abuse and unethical activities among officials (both politicians and appointed government servants) are inevitable and incurable. This pessimism is justified because people know that the custodians of state administration are under the unholy grip of corruption, and nothing moves smoothly without the help of influence, connections, bribery, extortion, or blackmail. Although the public is aware of the prevailing amount of corruption and lack of democracy in politics and administration, corruption and oligarchy continue.

Democratic deficit is not only limited to restricted freedom and public venality; it is also a question of socioeconomic and political inequity. Furthermore, liberal market reforms designed explicitly to enhance economic "freedom" often result in exclusion and in reduced ability to have a participatory process. Structural adjustment formulas tend to enhance the power of external constituencies and internationalized technocrats at the expense of internal democratic political process. The pervasive type of "receiver state" (Nef, 1992) – whose mission is to manage foreign debts and administer fiscal bankruptcy – favors at best restricted democracy, if not outright plutocracy.

It is hard to fathom the limit to which corruption and abuse may be tolerated by any society. It is important, however, that elected representatives and public servants are held accountable for the conduct of their tasks. Corruption among public officials does not mean that all of them or most of them are corrupt. The same goes for abuse of power. Even in some of the worst case scenarios, there are always honest and ethical public officials still in government and administrative offices, though they hold no influence in shaping the overall character and culture of their society. The tone for corruption, arbitrariness, and unethical behaviour is set by those in the commanding heights, and the quiescence of the many.

Moral leadership

Being in public office requires that its incumbents be willing not only to acknowledge the moral responsibility for their actions but also to accept accountability for what they do. Deflecting responsibility will not make action and its consequences disappear. Nothing is more damaging to public trust than justifying fraud and deception in the name of national security, government needs, or nation-building. Problems are more pervasive at the top simply because it is there where more is to be gained as well as lost. That is why moral leadership has to come from the top. The absence of such leadership breeds cynicism and generates tolerance of hypocrisy, greed, and self-indulgence. It could also create and sustain a culture of violence. The state (and finally society at large) becomes the victim of those public officials who are unable to put the public business above their selfish leanings.

If the public wants the state to show moral leadership, this proclivity is bound to have an effect sooner or later. Moral lassitude and abuse are as undesirable in the public place as in private life, if only for their consequences. It is difficult to draw a line between public and private morality, or between public ethics and private conscience. In some cases, ethical violations in public places may result partly from the absence of the fear of being caught, or impunity; partly from the increasing tendency to sidestep the voice of conscience; and partly from the view that if one is caught, there may be only a mild reprimand, or a lenient judgement. Nevertheless, a line will have to be drawn between what ought to be permitted and what not. That line can be drawn, maintained, and protected by an independent ethics commission or tribunal established for both elected and appointed public officials.

No country is immune to the moral disarray which we have seen recently. Whether the allegations regarding the "culture of corruption" in Washington, illegal spying, or torture, or the sponsorship scandals that brought down the Liberal government in Ottawa, corruption, deceit, and abuse are now center-stage. Even in the People's Republic of China, which was hailed as a paragon of public virtue and morality – though never for its respect for human rights – by those who visited in the 1970s, unethical activities and corruption have become widespread. Party rule has combined a huge democratic deficit with "capitalist-style" corruption. This pattern has become prevalent in many of the former communist societies in Russia and Central Asia. In many nations, a prevalent sense of moral disarray exists. Both industrial and non-industrial countries are at risk from this moral distemper. Everywhere, instances are on the rise detailing the collapse of standards and quality of service. Corruption, impunity, and disregard for the law have emerged as major threats to democracy and development everywhere. Globalization, far from making a dent in reducing the ethical and democratic deficits has only added to the depth and expanse of corruption and de-democratization. Newspapers are full of scandals; and abusive practices are becoming a way of life even at lower levels of bureaucracy.

This adversely affects the very tenets of democracy – equity, fairness, and the rule of law – as corrupt and authoritarian public life negatively impacts human development. State resources are diverted, absconded, or ineffectively utilized thus producing low public morale. Personal gains take prominence over "public good" leading to favoritism, inequity, and unfair treatment by those holding positions of power. In turn, this leads to human deprivation, generating a self-perpetuating vicious circle of corruption and authoritarianism. The pervasiveness of these dysfunctional traits has contributed to public cynicism worldwide; but at the same time the public is clamoring for a new basis for public morality, greater accountability, transparency, and ethical standards. To prevent drowning in a sea of dishonesty, authoritarianism, and self-centered hedonism, some sanctioned political consensus about the proper behavior of public officers has become paramount. The need to do so is clear. Modernization and globalization have created a vacuum: traditional and "old-fashioned" values have been discarded in favor of possessive individualism, often in the name of secularism. The strict separation between the secular and the "sacred" has weakened the protective layer of public morality which is left exposed to the onslaught of corruption, dishonesty, sleaziness, deception, and selfish individualism.

Reinventing the common good

Particularly relevant here has been the deconstruction of the common good idea brought about by the hegemony of neo-liberalism: private and public gains have become blurred. That protective ethical layer in the body politic is essential. There are some basic ethical values (drawn from the societal culture, traditions, religions, and even "common sense") which must be re-examined and reconsidered. However, the danger exists of the emergence of some kind of anti-democratic and fanatical fundamentalism, the copyright for which is now held by Taliban-like movements. Western societies are not immune to this kind of extremism rooted in the monopoly of truth and intolerance. To induce a return to ethics without fundamentalisms is not easy, but it is not impossible, as is the case with its unsavory opposite: fundamentalism without ethics. The key is in the education of both the public and public servants in ethical approaches from a critical and reflective perspective.

References

Caiden, G. E. (2001) "Corruption and Governance," in G. E. Caiden, O. P. Dwivedi, and J. G. Jabbra (eds), *Where Corruption Lives*. Connecticut: Kumarian Press, pp. 15–37.

Centre for Good Governance (2003) *A Guide to Developing and Implementing a Citizen's Charter.* Hyderabad, India: Centre for Good Governance.

Corry, J. A. and J. E. Hodgetts (1959) *Democratic Government and Politics.* Toronto: University of Toronto Press.

Dwivedi, O. P. (1988a) "Teaching Ethics in Public Administration Courses," *International Review of Administrative Science,* 54, 1, pp. 115–30.

Dwivedi, O. P. (1988b) "Bureaucratic Morality: Concluding Comments," *International Political Science Review,* 9, 3, pp. 231–9.

Dwivedi, O. P. (2001) "The Common Good and Good Governance," in K. L. Nandan (eds), *The Earth Has No Corners.* Delhi: Shipra Publishing, pp. 73–87.

Dwivedi, O. P. (2002) "On Common Good and Good Governance: an Alternative Approach," in D. Olowu and S. Sako (eds), *Better Governance and Public Policy.* Bloomfield, CT: Kumarian Press, pp. 35–51.

Dwivedi, O.P. and E. Engelbert (1981) "Education and Training for Values and Ethics in the Public Service: an International Perspective," *Public Personnel Management,* 10, 1, pp. 140–5.

Dwivedi, O. P. and D. S. Mishra (2007) "Good Governance: a Model for India," in Ali Farazmand and Jack Pinkowski (eds), *Handbook of Globalization, Governance and Public Administration.* New York: Taylor & Francis, pp. 701–41.

Frederickson, H. G. (1997) *The Spirit of Public Administration.* San Francisco, CA: Jossey-Bass Publishers.

Fukuyama, F. (2004) *State Building: Governance and World Order in the 21st Century.* New York: Cornell University Press.

Gawthrop, Louis C. (1984) *Public Sector Management, Systems and Ethics,* Bloomington: Indiana University Press.

Hyden, G. and J. Court (2002) "Comparing Governance Across Countries and Over Time: Conceptual Challenges," in D. Olowu and S. Sako (eds), *Better Governance and Public Policy.* Bloomfield, CT: Kumarian Press, pp. 13–33.

Jain, R. B. and O. P. Dwivedi (1990) "Administrative Culture and Bureaucratic Values in India," *Indian Journal of Public Administration,* 36, 3, pp. 435–50.

Narain, Jai (1996) "Political Corruption: Reversal of Gandhian Legacy," *The Tribune* (Chandigarh, India), November 30.

Nef, J. (with R. Bensabat) (1992) "Governability and the Receiver State in Latin America: Analysis and Prospects," in A. Ritter, M. Cameron and D. Pollock (eds), *Latin America and the Caribbean to the Year 2000.* New York: Praeger, pp. 161–76.

Nef, J. (2006) "Third Systems, Human Security and Sustainable Development," in Rebecca Harris (ed.), *Globalization and Sustainable Development: Issues and Applications.* Tampa: Dr. Kiran C. Patel Center for Global Solutions, University of South Florida, pp. 43–58.

Nye, Joseph S. et al. (2003) *The "Democracy Deficit" in the Global Economy: Enhancing the Legitimacy and Accountability of Global Institutions.* Task Force Report No. 57, The Trilateral Commission.

Redford, Emmette S. (1969) *Democracy in the Administrative State,* New York: Oxford University Press.

Rohr, John (1978) *Ethics for Bureaucrats: an Essay on Law and Values.* New York: Marcel and Decker.

Transparency International Report (2003) http://www.transparency.org/cpi/index.html (website of Transparency International).

UNDP (1997) Discussion Paper No. 3 on "Corruption and Good Governance," prepared by Management Development and Governance Division, Bureau of Public Policy and Programme Support, UNDP, New York, July.

UNESCAP (2004) http://www.unescap.org (website of United Nations Economic and Social Commission for Asia & Pacific (UNESCAP), Bangkok, Thailand).

World Bank (1992) *Governance and Development: the World Development Report.* Washington, DC: World Bank.

World Bank (1994) *The World Development Report.* Washington, DC: World Bank.

10
The Ethics of Development: Management in a Global Era

Ethics and development

The term "ethics" comes from the Greek word *ethos* which means accepted customs and traditions of a society; later, in Roman times, the term was translated into Latin as *mores*, which is the root of the words morals and morality. Sometimes, these two terms, "ethics" and "morality" are used as virtual synonyms. However, they mean different things. Ethics refers to fundamental values and principles underlying human action; morality refers to the observance of socially acceptable and customary practices. Nowadays, the common use of these terms is cast in terms of what is good or evil, right and wrong, as well as the appropriate conduct of people in a society (Engel, 1990: 6)

Of course, there are many social scientists who would like to avoid dealing with ethics and morality in the study of human affairs. Either they have a basic distaste for anything "moralistic," or they think that anyone talking about it must be acting out of self-interest while hiding behind a hypocritical facade of morality. They also allege that "the values referred to so frequently in ethical discourse are intangible, beyond measurement, often ambiguous and all too open to various interpretations" (Trompf, 1987: 103). And because of its alleged subjective or emotive language, ethical dimensions of development and governance have been rarely addressed.

But ethics and values have always been with us. Thus, the relevant question is whether or not the principles used in creating theories and models of social action – goal-oriented behavior – can be detached from the values of their creators. All human action (Karma) ever taken is susceptible to blame and praise, to being judged good or bad, or as having ethical implications. For instance, when the planet was conceptualized into First, Second, and Third Worlds, this taxonomy was loaded with ethical issues. In the 1950s and 1960s, the newly independent countries were termed "backward," "undeveloped," "less developed," or "underdeveloped" nations: this was a value-laden vision of the world. The very term "development" has an ethical connotation because it means a progress from small to big, bad to good, and poor to rich.

It is generally assumed in Western academic and international co-operation circles that their models of governance and development are universally applicable, in particular in the so-called developing nations. The opposite is hardly the case: we do not hear about non-Western models being used as a blueprint for governance structures and styles for the Western world. Culture, values, and prejudice, including the cultural construction of "the other," are important elements that make up the foundations of the origins and teleology of development. Until recently, overtly ethical vocabulary was seldom a part of any develop-ment theory dialogue; instead the thinking was that ideas, models, and technical solutions prescribed by the developed countries were value-neutral and uncontaminated by subjectivity. After all, these societies *were* developed.

One question that has been rarely raised is whether it is morally permissible to allow a distinct and inferior level of human dignity to be maintained for the poor. Are there no ethical compulsions and obligations that the governments and people of the North and the well-to-do in the South have towards exploitation, poverty, un-employment, disease, subhuman quality of life, environmental degra-dation, widespread corruption, and bad governance? Why has there been so little said about ethical issues when discussing development management? Nothing in the field of development is value-free. Impartial objectivity and value-neutrality are possible and practiced in the field of natural science. But when we discuss human activity and development, it is important to know and worry about the moral significance of prescriptions for bringing change in the human condi-tion. Thus, the *ethics of development* conjures an image of moral leaders like Henry David Thoreau, Albert Schweitzer, Mahatma Gandhi, and Wangari Maathai using ethics to empower themselves, and bring-ing changes in their societies by sharing their ideas with others. If development is to mean the emergence of a just society worldwide, then values and ethics cannot be fenced out of developmental planning and action. In this chapter, we attempt to examine some of these related issues.

The purpose of this chapter is not so much to elaborate on the theoretical foundations and practices of international development; rather, it is to explain and understand the historical, cultural, and moral factors affecting its leading ideas. In so doing, we will specifically explore the ethical sources and consequences of theory-building and discourses in development. Given the nature of the topic, a great deal of the analysis will be somewhat phenomenological, introspective, and prescriptive, yet grounded on our experience, reflection, observation, and interaction with academics, students, and practitioners in the course of decades of research, teaching, and international consultations. It will be presented from a standpoint and normative perspective reflective of the authors' personal values and observations.

Development and development theory

The idea of development has evolved considerably in the last two centuries. What was perceived as development in the early 1800s has been completely transformed in meaning and importance in today's society. Since the spread of colonialism, the birth of globalization, and the spread of modernization, development has encapsulated multiple and interconnected economic, political, social, and cultural changes. The concept of development itself cannot be separated easily from modernization, as the two terms are mutually connected when describing a given state of progress. One of the many definitions of development is the "act of improving by expanding or enlarging or refining" (HyperDictionary, 2004). Philosophers, thinkers, economists, and theorists viewed development in unique ways. For example, Hegel saw history itself as progression to the betterment of society. The birth of capitalism had in a manner forced people to view rationally facts of human, economic, social, political, and cultural development (Leys, 1996). Others viewed development in various contexts such as economic development, cognitive development, or human and social development.

The term "development theory" emerged in the late 1950s, primarily to deal with the economies of Britain, France, Portugal, and other European powers. Its aim was to provide grounds for policy (Leys, 1996). The first works on development theory began with the foundations built by economists influenced by the ideas of John Maynard Keynes and his state intervention economic policies. However, this slowly evolved to include development based on issues of production, the environment, and social conditions (Peet, 1999).

Development theories have also followed Marxist and neo-Marxist perspectives. It is imperative to distinguish between these two schools in terms of development theory. As Schuurman points out, although both schools regard social and political relations as determined by the primacy of productive forces, when it comes to development theory, they differ greatly (Schuurman, 1993). Marxism in its classical form is Eurocentric as it examines imperialism from the core and its function in the economic development of these core capitalist countries. Neo-Marxists examine imperialism from the periphery and study the consequences of imperialist penetration (e.g. world systems and dependency theory) (Schuurman, 1993). It is between these two schools of thought, that development theory was said to have originated in full scale. However, some theorists such as Colin Leys would argue that economic development theory began in the pre-Marxist era, while others would argue its beginnings originated after Marx.

There have been also development theories that emerged and evolved outside the Marxist and neo-Marxist matrix. Schuurman classified these theories that did not belong to either schools and are often ignored in discussions of development theories. He identifies the French regulation school, the actor-oriented approach, and post-imperialism. The French regulation school, led by Lipietz, assumes regularities in development theories and characterizes them into regimes of accumulation and modes of regulation which are observable through historical comparative research and concentrates on internationalism (Schuurman, 1993). The actor-oriented approach introduced by Norman Long is interested in the relationship between the meso and micro levels and where human reaction plays a central role in development. The post-imperialistic paradigm presented by Schuurman, Becker, and Skar comprises a set of ideas rather about the political and social organization of international capitalism (Schuurman, 1993). Although a more structuralistic approach, it has many similarities to the actor-oriented approach, in the sense that it focuses on the actors and the social and human involvement in development.

Other schools of thought include post-structuralism, post-colonialism and post-development. Post-structuralists, according to Peet, saw development as a strategy of modern power and social control (Peet, 1999). Post-colonialists sought to change the knowledge and social identities crafted by Western domination and colonialism. Peet suggests that "post-developmentalism," on the other hand, "entails the complete rejection of modern development rather than its modification or democratization" (Peet, 1999: 15). The theory of dualism is also another significant theory that follows a fine line between traditional and modern forms of development. It offers a split of economic and social structures in different sectors that differ in organization, level of development, and goals (Kuhnen, 1987). Theorists such as Eckhaus and Gannage have both added literature to the theory of dualism, particularly in communications and technology.

New currents in the broader literature on development are beginning to move towards the inclusion of voices previously unheard. For example, a paradigm shift seems to be occurring in feminist perspectives on sustainable development as the women-in-development discourse is replaced by a women–environment–development concept. The women-in-development literature emphasized the importance of women in the development process, but offered no basic questioning of the development enterprise itself. Women would be *included*, but would not change overall directions; more women administrators at all levels presumably would satisfy the participatory requirements, and gender *awareness* would assuage the demands of women's groups.

Alternative models of development

Until the 1980s, there were the two main models of development – capitalism and Soviet-style socialism – competing in the development race. Of these, communist collectivism, whose origins are as Western as Marx's dialectical materialism itself, left little room for the individual and ultimately failed politically, economically, and arguably socially too. The centrally planned economies seem to have been unable to offer an alternative and viable future, unless one accepts that one such alternative model is China. On the other hand, the capitalist model, which had been in competition with communism during most the last century, successfully extended Western materialist and consumerist values by requiring policy changes based on these values as a condition for development aid to the Third World. The combination of advertising, its success and better management gave capitalist ideology a hegemonic character. For all Western donors there is increased emphasis upon the private sector in this model, including privatization, removing impediments to business expansion, and generally using businesslike techniques to improve productivity. Moreover, hedonistic values emphasizing individual desire for economic and physical security are paramount. But besides these two Western materialist models, what are the alternative models of development? There appear to be many other types of alternatives, of which we will concentrate on three examples: Sarvodaya, Liberation Theology, and Islamic Revivalism. All of these have been implemented in some place, and all emphasize spiritual or religious values.

Sarvodaya

The Sarvodayan movement's original inspiration was Mohandas Gandhi. Sarvodaya signifies an awakening of spirit and therefore liberation of the individual as well as groups. The result of this personal awakening is intended to be a dynamic, non-violent revolution that results in a transfer of political, social, and economic power to all the people. Sarvodaya as a worldview has been practiced in Sri Lanka since the mid-1950s. Religion plays an important role in legitimizing the Sarvodayan movement, supplying its leaders with rhetoric and inspiration (Macy, 1985: 11). The religious aspects permeate the movement at every level, encompassing goals and tactics; it is based on a bottom-up, self-reliant approach, and many of its ideals are attractive to ethical administrators and those interested in good governance. Sarvodaya has grown in Sri Lanka from a brief work camp organized by science teachers for their students to a self-help movement active throughout the country. The social construct of the Sarvodayan model focuses on achieving equality and solidarity. In order to accomplish tangible results, it was necessary to focus first on such things as healthcare and education, ensuring that all citizens have access to both regardless of their social status. The economic component of the model is of integral importance, though it cannot be taken in isolation from other aspects. The Sarvodayan movement recognizes that the individual and the group require parallel development. Therefore, all efforts focus on projects that will accomplish both. This necessitates an awakening in people's spirits and consciousness, in the enhancing of skills, and development with minimum participation from outsiders. The participation of people is the basis for integrated economic development. Politically, the movement focuses on decentralized participation in decision-making.

Sarvodaya is non-partisan, which allows the movement to amass the needed trust of the population. The moral aspects of the Sarvodaya development definition are based on *Dharma* (virtue; right conduct in Hindu religion) but are applicable to other religious traditions as well. The basic premise is to enhance the dignity and self-respect of each other, which assumes that killing, stealing, lying, sexual misconduct, and drug abuse will be minimized and eventually eradicated at the village and higher levels. Culturally, Sarvodaya instills harmony in relationships, not only among human beings but also between humans and other living creatures. Lastly, the Sarvodayan movement is entrenched in the spiritual realm. The movement hopes to move people from a life of greed, hatred, and delusion into one of awareness, truth, and compassion (Dwivedi and Henderson, 1999: 35–8).

Liberation Theology

The roots of Liberation Theology stem not from the poor or those who work among the poor, but originally from Protestant and Catholic theologians. In 1962, a progressive Protestant group called Church and Society in Latin America (ISAL), inspired by the European and North American Social Gospel movement emerged in Latin America. In turn, progressive Catholic priests trained at Louvain University argued that the Christian message was not one of passivity and submission but of bringing social justice in the here and now. For some, political revolution was necessary to help the poor and Marxism offered one strategy to bring about desired goals. In the 1963 Episcopal Conference of Latin America, liberal theologians created a working paper on the subject, modifying the one originally formulated by the ISAL. This paper questioned a theology of liberation based on Marxist-materialist philosophy, but wholly supported its basic beliefs. More importantly, in 1968, in the ecumenical context of Vatican Council II the Latin American Catholic bishops' conference endorsed a radical Christian approach to the achievement of social and economic rights.

It called for the mobilization of the poor to struggle for their liberation. The pedagogical foundation of Liberation Theology is Paulo Freire's idea of "conscientization": adult learning as the practice of freedom (Freire 1971). It is from this intellectual core that Liberation Theology (Gutiérrez, 1973) received its impetus, upon which the concept would flourish far beyond the theological environment in which it was created. Later, Christian Base Communities (CBCs), and self-managed urban communities were established in many Latin American countries with the class-based purpose of reacting against oppression and seeking political rights along with self-help social and economic improvement. But its implications were not limited to Latin America. In a way, they also influenced Cesar Chavez's Farm Workers' movement in the United States and beyond. In South Africa, Liberation Theology assumed an important role in the struggle against apartheid, and also in Cabo Verde, Guinea Bissau, Angola, and Mozambique.

Liberation Theology finds itself centered primarily in Latin America because of the distinctive geo-political and cultural factors there. The role of the liberationist Catholic priests has been critical, with an opposition to government that they see as the source of corruption and exploitation being a key element. The emphasis is upon the class struggle of the poor against the landed gentry, the power elites, and political leadership, as emphasized by the Brazilian author Leonardo Boff: "What liberating potential is contained in the Christian faith, a faith that promises eternal life, but also a worthy and just life on earth" (Boff and Boff, 1987: 42).

Islamic Revivalism

Unlike Sarvodaya and Liberation Theology, Islamic Revivalism does not differentiate between religion and politics by sharing a common concern with the combining of state and society with strict adherence to the Qu'ran. Revivalism better captures the intent of reviving and reasserting the essence of the literal word of Allah, in the Qu'ran. To the Revivalist, Islam comprises a total belief system that provides direction for all aspects of life, including governance. Islamic Revivalists use the Shari'a law, the direct Qu'ranic rule over the society. Its objective is to develop the Islamic person; this is reflected in moral codes, education, family organization, and in other ways. Some countries maintain full rule by the Shari'a, but others (such as Pakistan) count themselves as Islamic states. Besides its use in Saudi Arabia, Afghanistan, and Sudan, Revivalism as a movement has asserted itself in countries as varied as Algeria, Egypt, Turkey, Kuwait, Bangladesh, and Malaysia. Muslims (both Shia and Sunni) believe that they have a perfect code of behavior that is true for all times to come.

Socially, Islamic Revivalism attempts to combine egalitarianism, militant puritanism, and an emphasis on the individual. The state acquires the right to rule and govern by the literal interpretations of the Qu'ran, which allows it to place social and ethical constraints on the individual. Revivalists believe that there are social limits to development, as illustrated in the "failures" of Western societies. Economics is of integral importance to the Islamic Revivalist mode of development. While Islamic philosophy supports and controls the sociopolitical superstructure, all traditional economic activities and enterprises may be privately owned and operated. Nevertheless, action in every field of human activity, including economics, is spiritual and should be in harmony with the goals and values of Islam. Politically, Islamic Revivalism requires that there be a judicious distribution of economic and political power among individuals.

This complements the principal aim of Islamic society, which is to maximize social welfare. The word Islam in Arabic means both submission and peace. A Moslem (Muslim) is a person who submits to the will of God and finds peace therein. In summary, the spiritual realm of Islamic Revivalism is all-encompassing. The state, its laws, and development practices are firmly rooted in scripture. Islamic Revivalism is an affirmation of religious authority as holistic and absolute, admitting neither reduction nor criticism (Lawrence, 1989; Ismael and Ismael, 1985; and Sayeed, 1995). With respect to state apparatus and administration, implicit in the model is the notion that civil servants will be trained in the Shari'a rather than the usual Western precepts of good administration.

These three alternate models of development have illustrated the need to consider that different theories may be operational in different cultural domains. For example, Islamic Revivalism would not be suitable for non-Muslim areas; similarly, the Sarvodayan model would be difficult to transplant in non-Hindu and non-Buddhist regions. Thus development models and theories should not be seen as totally universal in application although certain basic principles of governance (such rule of law, corruption-free service delivery, objectivity in applying rules and regulations, and independent judiciary) will have to be universally applicable.

Society and culture in development theory

There are key and recurring words and terms that have appeared in the explanation and definitions of development theories throughout the years. These include indicators to measure the level of development, the stages of development, variables of development and the different eras and schools of thought that influence and shape development theories. Richard Peet states that some development theories reach deep into a society's culture and meta-philosophy for explanatory and persuasive powers. This is a notion that has become rare in the study of development: cultural issues and ideology are generally lacking in many analyses of development. But culture and ideology are as important in development as are socioeconomic organizations and socioeconomic processes. Some crucial dimensions of culture that need to be addressed in development theory include religion, social networks and social capital, participation, values, and ethnicity.

There is, however, a more insidious and all encompassing misuse of "culture" in development. Jan Knippers Black noted that "one consequence of disappointment with political and economic trends in the Third World . . . has been a reversion to emphasis on the explanatory power of culture as an independent variable" (Black, 1999: 25). In turn, a cultural determinist like Samuel Huntington has noted that the concepts of modernization and Westernization are beginning to diverge. He maintains that if we fail to see development in Third World countries, it is because those goals are deemed as Western goals (Huntington, 1993). Huntington's argument for this is that Western culture perceives wealth, equity, democracy, stability, and autonomy in building development, whereas non-Western cultures prefer simplicity, austerity, hierarchy, authoritarianism, discipline, and militarism (Huntington and Weiner, 1987: 21–8). Human development theory, on the other hand, combines issues such as human development, the environment, feminist concepts, sustainable development theory, and the environment. Amartya Sen, a proponent of this theory, argues that development views should focus on human freedoms instead of gross national product, personal income, or technological advancement (Sen, 1999).

Elspeth Young, a prominent author on aboriginal development, developed a model adapted from Barbier in a 1987 work that she refers to as the aboriginal concept of development. The model consists of the integration of three systems: the social, environmental, and economic systems. Young added that "this holistic viewpoint accords well with dominant characteristics of aboriginal society, in which the people (the social system), their means to survival (the economic system) and the environment (the biolobical and resources system) are integrated so closely that none of these elements can be usefully studied in isolation" (Young, 1995: 12). It is important to note that theories such as that presented by Young are very rare. On the whole, as we said in earlier chapters, there is a persistent scarcity of perspectives from a non-Western viewpoint.

Tradition and modernity in development theory

Post-World War Two development theories tended to emphasize the transition between two poles: tradition and modernity. We need to identify and examine some of these conceptualizations in order to fully understand their analytical reasoning and their possible application in development planning, organization, and management. One major theory of development comes from Rostow's influential "stages of economic growth model" where all societies can be placed on a continuum between developed and underdeveloped levels (Rostow, 1960). Rostow claimed that developing societies had to go through five stages: traditional, pre-takeoff, takeoff, drive to maturity, and mass consumption.

McClelland who has also written on theories of modernization, particularly in the Malaysian context, saw development there as a function of an enlightened ruling class arising and awakening the people themselves in order to achieve development. For him, what was essential was changing the mentality of the people who are to be developed (McClelland, 1962).

Bjorn Hettne suggests that development "involves structural transformation which implies political, social and economic changes. Development theory is therefore also by definition *interdisciplinary*, drawing on, but questioning many theoretical and methodological assumptions in both Marxist and non-Marxist social science" (Hettne, 1982: 7). For him, one cannot describe development or modernizing theory without mentioning the role of Western society, and Hettne adds that one can assume that there is a specific image of reality, underlying the multiplicity of views within Western culture (Hettne, 1982). This suggests that Western culture is becoming more inclusive and therefore is imperative in the development of traditional non-Western cultures. Another sociologist, Rodolfo Stavenhagen, who did extensive work on Latin America, claimed that underdeveloped countries, and especially Latin American countries, were not dualistic societies, consisting of a traditional agrarian society and a modern urbanized society, where the former was often associated with feudalism and the latter with capitalism (Stavenhagen, 1966, quoted in Hettne, 1982: 34). Rather, the "modern" sector exploited the "backward" periphery for its own gain.

In relation to the term "development," a major author who has worked on the issue of underdevelopment and is said to be the first to introduce the term was Andre Gunder Frank. Frank claimed that modernization as described by McClelland and Rostow and others of the same theory, was empirically untenable, theoretically insufficient and practically incapable of stimulating a process of development in the Third World (Frank 1969 quoted in Hettne, 1982: 36). Instead Frank argued that the thrust of the modernization approach was to compare an underdeveloped country with a developed one by means of various indicators (Frank 1969 quoted in Hettne, 1982: 36). The difference from these indicators would reveal the essence of development. Mason, on the other hand, associates the term "development" with the term "Americanization" which in turn implies cultural and political changes (Mason, 1997).

There have been other writers who have focused more on the term "development" itself and its status in today's society, without paying particular attention to modernization or traditionalism. For example,

Mike Mason explains that the "By the 1990s, the 'Third World' had come to refer not just to countries but to conditions as well, especially conditions of destitution and disorder" (Mason, 1997: 39). As Arturo Escobar explains, development has become the main discourse or analytical convention for describing the history of the Third World in the half-century after World War Two, and attempts to overthrow, or at least renegotiate, the Western developmentalist idea evident throughout the Third World from the 1950s (Escobar, 1995). The next section will discuss the more contemporary theories or modernization theories of development.

Modernization theories

It is difficult to discuss development theories without mentioning the theories of modernization. Modernization theorists at the beginning directly critiqued the lack of evidence supporting the validity of dependency theory. The theory began with the assumption that there were two types of societies: traditional (relationships based on particularism, i.e. ties to particular groups of people) and modern (based on universalism in which achievement rather than ascription by birth was the main criterion in progression (Leys, 1996)). Based on this distinction, according to Leys, the term "modernization" therefore refers to the process of transition from traditional to modern forms of social organization (Leys, 1996). Modernization theories also distinguish factors such as illiteracy, traditional agrarian structure, the traditional attitude of the population, and the like that are responsible for underdevelopment of that particular country (Kuhnen, 1987).

The main critique was geared towards the differences in degree of dependency that were usually related to differences in economic development (Schuurman, 1993). Peet claims that modernization theories divided the global systems into modern progress (the core or the center) and traditional backwardness (the periphery) where the former leads the latter and paves the way for the future (Peet, 1999). Mike Mason explains that modernity "means inescapable globalization and homogeneity. It connotes the inevitability of 'MacWorld'" (Mason, 1997: 40). Samuel Huntington (1993) identified what other modernization theorists have ignored, the concept of social classes and revolutionary movements as central to the development of Third World politics.

Alternative development theories have taken a more practical outlook in approaching the concept of development and the underlying theme of modernization. For example, Michael Edwards looks at new directions in development studies such as participatory research and growing links between organizations and academics (Peet, 1999). Stuart Cobridge focuses on the ethics of development and how it might contribute towards the understanding of developing countries and their crisis. Peet, on the other hand, adds elements of social theory to the study of modernization. He discusses the effects of naturalism, rationalism, and structural functionalism on development thinking. Björn Hettne claims that modernization theory is inadequate from the point of view of concrete issues, like the food problem, since it deals with societal development in the abstract (Hettne, 1982). Hettne also adds that conventional modernization theories tend to put too much emphasis on industrialization and ignore agriculture (Hettne, 1982).

Thus, development theories from the late early 1960s began to evolve from the classical modernization theories presented by Rostow. Concrete and physical indicators called for a more specific definition of development and a conceptual framework to study what is in fact development and underdevelopment. Appropriate development strategies need to be grounded on sound theory, and good analysis of data.

Governance, management, and development ethics

For most countries, a persistent problem in governance is the absence of moral leadership. For lesser developed ones this is a hard felt scarcity. Moral decay and double standards are reportedly pervasive both in the public place and in primary groups. "Righteousness" in public office is, of course, extremely difficult to define, as it is hard to draw a line between public morality and private sin, or between public ethics and private conscience. In some cases, ethical lassitude in public offices may result partly from the absence of deterrence, and partly from the increasing tendency to moral relativism, resulting from rapid change and cultural disintegration. Political leaders frequently justify fraud and deception in the name of self-serving principles of national security, government needs, economic rationality, or community demands. Lack of moral integrity appears more pervasive at the top simply because it is there where more is to be gained, or lost.

The issue of moral leadership starts at the top, but its positive or negative effects extend to the entirety of the state and the civil society. The absence of such leadership generates hypocrisy, greed, and self-indulgence, ultimately breeding public cynicism and the acceptance of the inevitability of corruption. It appears that no governing process is immune to the growing moral disarray as people feel that dishonesty and corruption in public life are endemic. In other words, it may become a self-fulfilling prophecy. In lesser developed countries, poverty, failed states, authoritarianism, turmoil, disintegration, and growing human insecurity provide the context for the collapse of moral standards and quality of public service. Of course, the industrialized world is no paragon of ethical governance either, but the impact of corruption is less dramatic there.

Since culture and style of governance are the key to the understanding of what makes a country function, it is imperative that any public sector reform in developing nations draws on the local customs, societal values, culture, and traditions. When the local culture and traditions are discarded in favor of Western-style management practices, and when not enough time is given to these nations to see if such a transplantation has germinated, then, as noted earlier, a hotchpotch of value systems and contradictory ethical algorithms start operating simultaneously. There is no one specific standard left against which the conduct of public officials (as well as business people) could be assessed. The traditional "protective layer" in the body politic needs to be reaffirmed; for no nation or society, irrespective of its political and religious orientation, can live in a moral vacuum. For the West as well as for the "Other" world, a key to a just and sustainable world requires diversity in thought and action rather than the self-proclaimed universal relevance of West-originated paradigms. Only by bridging the gap between the Western demand for efficiency and accountability and taking into account the local traditions of community care and well-being, can the ethics of development be sustained.

The preservation and enhancement of the public good through governmental institutions has been an enduring concern in all cultures. While such was the case among many industrialized nations until the first half of the twentieth century, the need for good government is much more emphasized in the developing nations not only by its citizens but also, perhaps more vigorously, by the donors and various international agencies. Social science literature is full of information about bad government in developing nations: the stories about corrupt politicians, bribe-taking government officials, badly conceived and mismanaged public programs; a bloated bureaucracy and its disdainful attitude towards citizens are plentiful.

The prevalence of such pathologies bothers concerned mainstream thinkers in the West. Whether one refers to these intellectuals as neoliberal, the Washington consensus, or the public choice theorists, these establishment intellectuals favor a package of pro-business measures.

These include the retreat of the state, increased uses of private sector concepts in the government, and privatization of many governmental functions (Tendler, 1997). When one is bent upon looking for faults and bad performance, of course that is what one may find.

For example, the mainstream development community has looked at the style of governance in developing nations from the jaundiced eyes of the alleged superiority of their market mechanisms for solving governmental problems. Thus, the reforms ushered in by Thatcher in Britain, Reagan in the US, Chirac in France, Kohl in Germany, Mulroney in Canada, and Fraser in Australia appear to be panacea for all ills, not realizing that the poorer nations do not have such developed market mechanisms, a strong civil society, and alert citizenry which can fill the vacuum left by the retreat of the state. Their blind faith in the role of civil society, or consumer behavior which may monitor governmental performance or seek accountability, is badly placed mainly because such groups are either non-existent or controlled by a few elites. Moreover, without high standards of governance and oversight, the private sector itself is very likely to become corrupt.

If one has to look for the roots of bad performance by governments in both developed and developing countries, one should pay close attention to the opposite: that is, why certain functions get performed well in some nations and not others. For example, Japanese firms have performed so well compared to many American or Europeans industries. Is it perhaps because of the dedication, loyalty, and commitments of the workers along with a greater cooperation between labor and management, and a pride in their product? In the same manner, would it not be better if the reforms in developing countries emphasize government officials' dedication, loyalty, having a sense of "calling" and mission, serving the public as a patriotic duty, and being proud of serving their country? Instead of harping on government officials as corrupt, lazy, and venal, positive and complementary measures are required. There is no doubt that it will take time to establish good governance in developing countries; that is why the mainstream development community should not lose patience. The desire for good governance in developing nations is very strong; the means and political will are in short supply.

Finally, ethical ambiguity has been on the rise in many nations, thereby increasing the incidence of corruption and unethical behavior especially when officials are not afraid of being caught and swiftly punished. Two glaring examples are the Enron and WorldCom scandals, in which their top executives did not reveal the true financial state of their company affairs, and in the process shareholders lost billions of dollars, and thousands of people became jobless while individually company executives amassed millions. The challenge before public leaders, not only in developing nations but in all places, is to realize that they are there to perform a public duty, and that their every action must be ethically right and legally accountable.

Management ethics in an interdependent world

Sometimes one hears questions like: what's wrong with the Third World, and why do various efforts fail to bring about development? If we consider the history of developing nations and Western projects to "modernize" them, five misguided approaches to development can be identified. One is that in the dominant paradigm, development could only be attained by modernization (i.e. Westernization); that is to say, by the diffusion of Western values and technology. The second is that the predominant feature of development is economic development; the latter defined in terms of growth (i.e. the expansion of GNP per capita over a period of time). The third is the belief that quantitative change (economic change) will produce a critical mass leading to qualitative transformations. Sequentially, economic growth would bring about social changes that in turn would bring about political development. Structurally, an expansion of wealth in the hands of the investor elite would trickle down, bringing generalized prosperity and a higher standard of living. The fourth theme is that once a region becomes developed, capital, technology, and ideas would, in turn, bring development to other areas. The fifth main factor underpinning development and administration is the emphasis on attaining changes in the form of adaptation and systems maintenance, not radically altering the status quo.

In spite of much rhetoric, the emergent systems of governance have tended to be imitative and ritualistic. Practices, styles, and structures of administration generally unrelated to local traditions, needs, and realities succeeded in reproducing the symbolism, but not the substance, of a British, French, or American administrative system. Even where a relatively large contingent of trained functionaries existed, such as in India, Pakistan, Kenya, Nigeria, and Ghana, and arguably because of their existence, a continuation of colonial administrative culture prevailed. At the same time, a massive dose of political interference in the way of doing things stifled developmental initiative. Confronted with an ineffectual developmental bureaucracy, the Western solution was to call for even more of the same recipes that had previously failed. This was also the preferred option of the local elites. Technical and antiseptic solutions were more palatable than substantive political decisions to bring about real socioeconomic change. Administrative reorganizations and rationalizations for the sake of abstract principles soon became the ends rather than the means of development and administration. A number of signposts for managing development in a global age are outlined below.

(1) *Everybody has a personal worldview:* A worldview consists of a set of beliefs, attitudes, and values, a kind of individually developed paradigm and a specific way of looking at reality. Most theories and models of development have been influenced by the worldviews prevailing in industrialized societies. Conventional theories saw the developing world as a set of unfolding patterns such as GNP and industrial growth, fiscal and monetary issues, market flexibility and technical efficiency, clarity in rule-application, and a workable system of democratic governance. Terms such as progress, prosperity, development, improvement, and material growth were seen as synonymous. And when the rate of progress or prosperity does not reach the experts' level of expectation, a feeling of frustration and disappointment builds up, not realizing that material growth cannot remain a perpetual tool for development. An alternative view of development requires a different worldview, emphasizing the qualitative dimension of development, the removal of inequitable patterns of income distribution, dynamization of stagnant economic systems, alleviation of poverty, and protection of rights and freedoms. Furthermore, that worldview need not to be uniform; because as "in nature, diversity in a human society would be both a cause of and a result of sustainability" (Meadows et al., 2004: 258). How to seize the opportunity and how to bring into being a worldview that is not only sustainable but also *desirable* is a question of development ethics, vision, and courage.

(2) *Recognizing the world's cultural contradictions:* We must acknowledge that there is an unfocused and contradictory conditionality imposed on the developing nations. The World Bank has now acknowledged that the Bank and the International Monetary Fund supported programs "often include multiple objectives in civil service reform, which have occasionally been contradictory, and often not made explicit. In addition, there has been little consensus on what constitutes an acceptable approach to addressing each objective" (World Bank, 2002: 15). We must pay adequate attention to political factors and other institutional constraints faced by developing nations. For

example, reducing public service employment may be counterproductive if it undermines the stability of the very government which is being forced to institute reforms. Moreover, in several countries, government is compelled to provide employment as a safety net to some segments of the population. Thus, various models of reforms conceived in the West and applied blindly without recognizing the long-term nature of civil service reform are not going to succeed unless such reforms are made politically feasible. This means strengthening, not weakening, of political institutions. It also means sequencing and timing on a country-specific basis, with a judicious approach to conditionality, selectivity, and consistency of objectives, and adequate attention to culturally sensitive factors.

(3) *Prevalence of ethical deficit:* Besides the prevalence of democratic deficits (as examined in Chapter 9), many developing nations are also beset with the prevalence of an "ethical deficit" (to use an expression by the former Indian Prime Minister, Atal Behari Vajpayee). This means that members of the public would not hesitate in paying an official because they are more interested in the final result rather than the ethics of procedures, means, and consequences. Pavan Varma writes that in India, right from admission into prestigious schools, to the appointment through public service commission to government departments, or the transfer of government officials to "lucrative" posts where "extra" money can be made, to securing government contracts, or the willingness of street vendors to pay bribes to continue selling from their unlicensed stalls, corruption is rampant and systemic. The result is that in India black money accounts for as much as 40 per cent of the economy (Varma, 2004: 75–9).

For some, the above is a consequence of systemic corruption embedded in the cultural software; others explain corruption as a form of pure rationality of ends – the "ends justify the means." Still, for others it is a matter of simple expediency in an otherwise over-bureaucratized system. There are also those who explain ethical decay as a function of absent or weak moral leadership combined with a breakdown of basic values resulting from modernization and the upsurge of moral relativism. The fact of the matter is that all these explanations apply. Furthermore, ethical deficits and double standards are pervasive both in the public sphere, in business, and even in primary groups. One very practical question here is who is the most effective agent to take primary responsibility for closing the ethical gap. We have indicated earlier on that the responsibility always stops where the buck stops:

the top level of government and senior civil servants. Those who hold public office have the mandate and the responsibility – political, legal, moral, and fiscal – for governance and are accountable for their actions in the public domain. But as mentioned earlier, governance is not just commanding from the heights; rather it is the interface between those who rule and the ruled. Citizens share in the act of governing and are also responsible for their actions and inactions. When the public makes politicians and officials accountable for unscrupulous behavior, and when an outraged public does not permit officials to get away with misconduct, the ethical deficit will be reduced. When the "peoples' coups" took place in Argentina, Ecuador, and Bolivia, the popular cry was "let them all go." We are not suggesting that a fundamentalist notion of morality or the antiseptic definitions of rectitude common in the Scandinavian countries need to prevail in developing countries before deficit ethics is rolled back (Varma, 2004). Building ethical standards is a step-by-step process. Nevertheless, effective management for development and for the improvement of the human condition requires the menace of corruption be tackled immediately.

(4) *Mutual vulnerability in the global village:* It is now acknowledged that as we live in a global compact we are mutually interdependent. While one sector might appear more "secure" than others, whatever happens to another actor, no matter how seemingly insignificant, can have catastrophic effects upon the entire system, including those deemed less vulnerable. September 11, 2001 is a case in point. Events in distant lands brought about this terrible incident in the US; and from there it affected the entire world. Now we are just beginning to understand this vulnerability with regard to terrorism; for it is also applicable in the environmental, economic, social, and cultural spheres. The absence of good governance and leaders in these nations has bred insecurity, revolts, deprivation, corruption, and poverty. Although a kind of global integration in the economic and commercial sector has emerged, this has turned out to be quite unbalanced with uneven participation of poorer countries and their people. Before that unbalanced growth leads to further volatile situations and hostilities, income disparities, higher incidence of poverty, and civil strife, leaders will be needed to set the system straight. Those leaders will have to be trained, especially in democratic governance. And it is here where the West could do something concrete. The survivability and sustainability of our ever more interdependent global village requires international cooperation. Thus, it is in the best interests of everyone that effective

democratic institutions be nurtured worldwide, and that a reservoir of good leaders be in place to manage these institutions.

The ethical dilemma

The crux of the ethical dilemmas and the ethical crisis in international development has been the reluctance to challenge assumptions, to explore empirically, to raise probing issues related to the context, values, effects, and ethics of development. This ethical crisis is a cardinal manifestation of the underdevelopment of international development theory and practice. Once again, by design and default, in the absence of a unified and critical (Mestenhauser, 2002) paradigm, the assumptions of modernization theory, even its ethical inconsistencies and double standards, reign supreme. The irony is that these assumptions thrive in the very environment that once questioned their intellectual and ethical validity. All this translates into the insufficiency of the prevailing modes of analysis to address in any systematic, *systemic*, and explicit manner what Goulet has called development ethics (Goulet, 1995: 14). Ethics here does not necessarily mean a litany of prescriptive and lofty concerns, or a fortune-cookie-like recitation of fashionable recipes. Rather, it is the ability to ask probing conjectures about values, interests, choices, and consequences of development (Goulet, 1995). Ethics is mainly about the people who partake in the development process; not only decision-makers, intellectuals, national and international bureaucrats and experts, but also and especially those who experience deprivation, and are targeted in development schemes. What we are stressing here is that development has to be seen as a process by and for people, and therefore to be fully understood, it needs to be framed from the actors' perspective or their view of the world (a matter discussed above in this chapter).

From this vantage point the only possible goal of development is the reduction of risk, insecurity, and uncertainty, and the enhancement of the quality of life of people. This requires a holistic, multi-layered and comprehensive approach, in which multiple dimensions of development – environmental, economic, social, political, cultural, and ethical – can be integrated and analyzed. In sum, this view of development is synonymous with basic human rights and the well-being of all discussed later in the concluding chapter. Finally, approaching development management from this integrated human security and well-being perspective has important implications (Nef, 2004). One is the need to understand the dialectical interconnection between theory and praxis. A second important implication is the need for critical analysis applied to real life situations, leading to transformative engagement, before rushing to embrace ready-made solutions. A third implication is the need for a culturally sensitive perspective, devoid of the arrogance of power, wealth, and assumed knowledge extant in conventional "development-mongering." And, finally the fourth implication is the need to relate the micro to the macro – the "glocal" in Escobar's terms (Escobar, 1984–5), and the historical with the synchronic here-and-now. Above all, there is the implication of having to look at the context, the actors, and the effects of development processes and policies. This entails building the ethical "maps" of such processes and policies and bringing ethics back in an explicit, transparent, accountable, and rational manner.

Ethical implications of development

In the previous chapters, we have repeatedly encountered a number of common issues. (1) Western theories and practices of development and governance (basic concepts, assumptions, and values) do not have universal applicability. (2) Indigenously developed alternatives, perhaps more suited to tackling the satisfaction of people's basic needs, the eradication of poverty, and the protection of human dignity, are not part of the analysis, or prescriptions. (3) There is a growing recognition that the current crisis of governance – in the center and the periphery – is precisely a consequence of the inability to incorporate the substantive alternative paradigms into the prevailing conceptual mold. (4) Finally, before the dominant paradigm (and its attendant culture) is once again rehashed, there has to be a significant effort to critically assess its assumptions and results. Rather, some of the very same grand visions keep on multiplying, as each international institution tries to broaden its mission and scope of activities in the field of human development (Einhorn, 2001). The new century demands a new thinking to face the greatest dilemma before humankind: Why does a small group of nations, more specifically a small group within these nations, keep on "progressing" while the majority remains poor and deprived? This is perhaps the greatest ethical challenge for humankind.

References

Black, Jan Knippers (1999) *Development in Theory and Practice*. Boulder: Westview Press.
Boff, Leonardo and Claudius Boff (1987) *Introducing Liberation Theology*. New York: Orbis Books.

Dwivedi, O. P. and Keith M. Henderson (eds) (1999) *Bureaucracy and the Alternatives in World Perspective*, Basingstoke: Macmillan.

Einhorn, Jessica (2001) "The World Bank's Mission Creep," *Foreign Affairs*, 80, 5, September–October, pp. 22–35.

Engel, J. Ronald (1990) "The Ethics of Sustainable Development," in J. Ronald Engel and Joan Gibb Engel (eds), *Ethics of Environment and Development*. London: Belhaven Press, pp. 1–23.

Escobar, Arturo (1984–5) "Discourse and Power in Development: Michel Foucault and the Relevance of his Work for the Third World," *Alternatives*, 10, pp. 370–400.

Escobar, Arturo (1995) *Encountering Development: the Making of the Third World*. Princeton: Princeton University Press.

Frank, A. G. (1969) *Latin America: Underdevelopment or Revolution*. New York: Monthly Review Press.

Freire, Paulo (1971) *Pedagogy of the Oppressed*, trans. Myra Bergman Ramos. New York: Hearder and Hearder.

Goulet, Denis (1995) *Development Ethics: a Guide to Theory and Practice*. New York: Apex Press.

Gutiérrez, Gustavo (1973) *A Theology of Liberation: History, Politics, and Salvation*, trans. and ed. Sister Caridad Inda and John Eagleson. Maryknoll, NY: Orbis Books.

Hettne, Björn (1982) *Development Theory and the Third World*. Stockholm: Swedish Agency for Research Cooperation with Developing Countries.

Hood, Christopher and Michael Jackson (1994) "Keys for Locks in Administrative Argument," *Administration and Society*, 25, 4, pp. 467–88.

Huntington, Samuel P. (1993) "The Clash of Civilization?" *Foreign Affairs*, 72, 3, pp. 22–49.

Huntington, Samuel P. and Myron Weiner (eds) (1987) *Understanding Political Development*. Boston: Little, Brown & Co.

HyperDictionary (2004) Online at www.hyperdictionary.com.

Ismael, Tareq and J. Ismael (1985) *Government and Politics in Islam*. London: Pinter.

Kuhnen, Fritjof (1987) "Causes of Underdevelopment and Concepts of Development: an Introduction to Development Theories," *Journal of Development Studies*, 8.

Lawrence, Bruce (1989) *Defenders of God*. San Francisco: Harper & Row.

Leys, C. (1996) *The Rise and Fall of Development Theory*. London: Currey.

Macy, Joanna (1985) *Dharma and Development: Religion as a Resource in the Survodaya Self-help Movement*. West Hartford: Kumarian Press.

Mason, Mike (1997) *Development and Disorder: a History of the Third World since 1945*. Toronto: Between the Lines.

McClelland, D. (1962) *The Achieving Society*. Princeton: Van Nostrand.

Meadows, Donella, Jorgen Randers, and Dennis Meadows (2004) *Limits to Growth: the 30-year Update*. White River Junction, VT: Chelsea Green Publishing Company.

Mestenhauser, Josef (2002) "Creative, Critical and Comparative Thinking in Internationalization," in Sheryl Bond and Carl Bowry (eds), *Connections and Complexities: the Internationalization of Higher Education in Canada*. Winnipeg, Canada: Centre for Higher Education, Research and Development, University of Manitoba, pp. 53–77.

Nef, Jorge (2004) "International Development Studies and Ethical Dilemmas in Academia," *Canadian Journal of Development Studies*, 25, 1, pp. 79–99.

Peet, Richard (1999) *Development Theory.* New York: Guilford Press.

Rostow, W. (1960) *The Stages of Economic Growth.* Cambridge: Cambridge University Press.

Sayeed, Khalid Bin (1990) *Western Dominance and Political Islam: Challenge and Response.* Albany, NY: State University of New York Press.

Schuurman, Frans J. (ed.) (1993) *Beyond Impasse: New Direction in Development Theory.* London: Zed Books.

Schuurman, Frans J. (2001) *Globalization and Development Studies: Challenges for the 21st Century.* London: Sage.

Schwenke, Stephen G. (2006) "The World Bank's New Urban Strategy: an Assessment from Development Ethics," in Gedeon M. Mudacumura, Desta Mebratu, and M. Samsul Haque (eds), *Sustainable Development Policy and Administration.* Boca Raton, Florida: Taylor & Francis, pp. 571–89.

Sen, Amartya (1999) *Development as Freedom.* New York, NY: Alfred A. Knopf.

Stavenhagen, R. (1996) "Siete tesis equivocados sobre America Latina," *Desarrollo Indoamericano*, 4.

Tendler, Judith (1997) *Good Government in the Tropics.* Baltimore: Johns Hopkins University Press.

Trompf, Garry W. (1987) "The Ethics of Development: an Overview," in Susan Sontag and Philip J. Hughes (eds), *The Ethics of Development: the Pacific in the 21st Century.* Port Moresby: University of Papua New Guinea Press, pp. 102–29.

Varma, Pavan K. (2004) *Being Indian.* New Delhi: Penguin Books.

World Bank (2002) *Governance and Development: the World Development Report.* Washington, DC: World Bank.

Young, E. A. (1995) *Third World in the First: Development and Indigenous Peoples.* New York: Routledge.

Part IV
The Way Ahead

11
Some Reflections on the Well-being of Nations

At the onset of the new millennium and well into the UN Fifth Development Decade, most of humanity, including the two-thirds of the population living in poverty, have not yet reaped the benefits of development, although they have heard plenty of rhetoric, and some impressive statistics. For modern-day followers of the optimistic Dr. Panglos of Voltaire's *Candide*, even if the present is not the "best of all possible worlds," there have been some remarkable improvements. For instance, global life expectancy since the 1950s has moved from an average of slightly over 50 years to well over 60. This has been underscored by notable advances in sanitation, communication, and transportation technologies, and particularly in medicine and in combating perinatal and chronic diseases. Per capita incomes in constant dollars have risen more than three-fold. The most significant improvements have taken place in the area of basic education, in particularly literacy: in the twenty-first century illiteracy is much more the exception than the rule.

Today's population on average lives longer, is more literate and connected in networks of communication, has higher income levels, and is ostensibly much more urban, and less agriculturally based than it was half a century ago. Others in the same camp point to the beneficent impact of globalization, with freer trade and investment flows. They argue that gloom and doom scenarios, like the old "Asian drama," failed to materialize. Instead, the entire region is experiencing true economic miracles exemplified by the dynamism of the Indian and Chinese economies.

At a more structural level, however, the new era has compounded a continuation of past environmental, economic, social, political, and cultural challenges, combined with emerging threats, and multiplied by the velocity of change. Reflecting on the Braudelian *longue durée*, not only have change and development not corresponded, but they also seem to have been moving in opposite directions. A main issue for critics of globalization and capitalism is that averages fail to portray the reality of most people, as obscene and growing inequalities underpin and undermine statistical achievements. "Goods" and "bads" (liabilities) are inequitably distributed and are tied up to a spiraling cycle of poverty and deprivation. This process has ultimately negative systemic effects even for those who benefit from short run gain.

What is obvious, irrespective of which camp we are in is that both the achievements and the failures of the last development decades have been a function of the various strategies, structures, and mechanisms of development management. Some strategies, at least for a while, seemed to have produced results; others have exhibited modest outcomes at best, while others have failed. A broadly diachronic analysis of developmental experiences – from the Third, through the Second and even into the First World of development – suggests that structures and mechanisms to affect development outcomes are ostensibly failing. The once strong faith in the prescriptions of social planning, technology, and administration has been replaced by skepticism and a record of catastrophes. The former socialist world is a most telling example of induced modernization gone astray. But so is its Keynesian Cold War counterpart, whether the Latin American ISI, or the Asian "Tigers," or the various "social contracts" in the Western core.

This is not to deny that the record of the *laissez-faire* neoliberal formula, and that of NPM that replaced Development Administration and Management for Change, has been particularly successful. Quite the contrary. Marked-oriented restructuring, often associated with the Thatcherite determinism present in the "there is no alternative" (TINA) slogan has become hegemonic at the discursive level. However, this ideological primacy does not make it any more successful in terms of its real lasting impact. The environmental, social, political, and even economic consequences for most people have been quite devastating across the globe. The findings in our previous chapters regarding environment, poverty, and marginalization quite conclusively point towards a scenario of growing disparity and mutual vulnerability.

Whether in Africa, Latin America, the former Eastern European bloc, and parts of Asia, and the Middle East, the story is quite similar: extreme accumulation, contingent labor, and shattered lives. The environmental and political consequences of the development model have been intensive and extensive degradation, often accompanied by persistent and acute violence. As crises gather momentum and feed back on each other, it seems as if the current political leadership the world over has lost its ability to confront and arrest the impending breakdown. The Western core continues producing and exporting paradigms and ideologies of development, modernization, and globalization. A common feature of these exports is the compelling mantra that any problem can be solved by providing a technical blueprint, foreign aid, and a commitment to changing the existing political-economic configuration on the part of the recipient.

This is the current logic of regime-morphing and regime change that prevailed in the so-called Washington Consensus. What was once Lenin's NEP of soviets plus electrification has become nowadays neo-liberal structural adjustment combined with a form of meaningless low-intensity electoral democracy. In this "behavioral" sense, the new century has not been too different from its predecessor. The enormous difference is in the magnitude, the velocity, and interconnectedness of the problems faced by humanity in the global age. These challenges cannot be effectively faced by today's, let alone yesterday's, thinking. There is an urgent need for a new way of facing the challenges and asking the relevant questions. Part of the dilemma is the question of how sustainable is a mode of development in which an ever smaller group of people keep on "progressing" while the majority remains poor, marginalized, and deprived. Bold and decisive action requires sharp analysis and new ways of thinking beyond the repetitive cycles of "more of the same."

The discussion offered in the preceding chapters has attempted to highlight the problems faced not only by developing nations, but by the world as a whole. It is also a plea for bringing about a sustainable global order, i.e. one where rather than a limited quantifiable definition of development, the well-being of humankind is paramount. This means a state of affairs where the worst forms of poverty can be eliminated, the status of those generally excluded can be improved, and people all over the world can be provided with the cultural keys to take care of and improve their situation. In the final analysis, peace with justice demands more than just peace. Sustainable development for everybody also requires good governance. Such governance – in both the South and the North – goes beyond efficiency, effectiveness, and governability. Substantively, it involves respect and sensitivity to local customs, values, and culture, as well as compassion, and what Mathew Fox referred to as "deep spirituality." Only cultural humility – the opposite of the arrogance of power extant in the conventional development discourse – and empathy can bridge the gap between North and South, rich and poor, and usher in a new, more holistic and multicultural standpoint.

In all cultures and over the ages, philosophers and public intellectuals have debated the nature of living well and "the good life." Irrespective of the specific terminology and ideological intent, thinkers have concurred that happiness and well-being, individually and collectively, are the main indicators of such a good life. How people feel and think about their own existence as members of their families and of society constitutes a main indicator of their perceived quality of life. External factors such as income, educational background, family life, place of residence, and circumstances can have positive and negative effects on that feeling. But these and other demographic parameters are not the only determinants of the well-being of people (Diener et al., 2003). It seems that "intangibles," such as personality traits, inner peace, fulfillment, spirituality, satisfaction with one's existence, and above all, hope, play a central part in their well-being.

This is not to imply that wealth and material quality of life are irrelevant. They are; however, it is not only people living in wealthy nations, and wealthy people for that matter, who score high in the measurement of their satisfaction index. Empirical studies indicate that when poor people receive even a modest increase in their income, their satisfaction level grows. Such increases may be merely a temporary phenomenon, but they might help to fulfill their basic human needs. There are indeed variations across cultures; for example, Diener et al. (2003: 412) reported that Asian-American students were happier when they were closer to achieving academic goals "whereas Caucasian students were happy when engaging in an activity that was important to them at that moment." Satisfaction aside, some societies produce higher levels of both material and perceived well-being than do others; a factor that relates to each nation's unique cultural history, economic prosperity, and good governance.

To discuss this subject in some depth a number of threads discussed throughout this text have to be brought together. One is the relationship between individual well-being, happiness, and spirituality, and how it connects to "development." Another is the not always linear association between the well-being of people and the well-being of nation-states. A third notion is the centrality of good governance and how this concept is connected with human and ecosystem well-being. As stated in Chapter 7, the planet simply cannot sustain the ongoing patterns of current consumption and environmental degradation. Rather, and put in explicitly normative terms, a new model of development to ensure human security and the well-being of all people is essential. The future of humanity is inextricably connected with the progress of all, male and female, North and South, rich and poor.

What is well-being?

For some, human well-being is the same as human welfare; for others, they are quite different things. The OECD has defined human well-being as more than the sum of individual levels of well-being, which includes equality of opportunities, civil liberties, distribution of resources, and opportunities for further learning (OECD, 2001: 11). Human well-being in the OECD's study encompasses factors such as economic well-being (including the reciprocal value of social "regrettables" like pollution, crime, and divorce), social cohesion (or social capital), better health, and the quality of the environment. Although the OECD study did not consider in its measurements spiritual or personal fulfillment, virtually all human activity – whether by individuals or collectives – entails patterns of behavior, motivation, and some form of emotional involvement. Such activity affects the mental, physical, and spiritual "health" and well-being (or ill-being) of people. Spirituality, as a special factor, plays an important role in building the inner character of a person, as well as developing norms of behavior and sense of purpose, strengthening inherited culture and values, and supporting interactions within society. Specifically, cultural legacies, identities, practices, and religion play an important role in fulfillment. It should also be noted that even economic well-being cannot be based on a strictly economic calculation nor can it be determined simply on an aggregate cost-benefit analysis, or other consequential or "outcome" criteria (OECD, 2001: 14).

Scientists prefer to use the term "subjective well-being" instead of happiness because happiness means several different things (such as joy, satisfaction, etc.), which are difficult to standardize. Subjective well-being "is the scientific name for how people evaluate their lives" (Diener, 2005: 1). These evaluations can be specific (such as marital satisfaction, or satisfaction with one's job), or wide-ranging (such as satisfaction with the self). Measurement tools include asking people how satisfied or how happy they are. From various such measurements, it is seen that wealthier people are slightly happier on average compared to poor people. Also, good health plays a great part in being happy. Culture makes a difference because some cultures value a higher level of well-being than others. For instance, spirituality and religious beliefs make some people happier (Cohen, 2002). On the other hand, anxiety, anomic tendencies (such as powerlessness, social isolation, alienation, disorientation, and pessimism), and suicidal feelings relate to a low level of subjective well-being (Bulmahn, 2000). Bulmahn reported that in the mid-1990s, as expectations of the merger of East Germany (GDR) with West Germany increased, suicidal mortality in the DGR declined from more than 37 suicides per 100 000 to only 15 per 100 000 inhabitants (Bulmahn, 2000: 390).

Spirituality and well-being

Subjective well-being involves, among other things, life satisfaction, a sense of happiness, and a reduced level of anxiety and pessimism. For example, Bulmahn reports that when East Germany was amalgamated within the German Republic, the subjective well-being of the people improved considerably (Bulmahn, 2000: 391). The example of East Germany suggests that modernization and democratization may improve the quality of life, including life satisfaction, and increase the sense of well-being of people. Of course, life satisfaction here is seen as the expression of cognitive well-being, while happiness is an indication of emotional welfare (Bulmahn, 2000: 386).

One reason that many Western scholars consider the concept of well-being a highly subjective matter is because of the association between religious faith and happiness. However, it is not known which particular aspect of religiosity connects with life satisfaction and well-being. Of course, faith and religion are highly subjective matters, and thus the connection between well-being and faith is also seen as a subjective matter. Moreover, since there are significant differences among people belonging to different faiths and religions it is rather difficult to develop a universal model of such a co-relation which can be easily measured and analyzed in a systematic manner. Nevertheless, it has been argued very strongly that "religious people report being happier and more satisfied with life than irreligious people" (Myers and Diener, 1995: 16). Levin and Chatters (1998) have also concluded that religion appears to have a therapeutic effect on mental health outcomes, which ultimately relates to satisfaction with lifestyle.

Indeed, life satisfaction can also be operationalized and measured. The same goes for other related subjective factors such as religiosity and spirituality. Whereas religiosity may refer to one's relationship with the practice of religion (or the relationship with organized religion), spirituality (to paraphrase Adam Cohen, 2002) relates to satisfaction with life as people feel that their lives have purpose, understand events happening around them, find comfort in their beliefs, and are willing to help others. To use a Hindu term, they believe in good Karma. Of course, not all religious beliefs and practices may have the same impact on the spirituality of people including their impact on people's health. Yet, one major dimension of spirituality is that it helps to bring "goodness" – the reciprocal value of "badness" – into this world. Myers asserted that happiness also depends on what meaning and purpose people attach to life, their sense of humility, equanimity, grace, perspective, and lack of fear of death (Myers, 1992). These aspects help people to avoid hopelessness, depression, stress, and the negative impact of events, leading to a better sense of well-being, and managing their lives through difficult experiences (Cohen, 2002: 306).

Happiness and well-being

For many years, psychologists have been researching and writing about happiness (Hornby et al., 1948; Diener, 2005; Furnham and Cheng, 2000; Veenhoven, 1984). For some, happiness may imply a psychological state following the fulfillment or gratification of some human needs or desires. For others, happiness indicates prosperity and progress: looking ahead. But when it comes to measuring happiness, there are cultural, ethnic, and individual differences. For example, despite their often substandard living conditions, older Blacks in the US reported a higher level of happiness than older Whites (Campbell, 1976). Furthermore, a study about happiness, materialism, and religious experiences in the US and Singapore by William Swinyard and others (2000: 28) found that "less-materially-oriented people are happier than others – both in Singapore and in the United States." The study suggests that materialism is not the main source of happiness; instead, happy people look for happiness elsewhere although they might have and enjoy material possessions. That direction is generally towards their inner being, religious thoughts, becoming keenly aware of a spiritual presence, and trying to live by certain cardinal beliefs.

Those cardinal beliefs or values which may constitute the inner elements of well-being include five factors. (1) The most basic is meeting one's physical/biological needs. (2) Another is availability of freedom of action, and choices. (3) A third involves opportunities to develop and express intellectual and/or artistic abilities. (4) A commonality of norms and values being shared with others, especially trust (including

whether people trust others or whether people are considered trustwor-
thy, and whether they have trust in public and private institutions). (5)
Last but not least is the satisfaction of "higher" spiritual needs. Particularly important here is the existence of hope.

It is here where concepts such as Dharma and Karma in Hindu philosophy, as well as the Christian notions of providence and grace
become relevant. Dharma entails the principle of righteousness (doing
what is correct), while Karma involves the notion that there is a consequential ethic in any activity performed by an individual. In turn,
providence means the manifestation of transcendental values, purpose
(*telos*), and justice in everyday life, while grace involves inspirational
enlightenment in human agency.

Assessing the well-being of nations

Robert Prescott-Allen, in cooperation with the IUCN (the World Conservation Union), the International Development Research Centre
(Ottawa), and some other United Nations agencies, has prepared a
country-by-country index of the well-being of nations (Prescott-Allen,
2001). His contention is that as the human population and economies
have grown, "it has become impossible to improve one's own well-
being without affecting other people's" (Prescott-Allen, 2001: 1). For
example, nations with a high standard of living impose excessive pressure on the global environment while those nations which place low
demands on the ecosystem are desperately poor. Matters such as pollution, shortage of natural resources, and ever declining bio-diversity
have not only affected the well-being of the ecosystem, but also have
influenced the quality of life of people. Thus, the well-being of the
ecosystem and people is intertwined, and as such a sustainable society
and its development require not only the happiness of people but also
a resilient and rich ecosystem.

To measure the well-being of nations, Prescott-Allen used several
indicators such as the UNDP Human Development Report, the Ecological Footprint, Environmental Sustainability Index, World Resources
Report, and the Environmental Pressure Index (see Table 11.1). A
common framework of dimensions was prepared consisting of two
dimensions. One is the human dimension, including health and population, national and household wealth, education and culture, community and social capital, and equity. The other dimension is the ecosystem
dimension, including land and forests, water quality and diversity, air
quality, species and genetic diversity, and energy and resources use. He

Table 11.1: Ranking of selected countries by their HWI, EWI, and WI indices

Country		Human Wellbeing Index (HWI) Ranking	Ecosystem Wellbeing Index (EWI) Ranking	Composite Wellbeing Index (WI) Ranking
1	Sweden	79	49	64.0
3	Norway	82	43	62.5
7	Canada	78	43	60.5
12	Germany	77	36	56.5
18	Australia	79	28	53.5
24	Japan	80	25	52.5
27	United States	73	31	52.0
29	France	75	29	52.0
33	UK	73	30	51.5
38	Netherlands	78	22	50.0
55	Argentina	55	40	47.5
65	Russian Federation	48	42	45.0
79	Chile	55	30	42.5
87	Indonesia	36	48	42.0
89	Egypt	39	43	41.0
92	Brazil	45	36	40.5
99	Malaysia	46	33	39.5
116	Philippines	44	32	38.0
133	Nigeria	16	56	36.0
136	South Africa	43	27	35.0
143	Kenya	18	51	34.5
150	Mexico	45	21	33.0
160	China	36	28	32.0
167	Pakistan	18	44	31.0
168	Ghana	22	38	30.0
172	India	31	27	29.0
176	Saudi Arabia	31	23	27.0
180	Iraq	19	31	25.0

Total countries surveyed: 180. The highest and lowest scores for each of these three indices are 82/3, 68/14, and 64.0/25.0 respectively. *Source*: Prescott-Allen (2001). *The Wellbeing of Nations: a Country-by Country Index of Quality of Life and the Environment*. Washington, DC: Island Press (jointly with the International Development Research Centre of Canada, Ottawa), Table 27, pp. 267–8. Drawing on this conceptualization, the table has been constructed for 28 countries. The top range for the scale ("good") is a score of 100–81, in which all desirable conditions have been met. Next comes "fair," in the 80–61 range, in which most conditions have been nearly met. Then comes "medium," in the 60–41 range, in which some ecosystemic and human conditions have been met. "Poor" performance is in the 40–21 range, with undesirable environmental and human conditions. The lowest rank, "bad" is in the 20–1 range, where human and environmental conditions are threatening. Based on this scheme, the top-ranked state, Sweden, would be considered to be "fair" – with an acceptable performance in both forms of well-being – while most of the industrialized nations ranked as "medium," and the bulk of the developing nations generally scored poor or unacceptable.

defined human well-being as "a condition in which all members of society are able to determine and meet their needs and have a large range of choices to meet their potential." He understood ecosystem well-being as "a condition in which the ecosystem maintains its diversity and quality – and thus its capacity to support people and the rest of life – and its potential to adapt to change and provide a wide range of choices and opportunities for the future" (Prescott-Allen, 2001: 5).

Of course, while the well-being of nations and people can be measured in comparable indexes, the content of such feelings and attitudes may vary considerable. As Prescott-Allen noted in his own analysis, people in different cultures could aspire to different things. Examining common proverbial, or "common-sense" definitions and slogans of "happiness," different profiles emerge. For instance, the Chinese may seek the five Confucian blessings of the good life: "long life, riches, health, love of virtue, and a natural death in an old age." The French may aspire to "liberty, equality, and fraternity"; the British, "health, wealth, and wisdom"; Americans, "life, liberty, and the pursuit of happiness"; while Indians would perhaps prefer power, pleasure, morality, and emancipation of the soul (nirvana) (Prescott-Allen 2001: 1). In the case of the Chinese, another author has indicated that the traditional concept of happiness and well-being includes "material abundance, physical health, virtuous and peaceful life, and relief from death anxiety" (Luo, 2001: 409).

Despite the various teleologies, or desired states that people seek, when it comes to environmental quality, it is clear that those who have a high standard of living impose greater demands upon the environment. Yet, this relationship is neither linear nor simple. The poor can also place heavy demands on the environment precisely because they lack the means, infrastructure, and resources to control environmental damage. For instance, of the five countries (China, France, India, UK, and USA), whose proverbial cultural teleologies were mentioned earlier, the three more developed ones – France, the UK, and the USA – show a higher ecosystem well-being score, compared to the two poor nations of China and India.

Good governance and well-being

To achieve well-being by meeting human needs requires the presence of numerous objective and subjective factors. The most important of these factors to match needs with capabilities is good governance. There is no general agreement as to what precisely constitutes good governance. The specificity of such "goodness" depends upon existing differences in cultural norms, style of doing things, expectations of people from their governments, and the circumstances surrounding political and administrative practices. Nevertheless, high standards of governance are needed not only to deliver public services like education, health, and safety efficiently and effectively, but also to create conditions which enable civil society to pursue their own goals as they see fit.

A framework for analysis and prescription

The term "good" is a value-laden term that involves a comparison at least between two states of things or systems by using some standard of measure. A government, as a system of governance, is considered good if it exhibits certain fundamental characteristics. Perhaps the United Nations Development Programme (UNDP) offers the most comprehensive definition of the norm of good governance. For the UNDP, good governance is, among other things, participatory, transparent, and accountable. It is effective and equitable, and also promotes the rule of law. Finally, governance ensures that political, social, and economic priorities are based on a broad consensus in the society and that the voices of the poorest and the most vulnerable are heard in decision-making over the allocation of development resources (UNDP, 1998: 3). From the above characterization, an ideal model of good governance, with ten basic characteristics, can be constructed.

(a) *Public participation* in decision-making.
(b) The impartial enforcement of the *rule of law*.
(c) *Transparency* for access to governing processes (including institutions and information sources).
(d) The *responsiveness* of institutions to the needs of all stakeholders.
(e) *Consensus building* among different and often conflicting interests in society.
(f) *Equity and fair treatment* assured to all individuals so that they may improve their circumstances.
(g) Effective and efficient *responsibility and accountability* of institutions and officials.
(h) A *strategic vision of the public good* on the part of the leaders towards a broad range of long-term perspectives on sustainable human development.

(i) Substantive, *participatory democracy* – not merely formal electoral pluralism – based upon three basic values: fundamental freedom, equality for all, and universal suffrage.

(j) *Ethical governance* where governing elites dedicate their lives to service of the public, and where ethical violations are given zero tolerance.

Good governance and sustainable human development, especially but not exclusively in developing nations, also require conscientious attempts at eliminating poverty, sustaining livelihoods, fulfilling basic needs, and offering a delivery system that is open, "clean," and accessible. It is important that these characteristics are not only enshrined in a body of norms and discourses, but, most importantly, are also practiced in a persistent and consistent manner (Dwivedi, 2005: 271–3).

Values and good governance

As discussed earlier, spirituality plays an important part in the happiness and well-being of people. Similarly, it can play a crucial role in keeping the system of governance honest and transparent. Spirituality can provide a countervailing cultural "software" to base motivations such as greed, exploitation, abuse of power, and the mistreatment of people. It could also contribute to instill self-discipline, a sense of public good and service, and above all, the absence of arrogance in holding public office. Furthermore, it enables people to center their values on the notion that there is a higher order of things (providence) to frame human behavior. Spirituality serves both as an ethical code and an operative strategy for the transformation of human character by strengthening the genuine, substantive will to serve the common people. If the public goal is to serve and protect the common good, then spirituality can provide the incentive for public officials to serve the public with dignity and respect. Although spirituality is supposed to be an integral part of the religious traditions and beliefs and traditions of humankind, its impact upon secular public institutions (e.g. Weber's treatment of the Protestant ethic) is crucial in governance, especially with respect to the ethics and values of public service. Spirituality in governance requires officials not only to believe in Dharma (the concept of righteousness) but also to do good Karma (the concept of cause and effect of any activity performed by an individual).

Here again, we are faced with a delicate balance and dilemma. While moral righteousness is a fundamental component of civic duties, its divine-inspirational underpinnings often require the regular checks and balances of secular norms. Without it, messianism and intolerance, even fanaticism, can run rampant. On the other hand, a thoroughly secular legal-rational body of ethical norms faces the danger of creating merely instrumental and empty sets of principles, and moral relativism. Worse, it can lead to its substitution by extreme forms of fanaticized "civic religion." Rule by religious or secular zealots, as numerous tragedies in the last century illustrate, has basically the same effects: a possible reign of terror. Critical consciousness vis-à-vis ethical principles and concrete situations can provide an essential bridge between transcendental values and everyday practice.

A spiritually oriented public official knows that his or her sense of moral obligation enables him/her to serve others. In so doing, he/she will be fulfilling twofold duties: one to the self, whereby one seeks inner strength through spiritual action, and the other to the community-at-large whereby one works for the common good. As such, inner moral duty and a sense of consequential ethics regulate human conduct and cast individuals into a "character mold." This role-expectation framework induces in them values and social and moral virtues. The imbedding of normative and behavioral codes through socialization, reflection, and practice strengthens the public ethos of public servants. They become upholders of the social and moral fabric, and the public trust of a society, as role models of individual and group character.

Ethical education based on ethical reflection and spirituality may offer a common strategy from where a spirit of public service and good governance can be developed. Such a strategy depends upon three fundamental perceptions. One is how public officials as a group perceive a common future – a teleology – and hope for their society. Another is how far both individually and collectively they can take action to protect the common good: the relationship between means and ends. Last but not least is their belief that they as individuals have a moral obligation to support their society's goals since their acts will have consequences for the future of their society (Dwivedi, 2002: 48).

An ethically driven model of training strengthens good governance in numerous ways. First, it defines a normative goal-orientation in public policy-making and delivery. Second, it defines the direction towards which those who govern must channel their acts if they are to serve the common good. Third, public management includes a call for

individual sacrifice, compassion, justice, striving for the highest achievement, and defines public service, both as a profession and as a
vocation. Fourth, while the emphasis on secular government in liberal-
democracy assigns the place of morality to the individual's conduct
and behavior, it has, nevertheless, acknowledged a continuing tension
between the requisites of good governance (through its public policy
and programs) and the spiritual and moral standards by which they
can be measured. Thus, spirituality provides an important foundation
to the governing process, beyond legal rational calculation and self-
interest. Fifth, confidence and trust in liberal-democracy can be safe-
guarded only when the governing process exhibits a higher moral
standard, deriving from ethical and spiritual sensitivity. Finally, for
good governance, it is necessary that public officials (both elected
and appointed) know that there are correct (as well as incorrect) ways
of doing things and those standards and rules should be adhered to.
Having been entrusted with the stewardship of the state, officials owe
special obligations, have special expectations, and reside in a fiduciary
world. For them, accountability, responsibility, and compliance become
moral as well as technical or legal questions; and as such they are
serving a higher cause. It is here where spirituality and a sense of doing
one's duty acquire a holistic tone; a tone which may enable functionaries to dedicate their lives to the creation and maintenance of conditions
to further the well-being of their society. Material benefits, possessions,
and official privileges are going to be transitory illusions; their personal
fulfillment (as indicated by the Swinyard study of the US and Singapore) will come from how they perceive their inner world, i.e. their
spirituality, and their whole approach to life (Swinyard et al., 2001).
Good governance as an operational manifestation of satisfaction and
overall well-being is possible only when public officials perceive themselves behaving as such.

Final observations and reflections

Albert Einstein once stated: "The satisfaction of physical needs is indeed
the indispensable precondition of a satisfactory existence, but in itself
it is not enough. In order to be content men must also have the possibility of developing their intellectual and artistic powers to whatever
extent accords with their personal characteristics and abilities"
(Einstein, 1950: 12). Looking back at the exploration undertaken in the
ten preceding chapters of this volume from the prism of Einstein's
statement, we can advance four concluding propositions.

(1) *Poverty and inequity are still the greatest challenge*: Environmental stress is less the result of poor nations than the voracious style of consumption in the North. The pressure on natural resources increases with consumption. Consumption pressure is partly a matter of the number of people making demands, but it is also a question of consumption patterns. It has been estimated that every birth in the North puts as much pressure on resources as ten births in the South. Thus, in addition to the eradication of poverty in the South, lifestyles in the North will have to be modified. For example, the World Commission on Environment and Development has estimated that the cost of implementing Agenda 21 could be about $125 billion a year until the end of this century. And since most of the expenditures are related to managing commons and assisting poor nations, it helps to appreciate that "in 1990 developing nations transferred $140 billion in debt service payments, capital and interest, to creditor nations" (Ramphal, 1992: 253–4). If the North can divert a part of this sum towards global environmental protection and sustainable development, our world will be a better and safer place to live in.

(2) *Collaboration between North and South is crucial*: In the year 2004, the United States allocated $36 billion for homeland security, and about $360 billion for the military; contrast this with the $11.3 billion that the US sets aside for international aid each year (Brusasco-Mackenzie, 2004: 12). Billions more have been spent by the coalition of the willing in the Iraq war. On the other hand, only between $54 and $64 billion are needed annually to cut world poverty in half by 2015 (Devarajan et al., 2002). Clearly, there is a need to change the militaristic definition of security to the concept of the "well-being" of all. The world population is about 6.4 billion and it might rise to about 8.9 billion by 2050 (WWI, 2004). If 831 million people across the world remained hungry and malnourished in 2004, what will happen later when there is further loss of croplands due to degradation, soil erosion, and climatic changes as expected during the first half of the twenty-first century? If we take into account the water crisis facing the world, we should note that 1.1 billion people currently lack access to safe drinking water, and 2.4 billion people, mostly in Asia and Africa, do not have adequate sanitation. For these people, their well-being ought to be paramount rather than billions of dollars being used in militaristic ventures under the deceiving guise of "security." Clearly a new model of development – one that could ensure human security and planetary well-being – is needed. It is also clear that while the North has been able to achieve a modicum of environmental security at home, it has missed the opportunity to

promote sustainability and equity since the Rio Summit of 1992. Whether there will be any substantive change in this situation after the Johannesburg Summit of 2002 remains uncertain. It is in this area of concern where bridges of collaboration between North and South should be built by specifically assisting the achievement of the UN Millennium Development Goals (MDGs).

(3) *People live on the same planet but seem to belong to different worlds*: Demand for energy has outpaced the growth of population. For example, between 1850 and 1970, the population on earth tripled but energy consumption rose twelve-fold (Sawin, 2004: 25). Governmental agencies which manage energy supplies in developing nations are unable to meet demand with the result that people in India and other Asian nations have either no access or only limited access to energy use. At the same time, rich people in the West use, on average, 25 times more energy per person than do poor countries (Sawin, 2004). If the Chinese and Indians ever reach the level of energy consumption of the US (who use 10 times more than the average Chinese and 20 times more than the average Indian), the energy crisis would spin out of control. This has indeed disastrous planetary implications regarding global carrying capacity.

(4) *The challenge ahead is to arrest mutual vulnerability*: A fundamental premise of the dominant international paradigms which have emerged since the end of World War Two (and especially since the collapse of the Soviet Union) is the notion that the North is secure and the South is insecure (Nef, 1999). Instead, in an increasingly interdependent world, the weakness of the South increases the vulnerability of the North. There is a need to change the mental mode in the North which denies and resists any change to its age-old perception that developing nations are the problem. That is why there is a need to redefine a new global paradigm which supports human security and the well-being of all. If international cooperation is unable to reduce mutual vulnerability it makes little sense to talk about a common – or any other kind of – future.

References

Brusasco-Mackenzie, Margaret (2004) "Environmental Security: a View from Europe," *Environmental Change and Security Project*, Washington DC: Woodrow Wilson International Center for Scholars, issue 10, pp. 12–18.
Bulmahn, Thomas (2000) "Modernity and Happiness: the Case of Germany," *Journal of Happiness Studies*, 1, pp. 375–400.

Campbell, A. (1976) "Subjective Measures of Well-Being," *American Psychologist* (February), pp. 117–24.

Cohen, Adam B. (2002) "The Importance of Spirituality in Well-being for Jews and Christians," *Journal of Happiness Studies*, 3, pp. 287–310.

Devarajan, S., Margaret J. Miller, and Eric V. Swanson (2002) *Goals for Development: History, Prospects and Costs*. World Bank website, http://econ.worldbank.org/files/13269_wps2819.pdf

Diener, Ed (2005) "About Subjective Well-being (Happiness and Life Satisfaction)." http://www.psych.uiuc.edu/~ediener/faq.html (accessed April 28, 2005).

Diener, Ed, Shigehiro Oishi, and Richard E. Lucas (2003) "Personality, Culture and Subjective Well-being: Emotional and Cognitive Evaluations of Life," *Annual Review of Psychology*, 54, pp. 403–25.

Dwivedi, O. P. (1994) *Development Administration: From Underdevelopment to Sustainable Development*. Basingstoke: Macmillan Press.

Dwivedi, O. P. (2002) "On Common Good and Good Governance: an Alternative Approach," in Dele Olowu and Soumana Sako (eds), *Better Governance and Public Policy: Capacity Building and Democratic Renewal in Africa*. Bloomfield, CT: Kumarian Press, pp. 35–51.

Dwivedi, O. P. (2005) "Good Governance in a Multicultural World: Oceans Apart yet World Together," in Joseph G. Jabbra and O. P. Dwivedi (eds), *Administrative Culture in a Global Context*. Toronto, Canada: de Sitter Publications, pp. 265–84.

Dwivedi, O. P. and Renu Khator (2005) "Sustaining Development: the Road from Stockholm to Johannesburg," in G. M. Mudacumura, D. Mebratu and M. S. Haque (eds), *Sustainable Development Policy and Administration*. Boca Raton, FL: Taylor & Francis, pp. 113–33.

Einstein, Albert (1950) *Out of My Later Years*. New York: Philosophical Library.

Furnham, A. and H. Cheng (2000) "Lay Theories of Happiness," *Journal of Happiness Studies*, 1, pp. 227–46.

Gardner, Gary and Erik Assadourian (2004) "Rethinking the Good Life," *State of the World 2004 (A Worldwatch Institute Report)*. New York, NY: W. W. Norton, pp. 164–79.

Hornby, A. S., E. V. Gatenby, and H. Wakefield (1948) *The Advanced Learner's Dictionary of Current English*. Oxford: Oxford University Press.

Kagia, Ruth (2002) "Prospects for Accelerating Human Development in the Twenty-first Century," in Hans van Ginkel, Brendan Barrett, Julius Court, and Jerry Velasquez (eds), *Human Development and the Environment: Challenges for the United Nations in the New Millennium*. Tokyo, Japan: United Nations University Press, pp. 63–75.

Levin, J. S. and L. M. Chatters (1998) "Research on Religion and Mental Health: an Overview of Empirical Findings and Theoretical Issues," in H. G. Koenig (ed.), *Handbook of Religion and Mental Health*. Sau Diego, CA: Academic Press, pp. 33–50.

Luo, Lu (2001) "Understanding Happiness: a Look into the Chinese Folk Psychology," *Journal of Happiness Studies*, 2, pp. 407–32.

Myers, D. (1992) *Pursuit of Happiness: Discovering the Pathway to Fulfillment, Well-being, and Enduring Personal Joy*. New York, NY: Avon Publishers.

Myers, D. G. and E. Diener (1995) "Who is Happy?" *Psychological Science*, 6, 1, pp. 10–19.

Nef, Jorge (1999) *Human Security and Mutual Vulnerability: the Global Political Economy of Development and Underdevelopment*. Ottawa, Canada: International Development Research Centre.

OECD (2001) *The Well-being of Nations: the Role of Human and Social Capital*. Paris: OECD, Centre for Educational Research and Innovation.

Prescott-Allan, Robert (2001) *The Wellbeing of Nations: a Country-by-Country Index of Quality of Life and the Environment*. Washington DC: Island Press.

Ramphal, Shridath (1992) *Our Country, the Planet*, Washington DC: Island Press.

Saher, P. J. (1970) *Happiness and Immortality*. London: George Allen & Unwin.

Sawin, Janet L. (2004) "Making Better Energy Choices," *State of the World 2004 (A Worldwatch Institute Report)*. New York, NY: W. W. Norton, pp. 24–41.

Sen, Amartya (1999) *Development as Freedom: Human Capability and Global Need*. New York, NY: Alfred Knopf.

Swinyard, William R., Ah-Keng Kau, and Hui-Yin Phua (2001) "Happiness, Materialism, and Religious Experience in the US and Singapore," *Journal of Happiness Studies*, 2, pp. 13–32.

UNDP (1998) *Good Governance and Sustainable Human Development*. New York: UNDP. Online at http://www.undp.org/docs/un98-1.pdf.

UNDP (2004) *Human Development Report*. New York: United Nations Development Programme.

UNESCO (2002) "Enhancing Global Sustainability." Online at http://undesdoc. unesco.org/images/0012/001253/125351e.pdf. Report of the Preparatory Committee for the World Summit on Sustainable Development, New York, March 25, 2002.

Veenhoven, R. (1984) *Conditions of Happiness*. Dordrecht, Netherlands: D. Reidel Publishing Company.

World Watch Institute (WWI) (2004) *State of the World*. Washington DC: World Watch Institute.

Notes

1. A History of Development and Development as History

1. On sustainable livelihoods, see also Institute for Development Studies (IDS) and DFID, Livelihoods Connects (2002), "Frequently Asked Questions on the Sustainable Livelihoods Approach," electronic version, June 20, pp. 4–15, available at www.livelihoods.org/enquirydesk/enquiryfaq.html; also Susanna Davies and Naomi Hossain (1997), "Livelihood, Adaptation, Public Action and Civil Society: a Review of the Literature," IDS Working Paper 57. Institute of Development Studies, University of Sussex, Brighton, UK, pp. 1–48.
2. For a definition of "development models," see Helio Jaguaribe (1968), *Economic and Political Development: a Theoretical Approach and a Brazilian Case Study*. Cambridge MA: Harvard University Press, pp. 4–12.
3. For an overview of the critical literature emerging in the UN First Development Decade (1961–71) see E. K. Hawkins (1970), *The Principles of Development Aid*. Harmondsworth: Penguin, pp. 17–66; Frances Moore Lappe, Joseph Collins, and David Kinley (1980), *Aid as Obstacle: Twenty Questions About Our Foreign Aid and the Hungry*. San Francisco: Institute for Food and Development Policy, pp. 9–14, 158–75; C. R. Hensman (1975), *Rich Against Poor: the Reality of Aid*. Harmondsworth: Penguin, pp. 1–41, 233–87; Denis Goulet and Michael Hudson (1971), *The Myth of Aid: the Hidden Agenda of the Development Reports*. New York: IDOC Books, pp. 73–135.

2. Globalization and the Transnationalization of the State

1. This section is based upon the text of a lecture in a course for diplomats of the English-speaking Caribbean, organized jointly by the Andrés Bello Diplomatic Academy of the Ministry of External Relations, Chile, and the Organization of American States (OAS) on "Latin America and the Caribbean in the New World Order," Santiago, Chile, 13–29 October 1999.
2. Figures for 1991 are from the United Nations, *Human Development Report 1994*. New York: Oxford University Press, 1994, p. 35. The 1997 figures come from the United Nations (1999), *Human Development Report 1999*. New York: Oxford University Press, p. 3.
3. World economic growth per capita for 1990–2 declined on the average 1.1 percent per year. This hides extreme differences in performance in various regions. For instance, while the aggregate world GDP declined 0.5 percent, the developed market economies grew 0.8 percent and the developing economies (including here Asia) 3.4 percent. However, the "economies in transition" in Eastern Europe declined by 16 percent. See United Nations Department of Economic and Social Development (1993), *Report on the World Social Situation 1993*, p. xvi.

245

3. Poverty and Sustainable Livelihoods

1. However, recent corrections assisted by statistical refinements, and combined with the surge of India and China as trading giants, have suggested a departure from this historical trend.
2. Although the definition of *poverty line* is arbitrary and responds to overall economic profiles (for example, US$6393 per person in 1991 in the United States versus US$370 per person in the lesser developed regions in 1985), it is a useful device to appreciate a phenomenon that is relative and contextually structured.
3. This section is based upon Chapter 3, "Economic Insecurity," in Jorge Nef, *Human Security and Mutual Vulnerability: the Global Political Economy of Development and Underdevelopment*. Ottawa: IDRC, 1999, pp. 45–57.
4. Terrence Samuel "7,783,816,546,235 In Debt," *The American Prospect* (April 10, 2005), p. 1.
5. It has been estimated that during 1980 and 1986 the United States alone lost 15 billion USD worth of exports to Latin America. This meant 860 thousand fewer, mostly blue-collar, jobs in 1987. In total, the United States lost some 1.8 million jobs as a consequence of insufficient exports to the Third World, with at least half of these job losses directly attributable to the debt crisis. Estimates for Europe put the job losses for similar reasons at between 2 million and 3 million. In turn, Canada lost about 1.6 billion USD worth of exports to Latin America and the Caribbean during the same period (IDRC, 1992).

Index

256   *Index*

White , L.   91–2
Wilsonian Administrative Reform
   Movement   119
women
   -in-development   206
   marginalization of   63–8, **66**
World Bank   23, 26, 39, 70, 76, 88,
   98, 115, 128, 143, 148, 173,
   183–4
World Commission on Environment
   and Development
   (WCED)   140–1, 144, 145, 147,
   153, 241
World Conservation Union
   (IUCN)   234
World Health Organization
   (WHO)   22

World Resources Report   144, 234
World Social Forums   4
world trade *see* trade and labor
World Trade Organization
   (WTO)   39, 54, 59, 63, 76
   human rights and   81–4, 86–7,
   92–3, 97–102
   Trade and Environment
     Division   87
World War Two   107–8
World Watch Institute (WWI)   241
World Wide Web   71

Young, E. A.   211

Zia ul Haq, President
   Mohammed   113